LATINX BELONGING

LATINX BELONGING

Community Building and Resilience in the United States

EDITED BY

Natalia Deeb-Sossa AND
Jennifer Bickham Mendez

THE UNIVERSITY OF
ARIZONA PRESS
TUCSON

The University of Arizona Press
www.uapress.arizona.edu

We respectfully acknowledge the University of Arizona is on the land and territories of Indigenous peoples. Today, Arizona is home to twenty-two federally recognized tribes, with Tucson being home to the O'odham and the Yaqui. Committed to diversity and inclusion, the University strives to build sustainable relationships with sovereign Native Nations and Indigenous communities through education offerings, partnerships, and community service.

ISBN-13: 978-0-8165-4731-9 (hardcover)
ISBN-13: 978-0-8165-4100-3 (paperback)
ISBN-13: 978-0-8165-4537-7 (ebook)

Cover design by Leigh McDonald

Cover art: Soñaba con ser un ave by Alan Altamirano (MK Kabrito)
Typeset by Sara Thaxton in 10/14 Warnock Pro with Good Headline Pro and Californian FB

Publication of this book is made possible in part by financial support from University of California, Davis' Publication Assistance Fund, and by the proceeds of a permanent endowment created with the assistance of a Challenge Grant from the National Endowment for the Humanities, a federal agency.

Library of Congress Cataloging-in-Publication Data
Names: Deeb-Sossa, Natalia, editor. | Méndez, Jennifer Bickham, editor.
Title: Latinx belonging : community building and resilience in the United States / edited by Natalia Deeb-Sossa and Jennifer Bickham Mendez.
Description: Tucson : The University of Arizona Press, 2022. | Includes bibliographical references and index.
Identifiers: LCCN 2022008319 (print) | LCCN 2022008320 (ebook) | ISBN 9780816547319 (hardcover) | ISBN 9780816541003 (paperback) | ISBN 9780816545377 (ebook)
Subjects: LCSH: Hispanic Americans—Ethnic identity. | Hispanic Americans—Social conditions. | Community life—United States. | Belonging (Social psychology)
Classification: LCC E184.S75 L395 2022 (print) | LCC E184.S75 (ebook) | DDC 305.868/073—dc23/eng/20220509
LC record available at https://lccn.loc.gov/2022008319
LC ebook record available at https://lccn.loc.gov/2022008320

Printed in the United States of America
♾ This paper meets the requirements of ANSI/NISO Z39.48-1992 (Permanence of Paper).

Contents

Foreword

Readers of this volume are in for a treat. The chapters assembled here offer nothing less than a kaleidoscopic window into the multiple ways in which Latinx people find meaning, belonging, and inclusion in the United States. The book reflects the work of a talented group of scholars, guided by the ongoing collaboration and vision of Jennifer Bickham Mendez and Natalia Deeb-Sosa, sociologists informed by key ideas in Latinx Studies, and devoted to detailing the creative ways in which Latinx communities have persisted in spite of borders and exclusions. The big surprise is twofold. The book draws our attention to the numerous ways Latinx belonging unfolds, including through community building, political organizing, and performance and art, *and* it prompts us to consider that these multiple, dispersed, and radically different practices may continue even in this gloomy historical moment.

Our world faces three simultaneous, unprecedented crises: climate catastrophe, the COVID-19 pandemic, and struggles for belonging amid legacies of racial exclusion. Around the globe, decades of capitalist extraction and overconsumption have yielded extreme climate change, now causing catastrophic outcomes that we witness near and far. The outcomes include hurricanes, floods, mega-droughts, aridification, water scarcity, deep heat waves, and massive fire complexes. Climate refugees and migrations are predicted to escalate in coming years, especially afflicting the Caribbean basin, Central America, and Mexico. The coronavirus pandemic adds new complexity to this picture. As I write in August 2021, the World Health Organization counts over 198 million confirmed cases of COVID-19 and over 4.2 million deaths attributable to the virus around the globe. Public health experts, immunologists, and the World Health Organization cannot yet confidently predict when widespread vaccination and public health practices will eradicate the virus. Our contemporary movements for belonging unfold in this context. The rise of Black Lives Matter in the United States and Europe, antiracist struggles across the Americas, and the deep political polarizations witnessed in many nations are at the heart of the matter, struggles over the right to determine who belongs and who may be subject to exclusion and disposability. The struggle for immigrant rights and political opposition to refugee and immigrant rights, which we have seen arise in nations including England, Hungary, Australia, France, India, the Netherlands, and the United States (and this list is not exhaustive), also speaks to struggles over inclusion.

In this context, and well before the onset of the global pandemic, we have experienced unprecedented Latinx displacement in the United States. Deportation, detention, racist discrimination, incarceration, and the displacement wrought by gentrification processes are some of the key mechanisms of exclusion, familiar to all of us. This book, however, shifts the focus from Latinx displacement to the varied ways in which Latinx people push back to root themselves through placemaking, community engagement, organizing, and art.

It is important for us to recall that the politics and practices of Latinx belonging begin with struggles for survival and resistance against military violence and colonization. Latin America was first ruled and actively underdeveloped by Spanish colonization. The struggle over Latinx belonging in the United States is fundamentally a 170-year-long struggle for belonging while resisting oppression and maintaining a sense of sovereignty, and a 500-year-long struggle with Spanish colonialism and its after-effects. Today's early twenty-first-century geopolitics, racial dynamics, and demography are very different, but a brief revisiting of crucial moments in history offers us some important signposts. The year 1848 marks the end of the Mexican American War, and the U.S. colonization and acquisition of one-half of Mexico's territory. This includes the U.S. states that became California, Nevada, Utah, Arizona, New Mexico, and parts of Colorado, Kansas, Oklahoma, and Wyoming (Texas had already "migrated" to the United States in 1836). The year 1898 marks the end of the Spanish American War, between Spain and the United States, and the subsequent transfer of Puerto Rico and Cuba as U.S. colonies (also included in the bounty were the Philippines and

Guam). Recalling this war between Spain and the United States reminds us that Latin America begins with a double colonization. With vast territories of Latin America transferred to the United States as spoils of war in the nineteenth century, the scene was set for structured inequalities and the struggles for belonging that we see today.

The expansion of the United States as *the* global empire of the twentieth century, fueled by post-WWII economic growth and Cold War politics, set the stage for U.S. reliance on the extraction of Latin America's rich natural resources and on the maintenance of a system of exploitable, elastic, racialized labor. With this turn, the Caribbean and Latin America became known as "America's backyard," a shorthand trophy moniker. During the early twentieth century, to maintain these systems, the United States conducted military interventions and occupations in Haiti, Nicaragua, and the Dominican Republic, and in the late twentieth century, the United States sponsored military coups in Chile, Bolivia, and Paraguay, and civil wars in Central America. The resulting regimes were invariably favorable to small Latin American elites and U.S. economic and political interests, and always aimed at defeating revolutionary, redistributionist governments and social movements, including those established in Cuba, Nicaragua, Chile, El Salvador, and Venezuela. The list is long. To facilitate domination, the U.S. Department of Defense created the School of the Americas (later renamed the Western Hemisphere Institute for Security Cooperation) to train thousands of Latin American generals and military officials to put down popular insurgencies and Soviet-sponsored communism.

In the process, Latin America became a pawn of U.S. national security concerns, an expendable source of labor and place of extraction for natural resources. The movements of Latin American migrants and refugees to the United States are long and varied, but astute observers of the basic structural forces behind migration and refugee movements recognize that these occur when one society exerts economic and military involvement in another. Activists and advocates remind us of this truth with their pithy slogans, "We're here because you were there," and "We didn't cross the border, the border crossed us." And in many ways, these build on legacies and narratives of resistance established by activists in the Chicano and Boricua movement who struggled for sovereignty and belonging on their own terms in the 1960s and 1970s.

The Latinx population in the United States now numbers approximately sixty million. It's diverse in terms of origins and generation, and Latinx people live in all fifty states. It is racially diverse but principally nonwhite. An overwhelmingly young group, an estimated 900,000 Latinx youth are turning eighteen years old every year from now until 2028.

The context in which the research for these essays unfolds, as editors Deeb-Sossa and Bickham Mendez remind us, is now one of neoliberal globalization, and contested borders. Individually and collectively the chapters here draw our attention away from the deportation regime, to the quotidian experiences and life projects of Latinx communities in the United States. The subjects include Latinx families who have been in the United States since before the *Mayflower*, as well as recently arrived indigenous migrants and refugees. Diversity, intersectionality, and particular attention to place and region are critical vectors for understanding the diverse claims and practices of Latinx belonging today.

A mixed-methods study co-authored by myself and Manuel Pastor, *South Central Dreams* (2021), examines Latino immigrant homemaking in historically African American neighborhoods. Both Latino and Black residents have adapted innovative strategies of belonging, and these unfold inside the domestic dwelling, at neighborhood sites such as public parks and urban gardens, and through community organizing. Home and belonging are hard-won achievements, a long process of establishing a sense of security, familiarity, autonomy, and future-making. But like many hard-won gains, home must be vigilantly protected in the era of looming gentrification and displacement regimes. Race, place, and identity are fundamental to these projects of belonging.

No one can deny the power of detention, deportation, and other displacements in the current era. But *Latinx Belonging* helps inaugurate another line of research, reminding us that practices and politics of belonging may simultaneously occur in the face of powerful exclusions. It's not an either/or scenario. Alongside the powerful mechanisms of exclusion, we see many agentic and deliberate interventions and practices of belonging, inclusion, and homemaking. As we shift our gaze to these processes of inclusion, we can support, enact, and stand up to demand a better future.

—Pierrette Hondagneu-Sotelo

Acknowledgments

This book is the result of a long-standing, feminist, intellectual collaboration and *amistad* between the co-editors, which has sustained us over the last seventeen years and enriched our professional lives. The project slowly took shape over the course of many years through conference panels and workshops at the Annual Meetings of the Latina/o Studies Association and the Latin American Studies Association. Those sessions and our colleagues' critical engagements at them gave us the confidence to embark on this journey. We offer our deep thanks to our contributors who have stuck with us over this long haul. We are grateful for their dedication, patience, and collegiality through an extremely difficult time as we weathered a global pandemic and political turbulence.

We thank the faculty and staff in the Chicana/o Studies Department at the University of California, Davis, and the Sociology Department at William & Mary for their support and collegiality from which we have benefited tremendously. Jennifer is grateful for her colleague Amy Quark, who always encourages her and keeps her grounded through friendship and a shared commitment to social justice. Monika Gosin has offered not only her friendship to Jennifer but also her brilliant, deliberate mind to this project. Natalia acknowledges her chingona mentors, elders, colegas, and confidantes Angie Chabram and Yvette Flores for their pláticas of motivation, and for paving the way so that she and others like her could pursue community-engaged research with Latinx, farm-working communities. The University of California, Davis, and William & Mary provided generous financial support that allowed us to complete this book.

Kristen Buckles believed in this project from the beginning and handled every step of the process with grace. We are immensely grateful to her for her expertise and calm assurances as well as to two anonymous reviewers for their encouraging and enlightening comments. Elizabeth Snyder and Mayra Nunez Martinez provided expert assistance in preparing the book manuscript for submission.

Jennifer is grateful to Chuck Bailey for his love and support. He may be a geologist, but he is also her "rock," and she marvels daily that she gets to build a life with him. William Mendez Bickham and Sofia Mendez Bickham bring meaning to her life and work—and to this project, in particular. They are her guiding lights—always pointing her in the direction of what truly matters.

Natalia wishes to thank Caleb Caudle, her partner, for marching beside her, supporting her and her community projects, and loving her through her academic journey—particularly throughout the process of editing this book.

• • • • •

We dedicate this work to all Latinx people who have bravely faced the tumult, uncertainty, and danger of these times—especially the current generation of young people (our students and children) as they search for their place in the world. Their daily example and courage gave us the confidence to carry out this project.

LATINX BELONGING

Latinx Belonging and Struggles for Inclusion

JENNIFER BICKHAM MENDEZ
AND NATALIA DEEB-SOSSA

What does it mean to be Latinx? Asking this now—at the start of the third decade of the millennium—is also to raise pressing questions about national belonging in the United States and beyond. As we write these pages, the United States and indeed the world are gripped in the deadly clutches of twin "pandemics"—one recent and one long-standing. Even as the COVID-19 virus stealthily traverses the globe, its ongoing waves exacting their greatest toll on communities of color and the poor, activists of all backgrounds in the United States and across the world have poured into the streets to decry historic systems of racism. The rallying cry "Black Lives Matter" reminds us that questions of who belongs and who gets to decide can be a matter of life or death.

In this volume, we assert that the lives and experiences of people who trace their origins and heritage to Latin American contexts—Latinxs—hold important lessons about belonging, membership, and inclusion in the twenty-first century, not only for the United States but for culturally and racially diverse nations around the world. Latinxs have been hailed as the largest racial-ethnic group in the United States, surpassing African Americans in the 2000s (Clemetson 2003). The rise of this group, which in 2020 reached nearly 19 percent of the population (Jones et al. 2021), is representative of broader trends of demographic diversification in the United States. Indeed, in 2011, for the first time "minority" births outstripped those of whites, and demographers predict that sometime after 2040 a clear "racial majority" will no longer exist in the country (Frey 2015).

The 2016 election of Donald Trump as the forty-fifth president of the United States signaled a major backlash to this diversification, heralding a political era in which white supremacy, anti-Semitism, and xenophobia have gained widespread, public expression. Well before the 2020 killings of Black Americans George Floyd, Breonna Taylor, and numerous others at the hands of the police captured the nation's attention, racially motivated hate crimes had been on the rise (Eligon 2018; Federal Bureau of Investigation 2017). Critics have pointed to the Trump administration's propagation of dehumanizing racial discourse as emboldening the perpetrators of racial-ethnic violence. And, indeed, January 6, 2021, saw a massive, violent attack on the U.S. Capitol, leaving dozens of police injured and five dead after white, Trump-supporting insurgents armed with stun guns, batons, and bear spray stormed the building where Congress was in the process of certifying Joe Biden's electoral win. Some carried confederate flags, and others chillingly erected makeshift gallows (Godfrey 2021).

In the United States, racial dynamics have always been intertwined with immigration, and it comes as no surprise, then, that Trump made it the centerpiece of his campaign to "make America great again." He reserved some of his most virulent, racist, and xenophobic commentary for immigrants from Mexico and Central America—referring to Mexicans as "rapists," comparing Central American border-crossers to "animals" (Neuman 2018), and labeling immigrants' homelands as "shit-hole countries" (Costa and Rucker 2020; Dawsey 2018). At the same time, his administration ushered in a historically punitive immigration enforcement regime, canceling the Deferred Action for Childhood Arrivals (DACA) program,[1] which provides temporary deportation relief to approximately 700,000 young, unauthorized immigrants brought to the United States as children, and seeking to end Temporary Protected Status for immigrants from Haiti, Nicaragua, Sudan, and El Salvador.[2] In 2018, Trump's zero-tolerance policies at the U.S.-Mexican border drew national outrage when U.S. Border Patrol separated some 2,700 children from their asylum-seeking parents, placing many of them in foster care (American Civil Liberties Union 2018). Such affronts on the human dignity[3] of immigrants from Latin America and direct attacks on their families have exerted a powerful destabilizing force on Latinx communities, which despite Trump's loss at the polls in 2020 has been exacerbated by the deadly and disproportionate effects of the COVID-19 pandemic (Center for Disease Control 2020).

In light of these factors, as well as the anti-immigrant and anti-Latinx climate that has predominated in the United States for the last decades, a great deal of scholarly work has explored Latinx immigrants' deportability and exclusion.[4] While these are important considerations, we contend that an exclusive focus on Latinxs' marginalization runs the risk of discounting the agency and capabilities of Latinx people and further homogenizing the diverse experiences and identities encapsulated by this pan-ethnic designation.

Echoing the critique waged by Latino Studies scholars over twenty years ago, we recognize that too often social research is anchored "in the vantage point of the dominant social group" and reproduces dominant ideology by conceptualizing subordinate groups as a "problem" rather than as "people with agency—with goals, perceptions, and purposes of their own" (Rosaldo 1997). By centering our attention on the dialectic between collective agency and structural constraints, we seek to build nuanced understandings of the diverse, lived experiences of Latinx people, who are deeply and inextricably woven into the fabric of U.S. society—"Americans" in every sense of the word.

This anthology rests on the premise that Latinx people are not defined by their vulnerabilities, but should be instead understood as full-fledged, active members of U.S. society, whose realities and experiences hold significant lessons about contemporary social life in the "new America" and beyond. The authors who contribute to this volume center and theorize the perspectives, agency, and resilience of Latinx people in their sustained efforts to carve out a place for themselves in diverse spaces and sites in the United States. Their work renders visible the realities of diverse Latinx groups who go about the everyday work of sustaining their families and communities in efforts that sometimes take on politicized meanings. Several of the contributors to this book conducted their research while supporting or actively engaged in the struggles for recognition, inclusion, and resources of different Latinx communities (Bickham Mendez and Deeb-Sossa, Flores, Montes, Muñiz, Ochoa), and two contributing chapters (Téllez and Montoya, Kline et al.) are co-authored by academics and activist-practitioners, blurring the boundaries between these categories.

We situate this volume at the intersection of two contradictory realities: (1) the continuing and sustained anti-immigrant and anti-Latinx hostilities in the United States, and (2) the historic, evolving presence, and inextricable embeddedness of people of Latin American origin within communities across the country. This contradiction reflects what Rocco (2014) labels as "exclusionary inclusion." That is, despite the significant demographic presence and cultural influence of Latinxs and their inclusion in various aspects of social life, they face ongoing forms of exclusion and oppression that both regulate and restrict their participation in the primary institutions in U.S. society.

And yet, as our contributors illustrate through the case studies presented in this volume, the tension between Latinx marginalization and their rootedness in U.S. society manifests differently among diverse people of Latin American origin. For this reason, we argue for an intersectional approach to understanding *Latinidad* (or what it means to be "Latinx") that acknowledges and interrogates the array of intersecting social differences among Latinx people in the United States, as well as the corresponding power differentials, fissures, and contradictions within intra-Latinx relations (Aparicio 2019). Such an approach fully recognizes that relations both between Latinxs and other groups and among those identified as Latinxs are framed by intersecting hierarchies connected to race, gender, class, sexuality, and multiple colonialities.

Latinxs and Exclusionary Inclusion in the United States

Over the last 150 years persistent, and at times, accelerated levels of immigration—stimulated by a history of repeated U.S. military interventions and economic hegemony in the Western Hemisphere—have greatly shaped the U.S. Latinx presence, contributing to its rich and ongoing diversification. Contrary to popular perception, however, most Latinx people are not immigrants—65 percent of "Hispanics or Latinos," as the U.S. Census terms them, are U.S.-born (United States Census Bureau 2019). Latinx people, particularly those of Mexican descent, have enjoyed a rich and lengthy history in the United States, tracing their ancestry and citizenry back several generations and predating Anglos in the neocolonial territories of the U.S. Southwest (Sáenz and Morales 2015).

Since the 1990s, Latinx presence has become increasingly national, extending beyond concentrations in the Southwest, California, New York, and Florida, to all fifty states. Today suburbs, small towns, urban centers, and rural areas in the Mid-Atlantic (Montes this volume), Midwest (Licona and Maldonado 2014), American West (Schmalzbauer 2014), and across the Southeast (Deeb-Sossa and Bickham Mendez 2008), which until recently counted few people of Latin American origin among their residents, have become home to settled populations of Latinxs and to a new "second generation" (Noe-Bustamante, Lopez, and Krogstad 2020; Massey 2008).

Furthermore, major changes have occurred within regions and metropolitan areas with traditionally high concentrations of Latinxs. In New York City, Mexicans are now the third-largest Latinx group, while the Puerto Rican population has declined (Cordero-Guzmán 2019). On the other hand, in recent years Central Florida has seen a significant increase in its number of Puerto Rican residents (Kline et al. this volume). Meanwhile, on the West Coast, Central Americans, including various groups of Indigenous people, have added further cultural and linguistic diversity to the Latinx population, "transculturating Chicana/o spaces" and complicating notions of indigeneity (Aparicio 2019, 32; Canizales this volume). In Los Angeles, as Latinx people spread from traditional immigrant neighborhoods, they established themselves in those with a historically African American presence. As they have made South L.A. their home, these Latinx Angelenos have developed a new racial identity "based on affinity and experiences with African-American people, cultures and traditions" (Hondagneu-Sotelo and Pastor 2021, 11). As Latino Studies scholar Frances Aparicio (2016) notes, such diversification has produced new cross-cultural, cross-ethnic subjectivities that add complexity to "the Latinx experience" in these varied sites.

Scholars in Latino Studies trace the origins of contemporary contestations over Latinx membership and belonging in the United States to the colonizing efforts of Anglo settlers and political elites in the U.S. Southwest. Despite the 1848 Treaty of Guadalupe Hidalgo's classification of people of Mexican origin as citizens and thus legally white, during this period of westward expansion of U.S. settler colonialism Anglo settlers constructed Mexican populations as undesirable, racialized "outsiders" (Glenn 2015; Cobas, Duany, and Feagin 2009). Even as they engaged in a campaign of ethnic cleansing that targeted the Cherokee, Apache, Comanche, and other Indigenous nations, Anglo settlers dispossessed Mexican landowners and farmers through a combination of legal and extra-legal means, including taxation, boundary manipulation, outright theft, and the delay of land grant claims (Dunbar-Ortiz, 2021; Vélez-Ibañez 1996, 62). The first half of the twentieth century involved a continual process of social and political negotiation over the racial status of Latin American and Caribbean-origin individuals, setting into motion "social mechanisms of marginalization," which converge around an imaginary of a perennial, culturally deficient "foreigner," who is unfit for membership in a modern, liberal democracy (Rocco 2004, 12).

The continued legacy of Latinx status as alien citizens intersects in powerful ways with immigration policy to criminalize and construct them as a "threat" to the nation—regardless of their citizenship status (Chavez 2008). Importantly, the positioning of Latinxs as permanently foreign converges with racialization processes inscribed in the construction of the "illegal immigrant," "draw[ing] distinctions between who does and who does not belong within the boundaries of the state" (N. Rodríguez 2017, 10; Vaquera et al. 2014). Illegality operates not to physically exclude immigrants, but rather to differentially include them under conditions of vulnerability and deportability, ensuring the persistence of a precarious workforce, unentitled to rights and protections (De Genova 2002). Further, illegality exerts significant "spillover effects" that destabilize Latinx communities and hold particularly profound implications for the approximately 5.9 million U.S.-born children who live in mixed-status families, who must navigate a restrictive federal immigration system in which family members do not have the same rights or equal access to social services and healthcare (Singer et al. 2018; Mathema 2017). The deeply racialized socio-legal construct of illegality, signified by phenotype (brown skin), cultural attributes (spoken Spanish), and even Spanish-sounding surnames mark those culturally recognized as Latinxs as "not of this place" and as outside the law, casting the "worthiness" of Latinxs as citizens into perpetual doubt (Gosin 2019; De Genova 2006).

Notwithstanding, diverse Latinxs experience forms of social exclusion differently, as racialization processes intervene in specific ways in their daily lives. For example, as Gosin (2019) cogently demonstrates, Afro-Latinxs' navigation of ethnic-racial landscapes and experiences of institutional racism are framed by historic constructions of race in the United States as a "Black-white" binary (a construct, itself, built on settler logics of Indigenous elimination), as well as prevailing racial categorizations that define "Black" and "Latinx" as mutually exclusive identities. Thus, lighter-skinned Latinxs may police the boundaries of ethnic membership to enforce an anti-Black version of "Latinidad" (Gosin 2019).

One cannot comprehend the story of Latinx race-making in the United States, however, without looking beyond its borders to consider historical relations of U.S. and European colonialism in Latin America (Gómez 2020, 20). As Gómez (2020) and others have documented, the United States's overt and covert interventions in Latin America in its quest to extract natural resources, monopolize the production of global commodities, and achieve "manifest destiny" are deeply linked to the migration of Latin American people northward. And the systems of racial oppression and disadvantage that Latinx people (whether immigrants or not) encounter in the United States are, in turn, intimately connected to long-standing legacies of colonialism and white supremacy (Gómez 2020).

The struggles and experiences of the increasing numbers of Indigenous people who have migrated northward from Mexico, Guatemala, Bolivia, and other parts of Latin America are particularly revealing of the violent effects of enduring forms of settler-colonial power as they combine with intersecting structures of oppression (Canizales, this volume; Speed 2019; Blackwell, Lopez, and Urrieta 2017). As Indigenous migrants seek refuge from various forms of economic, gendered, and state-sponsored violence (Speed 2019)—in a country not only deeply stratified by race but also built on the elimination of Native people and theft of their land—they must navigate oppressive, ethnoracial hierarchies "as Latinx immigrants in an anti-Latinx and anti-immigrant American mainstream and as Indigenous within an anti-Indigenous Latinx community" (Canizales, this volume). Indigenous women experience specific vulnerabilities stemming from an overarching system of gendered, racial-ethnic, and what Shannon Speed (2019) dubs "settler-capitalist," state power. Canizales's chapter in this volume reveals how intersecting, structurally produced vulnerabilities play out in the lives of Mayan immigrant youth in the city of Los Angeles, California.

Scholars who have sought to bridge Indigenous Studies and Latino Studies perspectives have asserted that attending to Indigeneity is critical for understanding the complex effects of such intersecting structures of power on the lives of racialized people. Such an approach requires "thinking through the colonial legacies at play across transregions created by Indigenous migration" as well as challenging the settler colonial logic, reflected even in some immigration scholarship, that the United States is a "nation of immigrants" (Blackwell, Lopez, Urrieta 2017, 126–27; Dunbar-Ortiz 2021; see Wolfe 2006).

As we see in the case of Indigenous migrants from Latin America, while race and racialization strongly influence the lives of diverse Latinx people, other vectors of power and inequality, such as those tied to gender, sexuality, class, immigration status, and Indigenity, cross-cut these powerful forces. Accounting for such intersecting hierarchies of power among Latinxs, while also delineating the potential for alliances and community, remains of central concern in the field of Latino Studies, which this volume seeks to advance (Aparicio 2016, 2019). We understand Latinxs as conscious of and articulate about their desire and demands to be visible, to be heard, and to belong. An examination of the lived realities of Latinxs and their struggles for full membership and inclusion requires analytical attention to the constant tension between structure and agency, as well as an intersectional approach that fully acknowledges differences of power, identity, and social location, as well as the continuing impact of colonialism.

Labels and Latinidad

The reader will note that the contributors to this volume use a variety of labels to refer to people of Latin American origin. As Gutiérrez (2016) reminds us, members of subordinated and marginalized groups have always resisted and, indeed, defied the easy classifications of those in power. The various designations employed in this volume as well as in academic and public discourse reflect both the continually evolving and contestatory meanings surrounding Latinidad, as well as changes in Latinx communities in which youth, LGBTQ people, and Indigenous and Afro-Latinxs have increasingly found a political voice (Mochkofsky 2020; Aparicio 2019, 29).

The first official use of the classification "Hispanic" came in the mid-1970s with the passage of laws and policy directives for regulating the collection and publication of statistics about "Americans of Spanish origin or descent" (Lopez, Krogstad, Passel 2021, n.p.). Subsequently, the 1980 U.S. Census used "Hispanic" as a panethnic category to designate (and count) the segment of the U.S. population comprised of those of Latin American and Spanish ancestry. The government's adoption of this official codification, however, did not emerge from a vacuum, but was a direct response to the mobilization of ethnic communities during the civil rights era and their push for recognition and resources (Mora 2014).

In 1967 in an effort to moderate the militant demands of Chicanos, Boricuas, and other Latinx groups, President Johnson established the Inter-agency Committee on Mexican American Affairs, which Nixon later expanded to create the Cabinet Committee on Opportunities for Spanish Speaking People (CCOSSP; Gutiérrez 2016; Mora 2014). One of the first U.S. Senators of "Spanish-speaking descent," Senator Joseph Montoya (D-NM), co-authored the legislation to establish the CCOSSP and used the term "Hispanic"[5] to refer to the "Spanish Americans, Mexican Americans, Puerto Rican Americans, Cuban Americans and all other Spanish-speaking and Spanish-surnamed Americans," whose access to federal programs the Committee would work to ensure (Congressional Record 1969; Gutiérrez 2016, 48).

While the adoption of a panethnic designation, in this case "Hispanic," allowed for the aggregation of diverse ethnic groups, thereby increasing their numbers and garnering the attention of government actors and agencies, it also both racialized and officially homogenized those it classified, dividing them from potential allies and stimulating competition for scarce resources (Oboler 2006). In what Oboler (2006, 10) calls an "effective and time-honored method of social control," the classification also served to perpetuate the historic notion of Latinxs as "aliens in their own land" (Flores-González 2017; Vaquera et al. 2014; Flores and Benmayor 1997).

Nonetheless, panethnic labels have also acted as important platforms for people of Latin American ancestry to claim a public voice. By the 1970s, in their quests for resources and recognition Mexican-Americans and Puerto Ricans in Chicago forged coalitions, adopting a new identity label—"Latino"—which gained further currency in the ensuing decades as a term of resistance that rejected "Hispanic's" reference to Spain's colonial history of oppression in Latin America (Gutiérrez 2016; Oboler 1995). The umbrella label, "Latino," which was eventually included alongside "Hispanic" in the 2000 Census count (Lopez, Krogstad, Passel 2021), also served to both unite and recognize the diversity of nationalities and ethnicities that it encompassed, including those of "mixed" inter-ethnic parentage (Aparicio 2016).

By the late 1990s, new signifiers emerged to challenge gendered forms of linguistic exclusion. In Spanish nouns and corresponding adjectives are ascribed a gender—"Latino" is male, and "Latina" is female—with the masculine form applied universally. To signify greater gender inclusivity, the employment of a slash between the "a" and the "o," (Latina/o) gained widespread use. In the early 2000s a convention first originating in Queer, online communities began to use the *arroba*—a symbol that combines the "a" and the "o"—to create "Latin@," signaling the inclusion of those outside the gender binary. This term, according to Arlene Gamio (2016), "died down in popularity shortly afterward," perhaps due to its unpronounceability.

The continuing evolution of such identity terms speaks to the ongoing search for a collective identification that allows for inclusion and claims to heritage, but also the expression of diverse, intersecting identities. While there is some dispute over its origins, most attribute the initial emergence of "Latinx" to Queer communities of color in the early 2000s (see Vidal-Ortiz and Martínez 2018). In the mid-2010s the term gained resonance and circulation in various publics, with a number of celebrities and media embracing it and a 2018 adoption by the *Merriam-Webster Dictionary* (Mochkofsky 2020, n.p.).

The use of the "X" is intended as a gender-neutral alternative, which destabilizes the gender binary, while also recognizing the diverse identities rendered invisible by umbrella terms (Vidal-Ortiz and Martínez 2018; R. Rodríguez 2017). In an effort to expand the inclusivity of the label even further, some scholars have taken to using Latina/o/x (see Vidal-Ortiz and Martínez 2018). As Michael Muñiz notes in his chapter in this book, the use of this variant signals a recognition of "written language as malleable and an important and necessary site for disruption and experimentation." Notwithstanding, as critics point out, "Latinx" has enjoyed fairly limited usage within the general public and tends to be most widely recognized and used on social media, within academic circles and universities, and among young bilingual or English-speaking people between the ages of eighteen and twenty-nine (Noe-Bustamante et al 2020). Indeed, "Latinx," "Latinidad," and other labels remain heavily contested and fraught, with each containing its own contradictions and erasures (R. Rodríguez 2017). Critics, like the late Horacio Roque Ramírez (2007), have called some forms of Latinidad "dangerously essentializing" (281), while Tlapoyawa (2019) maintains that such umbrella terms "pay deference to a Eurocentric ideology that actively denies the Indigenous and African heritage of the people it claims to represent."[6] Others have criticized "Latinx" for its neocolonial centering of the English language, its association with elitist lexicons of academia, and its erasure of previous struggles of Mexican-Americans and Puerto Ricans (see Contreras 2017). Among Spanish-speakers the term "Latine" has gained recent traction as a gender-neutral designation that is more easily incorporated into spoken Spanish (Carbajal 2020).

Notwithstanding these critiques, the search for a collective identification that captures Latinxs' multiple identities and experiences continues unabated. Latino Studies scholars have pointed out that while the use of identity labels risks homogenization, it also allows for the production of scholarly work that "undermines [such] homogenizing tendencies" (Caminero-Santangelo

2007, 219). Some scholars have called attention to the potential for solidarity embodied in Latinidad as a "political rather than a descriptive category," noting that politicized deployments of the collective identification can serve to acknowledge shared experiences of marginalization and alienation from the state (Beltrán 2010, 9; see Aparicio 2019). Others have suggested the promise of Latinx as a site of inclusivity that "destabilizes in-group power dynamics" and invites the incorporation of previously excluded voices of sexual and gender minorities (Vidal-Ortiz and Martínez 2018). While we recognize the evolving and imperfect nature of identity labels, we have decided to employ "Latinx" in this introduction to signal inclusivity. And, in that spirit, we have asked each contributor to specify and explain their use of identity terminology.

Who We Are — Our Positionality in Relation to Latinidad

We write as two feminist scholars, friends/*amigas*, and longtime collaborators, who have studied and engaged as allies and advocates alongside Latinx communities for more than fifteen years in the places where we have lived and worked in Northern California and Southeastern Virginia. Natalia is a Colombian-born, light-skinned Latina who immigrated to the United States in 1995 to both continue her graduate studies *and* escape the Colombian violence, which at that time was perpetuated by the growing drug trade. She was finishing her degree in economics when the number of kidnaps, extortions, intimidations, and murders reached a grotesque and unprecedented level, even for Colombian standards. Her experiences eventually led her to sociology as a field of study. She claims the identity of radical, Xicana feminist to reflect both her racial-ethnic positionality and political orientation.

Jennifer is a white, U.S.-born scholar and educator who has traveled extensively in Latin America and conducted research in Mexico and Central America. Her research endeavors in the United States have involved her political positioning as an ally in Latinx, immigrant struggles for resources and inclusion in the spheres of health care, social services, and education. And her relationship with Latinidad has unfolded within her life experiences through her marriage into a Nicaraguan, immigrant family, a painful divorce from her children's father, and her experiences raising her two children in the former Confederate state of Virginia and accompanying them into young adulthood as they navigate complex, hybrid Latinx identities.

The contributors to this volume foreground Latinx agency and resilience, which we see as a corrective to an over-reliance on analytical frameworks drawn from immigration studies, which are employed in much of the literature on Latinx experiences in the United States. While immigration studies has produced extensive, invaluable contributions to collective understandings of immigrant incorporation,[7] as well as the detrimental consequences of immigration policy (and state-sanctioned or "legal" violence) on the lives of immigrants and their families (Menjívar and Abrego 2012); the predominant use of immigration frameworks to understand Latinxs' social realities risks reproducing the same conflation of Latinxs with immigrants that has plagued public discourse and even fueled anti-Latinx sentiments and hostilities.

Drawing inspiration from Patricia Hill Collins's (1990) notion of both/ and conceptualizations, we offer an analytical framework that recognizes the intersecting social locations and identities that comprise diverse Latinx experiences and positionalities. And taking up the refrain from the 2006 immigration protests in the United States, "*Aquí estamos y no nos vamos*," we seek to move beyond understandings of Latinxs as always "on their way" to one that conceptualizes them as *presentes*. In the next sections, we lay out a conceptual framework for capturing Latinxs' lived experiences and struggles for full inclusion.

Belonging and Intersectional Latinx Identities

Rapid societal changes brought on by neoliberal globalization and mass international migration have produced diverse, coexisting categories of membership within and across nation-states, leading scholars to rethink Western, liberal definitions of citizenship. Underlying these definitions is a concept of universal personhood, which is equated with a property-owning individual, assumed to be white, male, and heterosexual. All citizens are also presumed to enjoy equal (read: the same) rights and privileges (Yuval-Davis 1997). As Yuval-Davis (1991) cogently notes, this conflation of "sameness" with "equality" obfuscates the "differential access of different categories of citizens to the state and the implications this has on relations of domination" (58). That is, liberal conceptualizations fail to account for the distinctions among those who possess citizenship but are excluded from the rights and benefits it guarantees.

In an effort to overcome these limitations, scholars have called into question the meaning and value of citizenship—especially in the United States, where it has historically served as a proxy for race (Rosaldo 1993). Scholars have theorized citizenship in ways that move beyond an accorded, legally defined status to emphasize performance, placemaking, and cultural practice (see Bloemraad 2018). And such bottom-up conceptualizations are particularly relevant for Latinxs and other marginalized groups for whom citizenship has always been defined through struggle and an "active process of claiming rights" (Flores 2003, 295–96; Oboler 2006).

In their 1997 treatise, Flores and Benmayor (1997) and collaborators argue that it is through cultural resiliency and shared cultural expression that Latinx people define themselves, build community, and claim rights, space, and dignity. Cultural citizenship shifts analytical attention from formal, legal citizenship to "the ways people organize their values, their beliefs about their rights, and their practices based on their sense of cultural belonging" (Silvestrini 1997, 44). Cultural citizenship posits an understanding of oppositional social membership, since it is through community-building and cultural belonging that Latinxs cultivate resistance "to a larger world in which members of minority groups feel like aliens in spite of being citizens" (Silvestrini 1997, 43).

In the decades since Rosaldo, Benmayor, Flores, and collaborators published their pioneering work on cultural citizenship, a set of intensifying and emerging trends have raised new questions about the increasing complexities of Latinx experiences of agency, integration, and social exclusion. First, the growing precarity in the lives of immigrants and people of color across the industrialized world and their marginalization as racialized subjects of securitization and policing have intensified forms of social exclusion that transcend binaries of citizen/alien. Second, changing immigration and settlement trends have resulted in a national Latinx presence in the United States, producing new place-based identities in sites that diverse Latinxs call home. Finally, in addition to shifts in immigration patterns, racial and ethnic intermarriage and the changing demographics of regions and cities have given rise to complex processes of diversification and internal hybridity within U.S. Latinx communities (Aparicio 2016). Indeed, the 2020 U.S. Census shows a marked increase in the number of "Hispanics or Latinos" who identify as multiracial (Tavernise and Gebeloff 2021).

In light of these and other trends, some scholars have seized on the concept of "belonging"—social and affective connections to people and place produced through shared meanings—as central for understanding social membership (see Montes, this volume; Yuval-Davis 2011; Nelson and Hiemstra 2008). While in most cases scholarly conceptualizations of belonging have been coupled with citizenship, we follow others who theorize belonging on its own to argue for the concept's value in broadening the domain of understanding of social membership (Castañeda 2018; Shutika 2011; Coll 2004). Belonging is understood as both a subjective experience of "feeling at home" (Castañeda 2018; Montes, this volume) and something that is actively claimed—often in the face of exclusionary social boundaries (Antonsich 2010). Because it foregrounds subjective experiences and social attachments, belonging is a "thicker" concept than citizenship, better suited for capturing agentic, experiential dimensions of social membership and inclusion (Antonsich 2010; Crowley 1999). Its freedom from an association with a recognized legal status means that, as a concept, belonging readily extends across spheres of social life, allowing for the analytical centering of Latinx agency across social, geographic, and institutional contexts.

Feminist researchers have applied a gender lens in attending to community-building processes and claims to belonging, documenting how for Latinas seemingly "traditional" roles—including family and household responsibilities associated with motherhood—can form the basis for politicization and claims-making (Coll 2010; Moreno 2008; Pardo 1998). Latina mothers, especially from poor and working-class backgrounds, have used their cultural assets and knowledge to advocate for their children's education, challenging mainstream conceptions of Latinx families as uninvolved and disengaged in schools (Darder and Torres, 2014; Terriquez 2012; Dyrness 2011). As they create community in areas like the rural U.S. South, Latina mothers actively contest the deficit framing that depicts their families and childrearing practices as a "problem" (Villenas 2001).

In a recent study, Hondagneu-Sotelo and Pastor (2021) center analytical attention on Latinx immigrants' homemaking and belonging in historically Black neighborhoods in South Los Angeles, California. Hondagneu-Sotelo, Pastor, and colleagues (2021) demonstrate how Latinx and Black residents have engaged groundbreaking strategies of belonging in homes, neighborhoods, public parks, urban gardens, and through community organizing. For these researchers, homemaking and belonging are long processes of establishing a sense of security, building social connection and supportive relationships, and producing visions of a shared future. At the same time, home must be diligently safeguarded against the threat of gentrification and other systems of displacement and community destabilization.

In line with these and other scholars, we conceptualize belonging as attachments to people and place that are actively negotiated and produced as well as highly dependent on the quality of human relationships that people construct (Yuval-Davis 2011, 11; Shutika 2011, 15). And for us, belonging is deeply contoured by overarching, intersecting power structures, as well as by the effects of exclusionary state policies and the social disinvestment that has accompanied neoliberal capitalism (Yuval-Davis 2011). We contend that an approach to belonging that interrogates and recognizes the intersectional nature of systems of oppression related to gender, race/ethnicity, age, class, sexuality, and coloniality equips us to face the intellectual challenge and fruitful opportunity presented by shifting, hybrid, Latinx subjectivities and creative forms of agency that manifest in the twenty-first century.

In the chapters that follow, contributors to this volume explore how diverse groups of Latinx people lay claims to belonging, recognition, and inclusion in different realms of social life and across geographic contexts. From urban centers with a long history of Latinx presence, like Los Angeles (Canizales; Gosin), Chicago (Muñiz), and "sanctuary cities" in California (Gast et al.; Ochoa), to the highly contested U.S.-Mexican border region (Téllez and Montoya), to non-traditional Latinx settlement sites in the U.S. South (Kline et al. and Bickham Mendez and Deeb-Sossa) and Northeast (Montes), to agricultural areas in California that have long drawn on a Mexican and Mexican-origin labor force (Flores; Bickham Mendez and Deeb-Sossa); the case studies presented here illuminate the multiple ways that Latinxs in different contexts negotiate the boundaries of social membership to produce community and claim a place for themselves. Revealed in these contributions are the varied practices involved in such negotiations, claims-making, and productive processes, as well as how Latinx groups and communities across geographic locations "push back" individually or collectively against marginalization, the depletion of resources in their communities, and threats to their security. By centering and privileging diverse Latinx voices and their agentic experiences, these chapters highlight the role that communities play in responding to exclusionary policies and institutional practices and interrogate the power dynamics and interconnections that can lead to social justice and change.

Outline of the Book

Part I, "Intersectional Latinidades, Resilience, and Community Building," begins with Stephanie Canizales's "Ethnorace and the *Orientación* of Unaccompanied, Undocumented Indigenous Youth in Latinx Los Angeles." Through ethnographic research in two Catholic churches and a support group for Indigenous youth, Canizales focuses on Mayan, Guatemalan immigrant youths' experiences of *orientación*—the term they use to describe their process of social adjustment to social and cultural surroundings in Los Angeles, California. Her research demonstrates how ethnoracial hierarchies, including those that operate within the non-Indigenous, Latinx community, shape youths' experiences. Diverging from the existing research, Canizales finds that Church-based networks exclude Indigenous youth from social capital, while support groups offer a community in which they can recover and validate their Indigenous identities. Canizales' chapter highlights Mayan youths' agency, adaptability, and resilient Indigeneity as they traverse racist social structures in their process of social adjustment.

Co-authored by Nolan Kline, Andrés Acosta, Christopher Cuevas, and Marco Antonio Quiroga, Chapter 2, "Resilience in the Time of a Pandemic: COVID-19, LGBTQ+ Latinx Activism, and the Politics of Belonging," examines how in the wake of the brutal 2016 shooting at the Pulse night club, LGBTQ+, Latinx organizations emerged to advance an intersectional social justice movement focused on empowering people with LGBTQ+ and Latinx identities. Kline and collaborators describe how as part of this movement, newly formed LGBTQ+-Latinx organizations have responded to subsequent crises—including Hurricane Maria and the COVID-19 pandemic—by emphasizing unique vulnerabilities related to interlocking forms of oppression based on race, ethnicity, sex, gender identity, and sexual orientation. Their chapter examines the continued resilience among LGBTQ+, Latinx activist organizations in Central Florida during the 2020 COVID-19 pandemic, documenting how LGBTQ+ Latinx organizations mobilized financial resources and shifted their work online to challenge social divisions and advance their intersectional social justice agenda.

In Chapter 3, "No Choice but Unity: Afro-Cuban Immigrants Building Community in Los Angeles," Monika Gosin explores how Afro-Cuban immigrants living in Los Angeles insert themselves into this ethnically diverse gateway city where Cubans make up a small proportion of the population.

Gosin's respondents built on bonds that linked all Latinxs, regardless of country of origin and differences in immigration status, and developed connection with others who shared the experience of being an immigrant newcomer—as a matter of necessity. Gosin argues that given the unique constraints that Afro-Cubans encounter in finding a preexisting racial/ethnic community in the United States, "no choice but unity" reflects a necessary adaptation for pursuing inclusion and complex self-expression.

Part II, "Finding Home and Claiming Place Through Familia," begins with Verónica Montes's Chapter 4, "*Mujeres Luchadoras*: Latina Immigrant Women's Homemaking Practices to Assert Belonging in a Philadelphia Suburb." Montes analyzes community-building activities developed by the *Coalición Fortaleza Latina* that have enabled Latinx immigrants in Norristown, a suburb of Philadelphia, to cultivate a sense of belonging. She discusses the spatial as well as organizational dimensions of these activities, their specific structures and meanings, and their roles as vehicles for the social recognition and visibility of Latinx immigrants in the area. Montes argues that the social practices through which Mexican immigrants in Norristown have produced belonging occur through *haciendo familia* [making family], whereby immigrants deliberately created relationships that became as significant as their own families. She demonstrates how the group's community garden functioned as a site of *convivencia* [coexistence] and "restorative space of belonging" (Hondagneu-Sotelo 2014). Montes concludes that through the engagement of these social practices *Coalición Fortaleza Latina´s* members created a "*proyecto histórico de los vínculos*" (historical project of bonds) through which they created home and community.

In Chapter 5, "Creating Home, Claiming Place: Latina Immigrant Mothers and the Production of Belonging," we employ a gender lens to examine how in two distinct sites Latina, immigrant mothers make claims to place, belonging, and inclusion. We find that through their sustained individual and collective struggles to procure resources for their families, Latina mothers produce both subjective and politicized forms of belonging. Central American and Mexican immigrant mothers in Williamsburg, Virginia, created attachment to place through resilience in the face of restricted access to services and housing and overcoming fear to navigate unfamiliar physical and institutional settings. In Northern California, farmworker mothers made politicized claims to inclusion by advocating for educational and healthcare services in their community. In both sites, mothers developed and expanded support networks to assist them in procuring or collectively demanding re-sources and services for their families. We argue that mothers' responses to exclusionary conditions in these two contexts with differing histories of Latinx presence reveal gendered, place-specific dimensions of belonging and women's contribution to its production.

In the final chapter of this section, Chapter 6, "Finding Home/ Haciendo Familia: *Testimonios* of Mexican Male Farmworkers in Central California," Yvette G. Flores draws on the *testimonios* of ten Mexican men living and working in California's Central Valley to examine the psychological im-pact of migration and the ways in which immigrant men adjust to a new and often hostile country, negotiate transnational family relations, and cope with loneliness and isolation. The powerful *testimonios* shed light on Mexican-origin farmworker men's resilience and agency, and identify how the men created *familia* and community with each other, forging a sense of belonging out of alienation and experiences of discrimination, racism, and exploitation.

Part III, "Resistance Through Claims-Making and Cultural Expression," begins with Melanie Jones Gast, Dina Okamoto, and Jack "Trey" Allen's chapter "Belonging and Vulnerability in San Francisco: Undocumented Latinx Parents and Local Claims-Making." The authors focus on the city of San Francisco, California, a self-designated "sanctuary" city that has an es-tablished network of community-based organizations (CBOs) and activists working for immigrant and underserved populations. They examine how un-documented CBO participants, mainly mothers, begin to "make their rights real" by claiming entitlement to services and support afforded to other com-munity members in local programs and institutions. Through local claims-making acts and their participation in CBOs, these parents are expanding the boundaries of community membership.

In "Strategic (Il)legibility: The Marginalization and Resistance of Latina Community-Engaged Artists in Chicago," Michael De Anda Muñiz explores how Latina community artists are marginalized within the arts and how they resist such challenges to their inclusion. He finds that devaluation, contested access, stereotyping/pigeonholing, and illegibility place limits on Latina community-engaged artists' full inclusion and recognition in the arts. Muñiz argues that Latina community-engaged artists claim space and carve out belonging by strategically using legibility and illegibility. Muñiz contends that the ways in which they make themselves and their creative work legible at times and illegible at others allow them to create space in the arts for themselves and other marginalized groups.

In their chapter "Dance in the Desert: Latinx Bodies in Movement Beyond Borders," Michelle Téllez and Yvonne Montoya make a bold contribution to the scant literature on Latinx dance through the analysis of the creative practices of Dance in the Desert (DITD)—a regional gathering of Latinx dance makers unique to the U.S. Southwest. The authors argue that through the inclusion of diverse Latinx dancers, promoting and (re)imagining modes of Latinx identity, and enhancing community voices through storytelling DITD builds cultural citizenship in Arizona and the U.S. Southwest. Téllez and Montoya contend that DITD helps us understand Latinx communities' cultural expression and identity formation in response to the targeting of brown bodies by immigration enforcement, police brutality, and mass detention and incarceration. In this context, DITD offers a counter experience—one that centers Latinx's insistence on belonging in Arizona and in the field of dance. In so doing, Téllez and Montoya maintain that DITD is building a movement that advocates for the inclusion, visibility, and expression of Latinx's cultural traditions and creative practices.

Closing the section is Gilda L. Ochoa's chapter "A City of *Puentes*: Latina/o Cross-Generational Memories and Organizing in the 2016–17 Struggle for Sanctuary," which documents a local response to the Trump administration's anti-immigrant actions—community organizing efforts to establish La Puente, California, as a sanctuary city. Ochoa contends that generational memories, inclusive and intersectional lenses, along with public assertions of belonging were crucial components of community activism in La Puente. In her analysis, Ochoa argues that to assert belonging in the public spaces of city council and school board meetings, activists drew on multiple generations of knowledge—including frameworks developed by feminists of color and undocumented youth activists. This case study reveals the importance of trusted community relationships, cross-generational alliances, and inclusive and intersectional frameworks in exerting pressure on elected officials.

Part IV of this collection gives the last word to Suzanne Oboler, a leading, critical voice in Latino Studies. In this concluding chapter, Oboler offers reflections on Latinx belonging in the twenty-first century under conditions of crisis. For her, issues related to Latinx belonging and experiences of violence and precarity must be understood within a broader crisis of community within the United States and internationally. The current virulent political de-

bates about difference and the resulting fragmentation of U.S. society are prevailing symptoms of this crisis. Even as Latinxs—both immigrants and non-
immigrants—are being imagined as both disposable labor and less deserving
members of the community, under the current COVID-19 pandemic, they
are also paradoxically essential workers who are vital to the maintenance of
daily life in the United States. And herein lies hope during these dark times—
despite their invisibility and marginalization, through their commitment to
community Latinxs are (re)defining and reconstructing the very meaning of
community in the United States, grounded in mutual aid and solidarity.

Taken together, the chapters in this anthology present a rich and textured
picture of Latinx community-building, resilience, and belonging. These case
studies reveal how for different groups of Latinxs in varied geographical contexts intersections of race, ethnicity, class, gender, age, and other vectors of
difference produce nuanced experiences of social exclusion, but also distinct
practices for creating and sustaining communities and carving out spaces of
recognition. By foregrounding agency in the face of structural constraints
and exclusion, these studies contribute to an understanding of Latinxs as
diverse, multifaceted people with a rich and complex life experience whose
continued struggles for full inclusion offer important lessons about what it
means to be "American" in the twenty-first century.

Notes

1. In December 2020, in *Batalla Vidal v. Wolf*, a federal court ordered the Trump
    administration to restore Deferred Action for Childhood Arrivals (DACA) to
    its 2012 original form, reopening it to first-time applicants and restoring work
    authorization and renewals to two years (National Immigration Law Center
    2020). Seven months later, however, the program suffered a new blow when
    a federal judge in Texas ruled it unlawful, temporarily prohibiting the Depart-
    ment of Homeland Security from approving new applications and throwing the
    future of the program once again into question (Jordan 2021).
2. By 2019 the Trump administration had ended Deferred Enforced Departure
    (DED) status for Liberians and TPS for Salvadorans, Haitians, Nicaraguans,
    Sudanese, Hondurans, and Nepalese. At the time of this writing, multiple law-
    suits are challenging these terminations (see Cohn, Passel, and Bialik 2019).
3. Migrants' extended detention without a trial, several cases of children's deaths
    while in Border Patrol custody, as well as rampant abuse and disease-ridden
    conditions in U.S. immigration detention facilities have drawn heavy criticism
    from Human Rights and Immigrant Advocacy organizations (International
    Rescue Committee 2020). Under the current COVID-19 pandemic, advocacy

organizations as well as the Office of the Inspector General (2020) have cited concerns about improper quarantine, sanitation, and distancing measures, as well as inadequate testing.

4.   See, for example, Abrego (2014), Boehm (2016), and Golash-Boza (2015).

5.   Notably, in New Mexico the term "Spanish" or "*hispano*" has a history of widespread usage to designate New Mexicans who were descendants of the original colonial settlers of the formerly Mexican territory and later to differentiate New Mexican "natives" from Mexican immigrants (Gutiérrez 2016, 36). In a Senate floor speech in 1969, Montoya referred to himself as the "only U.S. Senator of Spanish heritage" (Congressional Record 1969).

6.   Notwithstanding, other Indigenous Studies scholars have embraced the term, highlighting its importance for drawing attention to the "the colonial nature of the imposition of gender binaries" (Blackwell et al. 2017, 129).

7.   Studies of this type are too numerous to list. For examples, see Alarcon et al. (2016), Jiménez (2009), and Vaquera et al. (2014).

References

Abrego, Leisy. 2014. *Sacrificing Families: Navigating Laws, Labor and Love Across Borders*. Stanford: Stanford University Press.

Alarcon, Rafael, Luis Escala, and Olga Odgers. 2016. *Making Los Angeles Home: The Integration of Mexican Immigrants in the United States*. Oakland: University of California Press.

American Civil Liberties Union. 2018. "Family Separation: By the Numbers." https://www.aclu.org/issues/immigrants-rights/immigrants-rights-and-detention/family-separation.

Antonsich, Marco. 2010. "Searching for Belonging: An Analytical Framework." *Geography Compass* 4(6): 644–59.

Aparicio, Frances R. 2016. "(Re)constructing Latinidad." In *The New Latino Studies Reader: A Twenty-First-Century Perspective*, edited by Ramón A. Gutiérrez and Tomás Almaguer, 54–63. Oakland: University of California Press.

———. 2019. *Negotiating Latinidad: IntraLatina/o Lives in Chicago*. Chicago: University of Illinois.

Beltrán, Cristina. 2010. *The Trouble with Unity: Latino Politics and the Creation of Identity*. Oxford: Oxford University Press.

Blackwell, Maylei, Floridalma Boj Lopez, and Luis Urrieta Jr. 2017. "Introduction: Special Issue: Critical Latinx Indigeneities." *Latino Studies* 15: 126–37.

Bloemraad, Irene. 2018. "Theorising the Power of Citizenship as Claims-Making." *Journal of Ethnic and Migration Studies* 44(1): 4–26.

Boehm, Deborah. 2016. *Returned: Going and Coming in an Age of Deportation*. Oakland: University of California Press.

Caminero-Santangelo, Marta. 2007. *On Latinidad: U.S. Latino Literature and the Construction of Ethnicity*. Gainesville: University Press of Florida.

Carbajal, Paloma Celis. 2020. "From Hispanic to Latine: Hispanic Heritage Month and the Terms That Bind Us." New York Public Library. September 29, 2020. www .nypl.org/blog/2020/09/29/hispanic-heritage-month-terms-bind-us.

Castañeda, Ernesto. 2018. *A Place to Call Home: Immigrant Exclusion and Urban Belonging in New York, Paris, and Barcelona.* Stanford: Stanford University Press.

Center for Disease Control. 2020. "COVID-19 Hospitalization and Death by Race/ Ethnicity." www.cdc.gov/coronavirus/2019-ncov/covid-data/investigations-dis covery/hospitalization-death-by-race-ethnicity.html#footnote01.

Chavez, Leo R. 2008. *The Latino Threat: Constructing Immigrants, Citizens, and the Nation.* Stanford: Stanford University Press.

Clemetson, Lynette. 2003. "Hispanics Now Largest Minority, Census Shows." *New York Times.* January 22, 2003. www.nytimes.com/2003/01/22/us/hispanics-now -largest-minority-census-shows.html.

Cobas, José A., Jorge Duany, and Joe Feagin. 2009. *How the United States Racializes Latinos: White Hegemony and Its Consequences.* Boulder, Colo.: Paradigm.

Cohn, D'vera, Jeffrey S. Passel, and Kristen Bialik. 2019. "Many Immigrants with Temporary Protected Status Face Uncertain Future in U.S." Pew Research Center. www.pewresearch.org/fact-tank/2019/11/27/immigrants-temporary-protected -status-in-us.

Coll, Kathleen. 2004. "Necesidades Y Problemas: Immigrant Latina Vernaculars of Belonging, Coalition, & Citizenship in San Francisco, California." *Latino Studies* 2: 186–209.

———. 2010. *Remaking Citizenship: Latina Immigrants and New American Politics.* Stanford: Stanford University Press.

Collins, Patricia Hill. 1990. *Black Feminist Thought: Knowledge, Consciousness and the Politics of Empowerment.* Boston: Unwin Hyman.

Congressional Record. 1969. Senate, 91st Cong., 1st sess. (25 September): 27119.

Contreras, Russell. 2017. "The X Factor: The Struggle to Get Latinos in US News Stories amid a Latinx Push and a Changing Journalism Landscape." *Cultural Dynamics* 29(3): 177–85.

Cordero-Guzmán, Hector R. 2019. "The Latino Population in New York City." *Footnotes* 47(3). www.asanet.org/news-events/footnotes/jun-jul-aug-2019/features /latino-population-new-york-city.

Costa, Robert, and Philip Rucker. 2020. "Trump's Push to Amplify Racism Unnerves Republicans Who Have Long Enabled Him." *Washington Post.* July 4, 2020. www .washingtonpost.com/politics/trump-racism-white-nationalism-republicans/2020 /07/04/2b0aebe6-bbaf-11ea-80b9-40ece9a701dc_story.html?utm_campaign=wp _politics_am&utm_medium=email&utm_source=newsletter&wpisrc=nl_politics.

Crowley, John. 1999. "The Politics of Belonging: Some Theoretical Considerations." In *The Politics of Belonging: Migrants and Minorities in Contemporary Europe*, edited by Andrew Geddes and Adrian Favell, 15–41. Brookfield, Vt.: Ashgate.

Darder, Antonia, and Rodolfo D. Torres. 2014. *Latinos and Education: A Critical Reader.* New York: Routledge.

Dawsey, Josh. 2018. "Trump Derides Protections for Immigrants from 'Shithole' Countries." *Washington Post.* January 12, 2018. www.washingtonpost.com/politics /trump-attacks-protections-for-immigrants-from-shithole-countries-in-oval -office-meeting/2018/01/11/bfc0725c-f711-11e7-91af-31ac729add94_story.html.

De Genova, Nicholas. 2002. "Migrant 'Illegality' and Deportability in Everyday Life." *Annual Review of Anthropology* 31(1): 419–47.

———. 2006. "The Legal Production of Mexican/Migrant 'Illegality.'" In *Latinos and Citizenship: The Dilemma of Belonging,* edited by Suzanne Oboler, 61–90. London: Palgrave Macmillan.

Deeb-Sossa, Natalia, and Jennifer Bickham Mendez. 2008. "Enforcing Borders in the Nuevo South: Gender and Migration in Williamsburg, VA and the Research Triangle, NC." *Gender and Society* 22(5): 613–38.

Dunbar-Ortiz, Roxanne. 2021. Not *"A Nation of Immigrants:" Settler Colonialism, White Supremacy, and a History of Erasure and Exclusion.* Boston: Beacon Press.

Dyrness, Andrea. 2011. *Mothers United: An Immigrant Struggle for Socially Just Education.* Minneapolis: University of Minnesota Press.

Eligon, John. 2018. "Hate Crimes Increase for the Third Consecutive Year, F.B.I. Reports." *New York Times.* November 13, 2018. www.nytimes.com/2018/11/13/us /hate-crimes-fbi-2017.html.

Federal Bureau of Investigation. 2017. "Incidents and Offenses." *Hate Crime Statistics, 2017.* https://ucr.fbi.gov/hate-crime/2017/topic-pages/incidents-and-offenses.

Flores, William V. 2003. "New Citizens, New Rights: Undocumented Immigrants and Latino Cultural Citizenship." *Latin American Perspectives* 30(2): 87–100.

Flores, William V., and Rina Benmayor, eds. 1997. *Latino Cultural Citizenship: Claiming Identity, Space, and Rights.* Boston: Beacon Press.

Flores-González, Nilda. 2017. *Citizens but Not Americans: Race and Belonging Among Latino Millennials.* New York: New York University Press.

Frey, William H. 2015. *Diversity Explosion: How New Racial Demographics Are Remaking America.* Washington, DC: Brookings Institution Press.

Gamio Cuervo, Arlene B. 2016. "Latinx: A Brief Handbook." Princeton LGBT Center. www .eachmindmatters.org/wp-content/uploads/2017/11/Latinx_A_Brief_Guidebook.pdf.

Glenn, Evelyn Nakano. 2015. "Settler Colonialism as Structure: A Framework for Comparative Studies of US Race and Gender Formation." *Sociology of Race and Ethnicity* 1(1): 52–72.

Godfrey, Elaine. 2021. "It Was Supposed to Be so Much Worse, and the Threat to the U.S. Government Hasn't Passed." *The Atlantic.* April 21, 2021. www.theatlantic.com /politics/archive/2021/01/trump-rioters-wanted-more-violence-worse/617614/.

Golash-Boza, Tanya Maria. *Deported: Immigrant Policing, Disposable Labor, and Global Capitalism.* New York: New York University Press.

Gómez, Laura E. 2020. *Inventing Latinos: A New Story of American Racism.* New York: New Press.

Gosin, Monika. 2019. *The Racial Politics of Division: Interethnic Struggles for Legitimacy in Multicultural Miami.* Ithaca, N.Y.: Cornell University Press.

Gutiérrez, Ramón A. 2016. "What's in a Name? The History and Politics of Hispanic and Latino Panethnicities." In *The New Latino Studies Reader: A Twenty-First Century Perspective*, edited by Ramon A. Gutierrez and Tomas Almaguer, 19–53. Oakland: University of California Press.

Hondagneu-Sotelo, Pierrette. 2014. *Paradise Transplanted: Migration and the Making of California Gardens*. Oakland: University of California Press.

Hondagneu-Sotelo, Pierrette, and Manuel Pastor. 2021. *South Central Dreams: Finding Home and Building Community in South L.A.* New York: New York University Press.

International Rescue Committee. 2020. "COVID-19 Escalating in ICE Detention Centers as States Hit Highest Daily Records—and ICE Deportation Flights into Northern Triangle Continue." www.rescue.org/press-release/covid-19-escalating -ice-detention-centers-states-hit-highest-daily-records-and-ice.

Jiménez, Tomás. 2009. *Replenished Ethnicity: Mexican Americans, Immigration, and Identity*. Oakland: University of California Press.

Jones, Nicholas, Rachel Marks, Roberto Ramirez, and Merarys Ríos-Vargas. 2021. "Improved Race and Ethnicity Measures Reveal US Population Is Much More Multiracial: 2020 Census Illuminates Racial and Ethnic Composition of the Country." U.S. Census Bureau. August 12, 2021. www.census.gov/library/stories/2021 /08/improved-race-ethnicity-measures-reveal-united-states-population-much -more-multiracial.html.

Jordan, Miriam. 2021. "Judge Rules DACA Is Unlawful and Suspends Applications." *New York Times*. July 16, 2021. www.nytimes.com/2021/07/16/us/court-daca -dreamers.html.

Licona, Adela C., and Marta M. Maldonado. 2014. "The Social Production of Latin@ Visibilities and Invisibilities: Geographies of Power in Small Town America." *Antipode* 46(2): 517–36.

Lopez, Mark Hugo, Jens Manuel Krogstad, and Jeffrey S. Passel. 2021. "Who Is Hispanic?" Pew Research Center. September 23, 2021. www.pewresearch.org/fact-tank /2021/09/23/who-is-hispanic/.

Massey, Douglas S., ed. 2008. *New Faces in New Places: The Changing Geography of American Immigration*. New York: Russell Sage Foundation.

Mathema Silva. 2017. "Keeping Families Together: Why All Americans Should Care About What Happens to Unauthorized Immigrants." Center for American Progress. March 16, 2017. www.americanprogress.org/issues/immigration/reports/2017 /03/16/428335/keeping-families-together/.

Menjívar, Cecilia, and Leisy Abrego. 2012. "Legal Violence: Immigration Law and the Lives of Central American Immigrants." *American Journal of Sociology* 117(5): 1380–421.

Mochkofsky, Graciela. 2020. "Who Are You Calling Latinx?" *The New Yorker*. September 5, 2020. www.newyorker.com/news/daily-comment/who-are-you-calling -latinx.

Mora, Cristina. 2014. *Making Hispanics: How Activists, Bureaucrats and Media Constructed a New American*. Chicago: University of Chicago Press.

Moreno, Melissa. 2008. "Lessons of Belonging and Citizenship Among Hijas/os De Inmigrantes Mexicanos." *Social Justice* 35(1): 50–75.

National Immigration Law Center. 2020. "Federal Court Orders DACA Program Restored: Immigrant Youth in Class-Action Lawsuit Celebrate Victory." Press release. December 4, 2020. www.nilc.org/2020/12/04/federal-court-orders-daca -program-restored/.

Nelson, Lise, and Nancy Hiemstra. 2008. "Latino Immigrants and the Renegotiation of Place and Belonging in Small Town America." *Social & Cultural Geography* 9(3): 319–42.

Neuman, Scott. 2018. "During Roundtable, Trump Calls Some Unauthorized Immigrants 'Animals.'" *National Public Radio.* May 17, 2018. www.npr.org/sections/the two-way/2018/05/17/611877563/during-roundtable-trump-calls-some-unauth orized-immigrants-animals.

Noe-Bustamante, Luis, Mark Hugo Lopez, and Jens Manuel Krogstad. 2020. "U.S. Hispanic Population Surpassed 60 Million in 2019, but Growth Has Slowed." Pew Research Center. www.pewresearch.org/fact-tank/2020/07/07/u-s-hispanic -population-surpassed-60-million-in-2019-but-growth-has-slowed/.

Oboler, Suzanne. 1995. *Ethnic Labels, Latino Lives: Identity and the Politics of (Re) presentation in the United States.* Minneapolis: University of Minnesota Press.

——. 2006. "Redefining Citizenship as a Lived Experience." In *Latinos and Citizenship: The Dilemma of Belonging,* edited by Suzanne Oboler, 3–30. New York: Palgrave Macmillan.

Office of Inspector General. 2020. "Early Experiences with COVID-19 at ICE Detention Facilities" (Report No. OIG-20-42). Department of Homeland Security.

Pardo, Mary. 1998. *Mexican American Women Activists: Identity and Resistance in Two Los Angeles Communities.* Philadelphia: Temple University Press.

Ramírez, Horacio Roque. 2007. "'Mira, Yo Soy Boricua y Estoy Aquí': Rafa Negrón's Pan Dulce and the Queer Sonic Latinaje of San Francisco." *Centro Journal* 19(1): 275–313.

Rocco, Raymond. 2004. "Transforming Citizenship: Membership, Strategies of Containment, and the Public Sphere in Latino Communities." *Latino Studies* 2(1): 4–25.

——. 2014. *Transforming Citizenship: Democracy, Membership, and Belonging in Latino Communities.* East Lansing: Michigan State University Press.

Rodriguez, Naomi Glenn-Levin. 2017. *Fragile Families: Foster Care, Immigration, and Citizenship.* Philadelphia: University of Pennsylvania Press.

Rodríguez, Richard T. 2017. "X Marks the Spot." *Cultural Dynamics* 29(3): 202–13.

Rosaldo, Renato. 1993. *Culture and Truth: The Remaking of Social Analysis.* Boston: Beacon Press.

——. 1997. "Cultural Citizenship, Inequality, and Multiculturalism." In *Latino Cultural Citizenship: Claiming Identity, Space, and Rights,* edited by William V. Flores and Rina Benmayor, 27–38. Boston: Beacon Press.

Sáenz, Rogelio, and Maria C. Morales. 2015. *Latinos in the United States: Diversity and Change.* Malden, Mass.: Polity Press.

Schmalzbauer, Leah. 2014. *The Last Best Place? Gender, Family, and Migration in the New West.* Stanford: Stanford University Press.

Shutika, Debra Lattanzi. 2011. *Beyond the Borderlands: Migration and Belonging in the United States and Mexico.* Oakland: University of California Press.

Silvestrini, Blanca G. 1997. "World We Enter When Claiming Rights: Latinos and Their Quest for Culture." In *Latino Cultural Citizenship: Claiming Identity, Space, and Rights,* edited by William V. Flores and Rina Benmayor, 39–53. Boston: Beacon Press.

Singer, Margaret A., Manuela Gutierrez Velez, Scott D. Rhodes, and Julie M. Linton. 2018. "Discrimination Against Mixed-Status Families and Its Health Impact on Latino Children." *Journal of Applied Research on Children: Informing Policy for Children at Risk* 10(1): 6.

Speed, Shannon. 2019. *Incarcerated Stories: Indigenous Women, Migrants, and Violence in the Settler-Capitalist State.* Chapel Hill: University of North Carolina Press.

Tavernise, Sabrina, and Robert Gebeloff. 2021. "Census Shows Sharply Growing Numbers of Hispanic, Asian and Multiracial Americans." *New York Times.* August 12, 2021. www.nytimes.com/2021/08/12/us/us-census-population-growth-diversity.html.

Terriquez, Veronica. 2012. "Civic Inequalities? Immigrant Incorporation and Latina Mothers' Participation in Their Children's Schools." *Sociological Perspectives* 55(4): 663–82.

Tlapoyawa, Kurly. 2019. "Erasing the Indigenous Roots of the Chicano Movement." *Indianz.com.* www.indianz.com/News/2019/11/25/kurly-tlapoyawa-erasing-the-indigenous-r.asp.

U.S. Census Bureau. 2019. "Table 8: Nativity and Citizenship Status by Sex and Hispanic Origin Type." Current Population Survey, Annual Social and Economic Supplement. www.census.gov/data/tables/2019/demo/hispanic-origin/2019-cps.html.

Vaquera, Elizabeth, Elizabeth Aranda, and Roberto G. Gonzales. 2014. "Patterns of Incorporation of Latinos in Old and New Destinations: From Invisible to Hypervisible." *American Behavioral Scientist* 58(14): 1823–33.

Vélez-Ibañez, Carlos G. 1996. *Border Visions: Mexican Cultures of the Southwest United States.* Tucson: University of Arizona Press.

Villenas, Sofia. 2001. "Latina Mothers and Small-Town Racisms: Creating Narratives of Dignity and Moral Education in North Carolina." *Anthropology & Education Quarterly,* 32(1), 3–28.

Vidal-Ortiz, Salvador, and Juliana Martínez. 2018. "Latinx Thoughts: Latinidad with an X." *Latino Studies* 16: 384–95.

Wolfe, Patrick. 2006. "Settler Colonialism and the Elimination of the Native." *Journal of Genocide Research* 8(4): 387–409.

Yuval-Davis, Nira. 1991. "The Citizenship Debate: Women, Ethnic Processes and the State." *Feminist Review* (39): 58–68.

———. 1997. *Gender & Nation.* London: Sage Publications.

———. 2011. *The Politics of Belonging: Intersectional Contestations.* London: Sage Publications.

PART I

Intersectional Latinidades, Resilience, and Community Building

CHAPTER 1

Ethnorace and the *Orientación* of Unaccompanied, Undocumented Indigenous Youth in Latinx Los Angeles

STEPHANIE L. CANIZALES

Over the last several decades, the numbers of Central American, Indigenous refugees and asylum seekers have dramatically increased, calling attention to the unique, migratory experiences of Indigenous diaspora (Barajas 2014; Loucky and Moors 2000; Popkin 1999). By the 2010s, the influx of unaccompanied youth from Central American countries to the United States garnered national attention. And yet, with some exceptions (Canizales 2021, 2019, 2015; Heidbrink 2020, 2014), research with unaccompanied Central American minors has largely excluded the experiences of Indigenous youth, focusing instead on the migration of Central American youth more generally (Lorenzen 2017; Donato and Sisk 2015). While some scholars have highlighted the need for more research on the integration of unaccompanied minors in the United States (Cardoso et al. 2017), critical Latinx and Indigenous scholars call attention to the erasure that existing integration frameworks produce by ignoring the unique vulnerabilities and histories of Indigenous youth (Casanova 2019; Boj Lopez 2017).[1] In this chapter, I employ the term *orientación*, used by Guatemalan Maya young adults to describe their process of social adjustment as unaccompanied youth in the United States, and examine how ethnoracial hierarchies shape *orientación* to social and cultural surroundings in Los Angeles, including those that operate within the Latinx community.

The Guatemalan Maya youth in this study migrated to the United States fleeing political and economic instability, with the goal of supporting the families that they left behind in their communities of origin. Unlike those migrants under the age of eighteen who are formally categorized by the Department of Homeland Security as "Unaccompanied Alien Children" (UAC), apprehended at the U.S. border, and subsequently held by the Office of Refugee and Resettlement until they can be released into the custody of a suitable legal guardian (Administration for Children and Families 2019), the youth of this study settle into life in the United States without parents or legal guardians. Undocumented youth who migrate as unaccompanied minors—and who remain unaccompanied throughout settlement—must learn to navigate life in the United States independently, entering social domains dominated by adults, such as the workplace, without the benefit of familial support (Canizales 2021; see also Zelizer 1985; Aries 1960). Their social *orientación* is marked by ethnoracial hierarchies that marginalize Guatemalan Maya youth both as Latinx immigrants in an anti-Latinx, anti-immigrant U.S. society *and* as Indigenous youth within an anti-Indigenous Latinx community. This chapter examines how unaccompanied Guatemalan Maya youth navigate this complex socio-cultural terrain.

Participant observations and in-depth interviews with Guatemalan Maya young adults in Los Angeles demonstrate that as unaccompanied minors, youth possess a strong, collective desire for *orientación* to guide their navigation of an unfamiliar U.S. *"sistema"* (system) that includes ethnoracial hierarchies. In search of such support, youth turn to churches, often lauded as safe havens that operate as spaces of refuge and solidarity for immigrants (Hagan 2008; Hondagneu-Sotelo 2008). Yet my observations within two Catholic churches and interviews with churchgoers reveal that although Guatemalan Maya youth find *"ánimo"* (encouragement) in these spaces, they also encounter marginalization that contributes to experiences of socioeconomic and socioemotional *"retraso,"* or setback. Some Guatemalan Maya youth defect or distance themselves from their churches and, through peer networks, turn to informal groups, including self-help, support groups. In these groups, youth are exposed to and adopt western ideologies of individualism and personal responsibility. Rather than exerting divisive and harmful effects on collectivism within the immigrant community, unaccompanied Guatemalan Maya youth leverage self-help ideologies for the collective good, drawing on their experiences to mentor other unaccompanied youth, including their Maya peers, through their own, socio-cultural *orientación*.

Like other unaccompanied youth, Guatemalan Maya youths' *orientación* includes learning to navigate work and school systems (Canizales 2021), a new language (Canizales and O'Connor 2021), and transnational family life (Martinez 2019). However, Guatemalan Maya youth are unique in that they must learn to navigate ethnoracial hierarchies that disadvantage their social position and thus access to resources within the Indigenous-disparaging Latinx community. While reliance on informal networks within resource-impoverished communities can exert negative effects on socioeconomic mobility (Hondagneu-Sotelo 2001; Menjivar 2000), co-ethnic networks can cultivate ethnoracial pride and a sense of community (Barajas 2014; Batz 2014; Kearney 2000), thereby bolstering socioemotional well-being (Canizales 2019). In this chapter, I argue that youth's movement from traditional immigrant-serving institutions that cause *retraso* to informal peer networks that promote individual and collective well-being evinces their agency, adaptability, and ultimately their "resilient Indigeneity" (Casanova 2019). Understanding how unaccompanied Guatemalan Maya youth navigate ethnoracial hierarchies in the U.S. context is important, because while ethnicity is considered a critical tool for "inclusion projects" (Valdez and Golash Boza 2017) and is often grounds for collective action and solidarity, racialization and structural racism produce socioeconomic and socioemotional inequities (see Treitler 2015; Canizales 2019) across macro, meso, and micro levels of interaction (Aranda and Vaquera 2015). This research offers insight into how enthnoracial hierarchies shape Indigenous youth's agency in response to inequities by elucidating whether or not resources—in the form of social and cultural capital—are accessible to Indigenous communities, along with how access to them can promote socioeconomic and socioemotional well-being in the United States.

Ethnoracial Hierarchies and Social Orientación

Recent studies find that Latinxs in the United States feel excluded from "Americanness" due to their racial and cultural incompatibility with normative identity markers, such as whiteness or Anglo-Saxon Protestant heritage (Flores-González 2017). At the same time, embedded within systems of racialization are ethnoracial hierarchies that advantage non-Indigenous Latin American origin immigrants and their descendants. Thus, as Latinxs in the United States navigate externally imposed racial labels (or racialization), Indigenous communities are subject to multiethnic structures that position them in the "margins of multiple racial, ethnic and national spaces" (Casanova 2019; see also Blackwell, Boj Lopez, and Urrieta, 2017; Casanova, O'Connor, and Anthony-Stevens, 2016). Extreme racism, rooted in "anti-Indian hatred enacted by mestizos and Ladinos (non-indigenous people)" contributes to Indigenous people's social, spatial, political, and economic marginalization, resulting in the genocidal erasure of Indigenous communities (Blackwell, Lopez, and Urrieta 2017). It is not confined to the home country but still accompanies Indigenous people across Latin American diasporas (Canizales 2019; Herrera 2016).[2]

Latinx and immigration studies scholars have long touted the benefits of social networks based on kinship (Suarez-Orozco et al. 2010; Portes and Zhou 1993), as well as ties to immigrant community-based and co-ethnic institutions (Zhou and Bankston 1998) in buffering immigrants from discrimination and exclusion in the host society by reinforcing ethnic pride and creating socially inclusive spaces. Others find that co-ethnic networks can be a source of oppression as they exclude based on gender, ethnicity, and generation (Cranford 2005; Menjívar 2000). Unaccompanied Guatemalan Maya youth who migrate to the United States in search of work typically have limited access to social networks—both in the United States and transnationally—resulting from intersectional disadvantages associated with race, legal status, age, and family dynamics. Thus, unaccompanied Guatemalan Maya youth face a dual disadvantage in that they are largely detached from familial ties and limited in their ability to access social networks dominated by Ladinos (Canizales 2015; Menjívar 2001). Their *orientación* thus involves confronting disadvantages as well as acquiring knowledge and resources to navigate them.

This chapter focuses on unaccompanied Guatemalan Maya youth's experiences of *orientación* within two institutions: the Catholic church and a support group. I focus on churches because much of the existing scholarship posits that church and religious beliefs provide a series of important functions for migrants as they leave their homes and begin to settle in the host society (Hagan 2008; Levitt 2007). Immigration researchers agree that churches and religious organizations play an important role in the creation of community and offer significant social and economic assistance to those in need (Hagan and Ebaugh 2003). Churches are often characterized as advocates for immigrant rights (Hondagneu-Sotelo 2001) and as an "urban service hub" (Ley 2008) or "surrogate family" (Cao 2005) for immigrants. Churches are said to promote fellowship, social services, and social status for those who are excluded from mainstream institutions (Min 1992), such as unauthorized immigrants and unaccompanied minors.

Although churches are considered institutions that promote ethnic transcendence through shared religious identities (Marti 2009), researchers find that Latinx immigrants' religious incorporation can differ based on ethnicity (López-Sanders 2012; Lopez 2008). Indigenous churchgoers' relationship with religious institutions is characterized by a violent history of death, disappearance, and erasure of Indigenous culture and identity by Western missionaries. The Catholic church historically implemented systems, such as the requirement that Indigenous people pay tribute to Spanish colonizers, that continue to oppress and exploit Indigenous people in Latin America (Schwaller 2011). In the United States, intragroup tensions heightened within the hierarchical structure of the Catholic Church can hinder inclusion, as Catholic parishes have not adequately embraced Guatemalan Maya migrants (López-Sanders 2012). Thus, although churches are commonly understood to be supportive of immigrants, the experiences of Indigenous churchgoers in diaspora are framed by a history of violence that manifests as marginalization in contemporary society. This same marginalization causes youth to withdraw from the church physically or socially.

Support groups are often thought of as the antithesis of community-building institutions and a threat to collective orientations, as they promote individualism through notions of self-help and personal responsibility (Wuthnow 1994). Sociologists debate the social benefits of therapeutic cultures of self-responsibility for communities. Some consider collectivism and individualism as diametrically opposed to each other, or as two riders on a see-saw (Etzioni 1996; Lichterman 1995; Wuthnow 1994). In this vein, migration scholars have argued that American values of individualism can undermine a sense of community, threaten family unity (Loucky 2000, 221), and heighten youths' "apathy" toward their Indigeneity (Batz 2014). However, some find that individualism learned and practiced within community settings can facilitate the process of developing the self in community (Lichterman 1994) and "identify[ing] a personalized form of public commitment" (Lichterman 1995, 276). That is, just as scholars have argued that the "recovery" and "reconstruction" of one's identity can enhance self-worth (Batz 2014; see also Lopez 2017), doing so in a community setting can instill feelings of community worth.

Unaccompanied Maya youth workers' *orientación* to the U.S. *sistema* entails dual processes of exposure to ethnoracial hierarchies, embedded in social institutions in U.S. society and Latinx communities, and learning how to navigate the social networks and cultural ideologies made accessible through those institutions to attain individual and collective interests. In contrast with existing research, I find that church-based networks can exclude youth from social capital, and in some cases extract limited resources from them. Support groups offer youth social and cultural capital while providing a community in which they can recover and value their Indigenous identities. Youth demonstrate agency, adaptability, and resilient Indigeneity as they navigate marginalization within racist social structures through their *orientación*.

Indigenous Guatemalan Communities in the United States

The migration of Guatemalan Mayas began during the colonial era but escalated dramatically during the armed conflict (1960–96) that killed or disappeared over 200,000 people and internally displaced 1 million people. Since then, migration patterns have been characterized by labor migration to the Pacific coast of Guatemala, to Southern Mexico, and to the United States. Today, approximately 1.2 million Guatemalans live in the United States, and Los Angeles is home to the largest Guatemalan community outside of Guatemala (U.S. Census Bureau 2016). Concentrating in Pico-Union/MacArthur Park, a neighborhood west of Downtown, 50–60 percent of Guatemalans in Los Angeles are Maya (Estrada 2013). Youth-driven migratory flows are a significant component of Guatemalan Indigenous migration and represent a "survival strategy that responds to their past experiences of violence and marginalization and to their present and future needs" (Heidbrink 2020). Established migration networks and proximity to the low-skilled, low-wage labor market in Downtown Los Angeles draw many unaccompanied Guatemalan youth workers to the city.

Unaccompanied Guatemalan Maya Youth in Los Angeles

Data for this chapter come from a four-year-long study that explores the migration and coming of age experiences of unaccompanied, undocumented Latinx youth in Los Angeles. In early 2012, I first met the coordinators of

Voces de Esperanza, an informal support group for Guatemalan indigenous youth in Los Angeles. Wilfredo, a Salvadoran first-generation immigrant in his early fifties, joined with Jorge, a Mexican 1.5-generation immigrant in his early twenties, to form *Voces* after noticing the concentration of unaccompanied Guatemalan Maya youth and the "*retraso*" (setback) that they experienced in Catholic churches in Los Angeles. During their time living, working, and volunteering in immigrant-serving organizations in the Westlake/ MacArthur Park community, they learned of how Indigenous communities in Los Angeles, and Mayas in Pico-Union, uniquely experience life, labor, and community participation. Their shared commitment to supporting Guatemalan Maya youth drove them to form *Voces*. In 2012, at the invitation of these men, I began attending and conducting participant observation at *Voces de Esperanza* meetings. I supplemented these observations with fifteen in-depth interviews with group members (thirteen men and two women). In addition, I conducted participant observation at two Catholic churches (*Iglesias Divina* and *Sagrada*) and their respective youth groups and small groups, or *comunidades*. I observed these events and group meetings between 2013 and 2015. I interviewed twenty-three youth churchgoers (twenty men and three women; Canizales 2019). The overrepresentation of men here may contribute to the emphasis on *orientación*, leadership, financial provision, and emotion management among research participants whose identities are constrained by ideologies of hegemonic masculinity (Ruehs 2016; Montes 2013).

In 2013, one of the *Voces de Esperanza* participants invited me to *Iglesia Divina* to attend an annual festival in honor of the Black Christ, *El Cristo Negro*, patron saint of the Guatemalan town of Esquipulas. Such festivals take place in Catholic churches throughout Los Angeles. After attending this celebration, I was invited to attend a second festival at *Iglesia Sagrada* the following week, where I made additional community contacts. While I alternated site visits throughout two years of ethnographic observations, I immersed myself most in *Iglesia Divina's* community life, where seventeen (74 percent) of my interview participants were members of the congregation.

Study participants arrived in Los Angeles as minors between 2003 and 2013. *Voces* participants migrated to Los Angeles between the ages of twelve and seventeen. Participants from *Iglesias Divina* (seventeen) and *Sagrada* (six) migrated between the ages of fourteen and seventeen. All participants were between the ages of eighteen and twenty-six at the time of the interview.

Research participants at both sites refer to themselves as *jóvenes*, or "youth," and thus I refer to them as such throughout this chapter. All Indigenous youths shared experiences of familial poverty in Guatemala. While their educations were incomplete (averaging about four years of formal schooling), they all had significant work experiences prior to migration, having worked alongside parents or caregivers in Guatemala. Upon arriving in Los Angeles, these young people found work in manufacturing and domestic work.

Access to these groups was facilitated by my family background and social identity. As the daughter of Salvadoran immigrants who grew up in the Westlake/MacArthur Park neighborhoods, I was easily able to discuss the local neighborhood and the excitement and anticipation of community, cultural events that facilitated introductions, and informal conversations with youth participants. My father, who migrated from El Salvador as an unaccompanied, undocumented seventeen-year-old, worked in garment manufacturing for several years after his arrival in Los Angeles. Sharing this with youth provided a framework of common experience and facilitated relationship-building and rapport with my respondents. I conducted fieldwork while I was also moving through young adulthood, between the ages of twenty-four and twenty-eight. I shared similar interests in music, technology, food, and neighborhood events as the study participants. Despite being a monolingual Spanish-language speaker until the age of five, I entered the field with limited Spanish fluency—much of which was lost during my K–12 education—and with considerable insecurity related to my linguistic abilities. During fieldwork, I learned that many of the Maya youth also felt insecure about their Spanish-language proficiency. My limited language abilities allowed me to assert that I was not the expert but was positioned to learn. All interviews were conducted in Spanish. I use pseudonyms here to protect participants' identities.

Orientación in Latinx Los Angeles

Guatemalan Maya youth experience ethnoracial discrimination in their home countries, during migration, and upon arrival in Los Angeles. For Aarón, who was a steadfast *Iglesia Divina* member for eight years prior to attending *Voces*, discrimination caused low self-esteem and depression. Aarón says, "*Empecé a caerme. Me caí en la depresión* [I started to fall. I fell into depression]. I would ask myself why and I didn't accept that I was Guatemalan. I felt rejected. I couldn't find help. I didn't see anything good in the world." Aarón's experience, like that of many unaccompanied Guatemalan Maya youth I met, led him to pursue guidance from formal and informal community-based organizations.

Animo and Retraso in Latinx Churches

As financially independent youth who are unable to attend school because of highly flexible work schedules in the low-wage employment sectors in which they work, the church is among the first formal institutions in which they participate. For Guatemalan, Indigenous youth even before migration churches played a supportive role in their families' lives, and they continued to see both churches and their religious faith as a source of refuge and support during their migratory journey and eventual settlement in Los Angeles. For example, Ismael explained that his mother emphasized church attendance as he grew up in Guatemala. He said, "My mom would tell me, 'Go to church and there is a God who will give you everything you ask for.' Since I was a child, I would ask God for my trip here. It was difficult but I passed through."

Researchers find that religion is often used by individuals and families who face severe and consistent impoverishment and hardship to "fill the gap" in their economic and emotional stability (Cooper 2014). Likewise, religion and religious beliefs are central to motivating and making sense of the migration experience among recently arrived immigrants (Hagan 2008). Religiosity offers youth hope for a successful migration journey and, in a similar fashion, success in the United States. Additionally, one of the ways that youth receive support through their struggles of depression, fear, anxiety, and isolation is through engaging with practices that promote "inner strength." Oswaldo arrived at age fourteen and described how he found emotional support through regular participation in his local church as he struggled with the depression of being away from his family. He said:

> Being in the church helps me to be at peace when I feel challenges because my emotions sometimes go up and go down. And when they are down sometimes, I can't find what to do. Prayer helps me a lot. It gives me hope. It gives me *inner strength*. My emotions go up and go down and when they are down, I don't know what to do so it helps me a lot. Sometimes I cry and start to cry out to God and I feel at peace. I feel free. That helps me.

Oswaldo repeatedly spoke of his emotional instability, perhaps more severe for an unaccompanied fourteen-year-old than someone who migrates at a later age. Various others also spoke about feelings of *ánimo*, or encouragement, through their participation in religious organizations and practices.

Joining groups that invest in the growth and development of young people is especially important for youth who do not attend school in the United States. Religious seminars and classes also expose youth to similarly situated peers who may comprise a support network, offer companionship, and cultivate fictive kinship. In 2006, at the age of fifteen, Juan arrived in Los Angeles from Guatemala with the intention of working to build a home for himself and his family. He recalls one of the lowest moments in his early years in the United States, in which he became extremely ill and the support of his friends from church intervened. He said:

> I was left without money because I got sick one Christmas and I had sent all my money to my family. I was thinking about my house, and I wanted to put floors down. I was left without money here because I had someone working there (Guatemala). So, when I got sick and was without money, I only had my friends from church. They helped me get ahead. That's when I realized that you can have a lot of money in life, you can be a billionaire, but when you die you have nothing.

Juan's friendships and the support he received through his church networks helped him overcome his feelings of loneliness and despair.

Reliance on and commitment to church organizations can also contribute to exposure to *retraso*—or emotional and financial setback. This is because social interactions in the church community are shaped by ethnic hierarchies—a mechanism that contributes to *retraso*. At *Iglesias Divina* and *Sagrada*, sharply drawn ethnic boundaries between Ladinos, the Hispanicized population, and the Indigenous population create community cleavages (Vanthuyne 2009), disenfranchise Indigenous youth, and shape Ladinos' perceptions of and interactions with Guatemalan Maya members. A common form of exclusion that reflected Maya youth's outsider status was their assignment to lower-status, volunteer tasks. It was common for Maya youth to be assigned the tasks of guarding the church parking lots, maintaining restrooms, moving furniture, and setting up and tearing down events. In contrast, event organizers were more likely to assign Ladino parishioners to more prestigious, leadership positions, such as volunteering inside the sanctuary as ushers, worship leaders, and teachers, where they acted as the public face of the institution. As a result, rather than strengthen the ethnic affiliation between Guatemalan Maya youth and other Latinxs in the church community, the churches' differential treatment and racial-ethnic marginalization of Indigenous youth caused them to feel a sense of embarrassment and even to conceal their Maya identity within the church.

Guatemalan Maya adult and young-adult churchgoers commented that they did not feel fully accepted in the parish, but were looked down upon by Guatemalan Ladinos, as well as other Central Americans and Mexicans. To ameliorate this and retain membership, *Iglesias Divina* and *Sagrada*, along with others in the Pico-Union/MacArthur Park district, encouraged the formation of *comunidades*, similar to traditional Bible studies or prayer groups, for members of all ages and small groups for young adults. Since *comunidades* were not sponsored or financed by their parishes, they had to rely on the financial support of already economically strained group members to keep their doors open. Ranging from twelve to about sixty-five members, *comunidades* differed in location, building infrastructure, the equipment they utilize, and their financial need.

Recognition as a leader within church groups required the dedication of personal resources to the community, which reinforced the "self-initiated, production-oriented nature of traditional Meso-American religious cargo systems" (Wellmeier 1998, 107). In the context of Los Angeles, the financial expectations of the *comunidades* produced considerable economic hardship for Maya immigrant youth. Young adults, such as Mauricio, a twenty-seven-year-old who spent eight years volunteering in *comunidades* and youth groups at *Iglesia Divina*, described the mismatch between youth's needs and the resources they were asked to contribute as causing *retraso*, or setback. While at a coffee shop with a group of eight youth who attend *Iglesia Divina*, Mauricio explained with frustration, "*Uno pasa años sirviendo, dándole a la iglesia, pero no nos ayuda. Nomás es un retraso.*" (You spend years serving, giving to the church, but it does not help us. It's only a setback.)

The experiences of Victor, a young man whom I briefly met in 2014, further demonstrate the deleterious effects of *retraso*. Victor diligently organized a Sunday afternoon youth group event at *Iglesia Sagrada*. In September 2014, I was formally introduced to him at a smaller youth group meeting where he explained that he had decided to attend the group as a last resort.

He shared his story with me before the group meeting and later reiterated it to the others present with a tone of sadness. Others commiserated with him, sharing similar experiences:

> I am thankful to God for everything he has done for me. But now what is happening to me is ... what is ... umm ... in this group they told me I had to pay. I was willing to pay the rent, the bills, and I paid. I took guitar classes, but they asked us to sell ... to pay ... buy speakers. Every time there is an activity, we did all of these things. I paid my tickets, I paid the light bill, but I cannot tolerate it anymore. "No more," I said. "I cannot give anymore." They didn't listen to me, so I said, "Oh well, I have to give." They called me again. I cannot tolerate it anymore. [The stress] came to me little by little and like two weeks ago I had a pain in my stomach, it pulsated. I felt the stress. The doctor told me it's ulcers. I felt like my stomach was pulsating. I felt the stress. I have stress. I feel stress.

The financial expectations of Victor's *comunidad* had detrimental effects on his health. As Victor spoke, he shook his head and rubbed the back of his neck, signaling the disappointment and anxiety caused by his financial, emotional, and mental health instability. Victor continued to talk about a recent visit to a local clinic where he was given various supplements to *"calmar los nervios"* (calm his nerves). When I asked if he remembered their names, Victor retrieved seven containers from his backpack, none of which had recognizable brands but whose labels read such names as, "Mood Support," "Calming Essence," and "Adrenal Support." The combination of these substances was causing drowsiness, headaches, shakiness, and vomiting, all of which were impinging on Victor's ability to work. As a garment worker paid a piecemeal rate, the inability to work quickly and consistently affected his earnings. Victor had now not only spent his limited resources on finding a remedy for his ailments, but also reported having left school until he was able to "overcome."

Resilient Indigeneity in Support Groups

To counter feelings of *retraso*, youth engaged in various activities across multiple organizations, including entering existing organizations such as English-language night schools and recreational groups like soccer clubs or Zumba classes. In some cases, such as *Voces*, youth might work together in developing new community spaces. *Voces* is a support group that promotes self-help and community connectedness among unaccompanied Guatemalan Maya youth in Pico-Union by offering a space for youth to gather with similarly situated peers and discuss their challenges and triumphs of the week. The group met once a week for two hours, during which participants were encouraged to "develop" in seven areas: physical, intellectual, moral, emotional, spiritual, social, and sexual. Dialogue opens with the simple question: "How was your week?" Responses varied from descriptions of experiences at work to more intimate discussions of family, physical, mental, or emotional health. *Voces* did not offer financial support and only occasionally invited guest speakers who worked as therapists, lawyers, teachers, researchers, or recreational instructors. Thus most of the coordination and support came from the participants themselves. During the height of media attention to unaccompanied minors at the U.S. southern border in 2014 and 2015, *Voces* included about forty members, aged eighteen to thirty-one, who migrated as minors (between the ages of eleven and seventeen). *Voces* support group structure played an important role in cultivating social capital among its participants (Moya 2005). As opposed to churches, youths' ethnic identity was mobilized as a resource for community collectivism and knowledge through their support group participation (Popkin 1999).

For example, to reinforce a positive ethnic identity, youth are encouraged to speak to each other in K'iche, K'anjobal, and Mam during *Voces* meetings. This practice is common among all attendees regardless of background. The support group setting reinforces the value of the personal self and one's identities within a shared group setting that simultaneously bolsters solidarity. Having been an active member of *Voces* for several years, Aarón met various youth who participated in the group as well as other community leaders and mentors who excitedly discussed Guatemala, Guatemalan migration, Maya culture, and his native K'iche language.

Exposure to these practices and social ties increased youths' ethnic pride. Aarón, who is twenty-five years old and had been living in the United States for nine years, articulately described how this transition occurred in his life. Upon arrival in Los Angeles, he did not identify as Guatemala Mayan. During our interview in 2014, he explained, "*Antes no sabia quien era yo. Yo pensaba que simplemente era un ser humano sin valor* [I didn't know who I was before. I simply thought I was a human being without value]. Now I know what my value is. I know we are all the same whether white, Black, or whatever it may be. Mayas, too. We are all the same." Through what he describes as "education" and "self-preparation," he began to awaken to a new reality: "I did not accept that I am Guatemalan. I felt that I am rejected there. I am rejected here. I could not find help. I fell into depression and everything was bad; nothing was good. I asked myself why other people are okay, and I am not. I would tell myself, 'Well, it's because I am an *indio.*'"

Aarón recalls meeting Wilfredo and Jorge, admiring how they constantly spoke of learning new things. He enrolled in English-language learning courses and began reading books about Maya history. Aarón described "awakening" to the reality that "a bunch of youth from my culture and my country are suffering. Many youth are here but they are not studying and they just work and work. I started studying and noticed we don't have leaders. We don't have anybody." I asked Aaron to elaborate on what he was "awakening" to. He responded:

Well, before I thought I was someone without value. . . . Before I thought that I was *indio*, now I know I am not *indio*. I am Maya. Why am I Maya? Because my grandparents and great grandparents are Maya. My language is K'iche. Now I am seeing the reality, I am waking up. It does not affect me now when people say, "You are Maya." I say, "Yes, yes I am," because I know who I am, but the youth who do not know think that they are being humiliated. It's not like that.

Through Wilfredo and Jorge, Aarón met other community leaders and role models who spoke with him about Guatemala and Maya culture and language, which gave Aarón a sense of cultural pride. Many youths described moving from thinking of themselves as *indio* to feeling pride in identifying as Maya. Indeed, symbols of Maya identity were incorporated into *Voces* meetings. It became customary for a table at *Voces* meetings to be decorated with textiles in vibrant red, purple, blue, and green with the word "Guatemala" embroidered in yellow, a Maya calendar, and images of the Guatemala highlands. During special events, youth dress in *traje*, traditional Maya clothing that includes embroidered shirts and slacks for men and white ruffled tops with floor-length skirts for women. Maya youth individually adopt a thickened Indigenous ethnic identity, yet this process also occurs collectively; thus a culture that emphasizes individualism can be blended with cultural notions of the collective.

Maya youth adopt these interlinked ideologies of individualism and collectivism in innovative ways that contribute to the dissemination of community knowledge. For example, Aarón encourages those within his social network to pursue opportunities to increase their understandings of their histories and social positions. He mentions books, *Voces*, and church groups as options for having "time for themselves" and cultivating a personalized self. As he does this, Aarón is also encouraging the accumulation and dissemination of human and social capital, which were sparse to youth upon arrival in Los Angeles. He is motivated by his own "awakening" to serve as a mentor and a source of social and cultural capital for the *orientación* of others: "I suffered a lot. And I would say that I am delayed many years because no one helped me. Other people think this is normal, but I tell them, 'You have to read this book, this book, this book. . . .' And now we are advancing. They will say, 'Okay, you make sense. I have to prepare myself in these areas.' I see this happening."

Toward the end of my four years of fieldwork, Jorge entered a graduate program and no longer regularly attended the weekly meetings. Wilfredo fell ill frequently, experienced a stroke, and began warning youth that he would not be attending *Voces* for much longer. Given these shifts in group dynamics, Wilfredo encouraged youth to think of themselves as experts who not only take on self-responsibility but also offer community support. In a meeting in late December 2015, neither Wilfredo nor Jorge were present. Aarón became visibly frustrated when group participants did not share as openly as when the key figures were guiding the discussion. Years of learned self-help talk and role modeling came to the fore when Aarón began guiding the group:

> If there are things you want to talk about with us, your friends, it's one of the only ways to really heal. You have to make an effort, that's the key that we have to healing our wounds. We have to accept [our conditions] and then start to work on the areas we have. There are seven and those are the areas we focus on. We come here to talk about the physical, intellectual, moral, emotional, psychological, spiritual, social, sexual. And then we just have to accept ourselves.

Young people, like Aarón, develop individual narratives and practices within a collective. This setting motivates them to situate their understandings of themselves, including their marginalized identities, within a broader community. Rather than breeding divisiveness and individuation from their Guatemalan Maya community, self-help ideologies learned in community prompt youth to cultivate resilient Indigeneity within that community and among similarly situated peers. In this way, individualism and collectivism are not opposing orientations on a seesaw, but mechanisms of self- and community *orientación* that foster ethnic pride and the cultivation of community resources.

Conclusions

Though high rates of migration of Central American, unaccompanied minors drew researcher and policy attention in 2014 and the years following, youth-driven migration from the region is not new. Central American youths' pre- and post-migration experiences vary by such factors as country of origin and ethnoracial identity. This article aims to address the call by researchers to demonstrate how Indigeneity operates as an axis of inequality that shapes the outcomes of immigrant-origin children and youth, including unaccompanied minors, in diaspora.

This chapter has introduced the concept of *orientación* as an Indigenous youth-identified process that may facilitate the achievement of social, financial, and health well-being among unaccompanied minors who lack parental or a caregiver's guidance and support upon arrival in the United States. *Orientación* includes awareness about the role of specific institutions in social life, the potential for individual and collective participation within these institutions, and the accessibility of resources—financial, social, cultural capital—to support stability or mobility as youth come of age. With limited access to supportive adult figures and institutions and given their experiences of marginalization in Latinx Los Angeles, Guatemalan Maya youth turn to churches to access and develop networks of social, emotional, and spiritual support. Yet they also experience *retraso* as their marginalization within the Latinx Catholic community in Los Angeles is reinforced by racially motivated organizational practices and dynamics that impede financial, emotional, and mental health stability.

Recognizing their *retraso*, youth turn to forming and participating in alternative organizations, including support groups like *Voces de Esperanza*. *Voces* shares similar resource impoverishment as many other civil organizations serving Latinxs; thus the support group does not offer financial resources, jobs, or formal education that would drastically shift the incorporation trajectories of unaccompanied youth. *Voces* does, however, empower youth to view themselves, their narratives, ethnic identities, and cultural practices as resources and skills that they can individually harness for collective good. The fear of ridicule and mistreatment often causes Indigenous individuals to minimize their Indigenous identity (Castaneda, Manz, Davenport 2002). Yet support group participation and self-help talk fostered individuals' resilient Indigeneity. Expressing resilient Indigeneity in a group setting and across time was fundamental to constructing a positive ethnic identity. Beyond arguing that one organization benefits youth more than another, the findings here point to youths' ability to navigate community-based organizations and resources in ways that benefited them, advanced their well-being, and empowered their peers and community.

This study advances immigration and Latinx studies research by examining the experiences of unaccompanied Guatemalan Maya youth and the resilient Indigeneity that arises as they navigate Latinx Los Angeles without parents or primary caregivers. I also demonstrate that the social worlds of Indigenous youth in diaspora go beyond parent-led households and schools (Canizales 2021) and include spaces deemed the domain of adults, such as workplaces and support groups. The experiences of unaccompanied youth workers, and the intersecting identities that shape them, warrant greater consideration. In highlighting these experiences and social positions, this study raises questions about the existence of a homogenous, bounded "Latinx" community and who is able to participate in it. Finally, findings show that despite their dual disadvantage of being unaccompanied and youth workers, and the grip of hybrid hegemonies within U.S. institutions, youth possess agency, practice adaptability, and experience resilient Indigeneity as they independently navigate *orientación*. The eradication of anti-immigrant racism and xenophobia in the United States and anti-Indigenous discrimination and exclusion can increase the prospects for material and emotional well-being as unaccompanied Maya youth come of age in diaspora.

Notes

1. Socially constructed in the United States as a homogenous panethnic group identity, the term *Latino* is often used to refer to a population that is diverse in terms of Latin American national origins, class, race, and ethnocultural characteristics while giving preference to the masculine identifier. I use the gender-neutral term *Latinx* here to ensure gender inclusivity.

2. Throughout the chapter, I use the terms *Ladino, Indigenous,* and *Maya* to reflect the ethnoracial distinctions between non-Indigenous and Indigenous populations within the socially constructed ethnoracial hierarchy. Indigenous Mayas are descendants of the pre-Colombian inhabitants of southern Mexico and Central America, many of whom continue to follow traditional pre-Colombian sociocultural behaviors, beliefs, and practices. Ladinos are the descendants of Spanish conquistadores and follow a Spanish-derived way of life.

References

Administration for Children and Families. 2019. "Fact Sheet: Unaccompanied Alien Children." Washington, DC: Health and Human Services. www.hhs.gov.

Aranda, Elizabeth, and Elizabeth Vaquera. 2015. "Racism, the Immigration Enforcement Regime, and the Implications for Racial Inequality in the Lives of Undocumented Young Adults." *Sociology of Race and Ethnicity* 1(1): 88–104.

Aries, Philippe. 1960. *Centuries of Childhood: A Social History of Family Life.* New York: Vintage Books.

Barajas, Manuel. 2014. "Colonial Dislocations and Incorporation of Indigenous Migrants from Mexico to the United States." *American Behavioral Scientist* 58(1): 53–63.

Batz, Giovani. 2014. "Maya Cultural Resistance in Los Angeles: The Recovery of Identity Among Maya Youth." *Latin American Perspectives* 41: 194–207.

Blackwell, Maylei, Floridalma Boj Lopez, and Luis Urrieta Jr. 2017. "Introduction: Critical Latinx Indigeneities." *Latino Studies,* 15(2):126–37.

Canizales, Stephanie L. 2015. "American Individualism and the Social Incorporation of Unauthorized, Unaccompanied Mayan Young-Adults in Los Angeles." *Ethnic and Racial Studies* 38(10):1831–47.

———. 2019. "Support and Setback: How Religion and Religious Organisations Shape the Incorporation of Unaccompanied Indigenous Youth." *Journal of Ethnic and Migration Studies* 45(9): 1613–30.

———. 2021. "Work Primacy and the Social Incorporation of Unaccompanied, Undocumented Latinx Youth in the United States." *Social Forces.* https://doi.org/10.1093/sf/soab152.

Canizales, Stephanie L., and Brendan H. O'Connor. 2021. "From *Preparación* to *Adaptación*: Language and the Imagined Futures of Maya-Speaking Guatemalan Youth in Los Angeles." In *Refugee Education Across the Lifespan: Mapping Experiences of Language Learning and Use,* edited by Doris Warriner, 103–19. Switzerland: Springer Press.

Cao, Nanlai. 2005. "The Church as a Surrogate Family for Working Class Immigrant Chinese Youth: An Ethnography of Segmented Assimilation." *Sociology of Religion* 66: 183–200.

Cardoso, Jodi Berger, Kalina Brabeck, Dennis Stinchcomb, Lauren Heidbrink, Olga Acosta Price, Óscar F. Gil-García, Thomas M. Crea, and Luis H. Zayas. 2017. "Integration of Unaccompanied Migrant Youth in the United States: A Call for Research." *Journal of Ethnic and Migration Studies* 45(2): 273–92.

Casanova, Saskias. 2019. "*Aprendiendo y Sobresaliendo*: Resilient Indigeneity & Yucatec-Maya Youth." *Critical Latinx Indigeneities and Education* 13(2): 42–65.

Casanova, Saskias, Brendan H. O'Connor, and Vanessa Anthony-Stevens. 2016. "Ecologies of Adaptation for Mexican Indigenous Im/Migrant Children and Families in the United States: Implications for Latino Studies." *Latino Studies* 14(2): 192–213.

Castañeda, Xochitl, Beatriz Manz, and Allison Davenport. 2002. "Mexicanization: A Survival Strategy for Guatemalan Mayans in the San Francisco Bay Area." *Migraciones Internacionales* 1(3): 102–23.

Cooper, Marianne. 2014. *Cut Adrift: Families in Insecure Times*. Oakland: University of California Press.

Cranford, Cynthia J. 2005. "Networks of Exploitation: Immigrant Labor and the Restructuring of the Los Angeles Janitorial Industry." *Social Problems* 52: 379–97.

Donato, Katharine M., and Blake Sisk. 2015. "Children's Migration to the United States from Mexico and Central America: Evidence from the Mexican and Latin American Migration Projects." *Journal on Migration and Human Security* 3(1): 58–79.

Estrada, Alicia Ivonne. 2013. "Ka Tzij: The Maya Diasporic Voices from *Contacto Ancestral*." *Latino Studies* 11: 208–27.

Etzioni, Amitai. 1996. *The New Golden Rule: Community and Morality in a Democratic Society*. New York: Basic Books.

Flores-Gonzalez, Nilda. 2017. *Citizens but Not Americans: Race and Belonging Among Latino Millennials*. New York: New York University Press.

Hagan, Jacqueline. 2008. *Migration Miracle: Faith, Hope, and Meaning on the Undocumented Journey*. Cambridge, Mass.: Harvard University Press.

Hagan, Jacqueline, and Helen Rose Ebaugh. 2003. "Calling Upon the Sacred: Migrants' Use of Religion in the Migration Process." *International Migration Review* 37: 1145–62.

Heidbrink, Lauren. 2014. *Migrant Youth, Transnational Families, and the State*. Philadelphia: University of Pennsylvania Press.

———. 2020. *Migranthood: Youth in a New Era of Deportation*. Stanford: Stanford University Press.

Herrera, Juan. 2016. "Racialized Illegality: The Regulation of Informal Labor Space." *Latino Studies* 14(3): 320–43.

Hondagneu-Sotelo, Pierrette. 2001. *Doméstica: Immigrant Workers Cleaning and Caring in the Shadows of Affluence*. Oakland: University of California Press.

———. 2008. *God's Heart Has No Borders*. Oakland: University of California Press.

Kearney, Michael. 2000. "Transnational Oaxacan Indigenous Identity: The Case of the Mixtecs and Zapotecs." *Identities* 7(2): 173–95.

Lichterman, Paul. 1995. "Beyond the Seesaw Model: Public Commitment in a Culture of Self-Fulfilment." *Sociological Theory* 13(3): 275–300.

Levitt Peggy. 2007. "The Changing Contours of the Immigrant Religious Life." In *Citizenship and Immigrant Incorporation*, edited by Gökçe Yurdakul and Y. Michal Bodemann, 99–122. New York: Palgrave Macmillan.

Ley, David. 2008. "The Immigrant Church as an Urban Service Hub." *Urban Studies* 45(10): 2057–74.

Lopez, David. 2008. "Whither the Flock? The Catholic Church and the Success of Mexicans in America." In *Immigration and Religion in America: Comparative and Historical Perspectives*, edited by Richard Alba, Albert J. Raboteau, and Josh DeWind, 71–88. New York: New York University Press.

Lopez, Floridalma Boj. 2017. "Mobile Archives of Indigeneity: Building *La Comunidad Ixim* Through Organizing in the Maya Diaspora." *Latino Studies* 15: 201–18.

López-Sanders, Laura. 2012. "Bible Belt Immigrants: Latino Religious Incorporation in New Immigrant Destinations." *Latino Studies* 10(1–2): 128–54.

Lorenzen, Matthew. 2017. "The Mixed Motives of Unaccompanied Child Migrants from Central America's Northern Triangle." *Journal on Migration and Human Security* 5(4): 744–67.

Loucky, James. 2000. "Maya in a Modern Metropolis: Establishing New Lives and Livelihoods in Los Angeles." In *The Maya Diaspora: Guatemalan Roots, New American Lives*, edited by James Loucky and Marilyn M. Moors, 214–22. Philadelphia: Temple University Press.

Loucky, James, and Marilyn M. Moors. 2000. *The Maya Diaspora: Guatemalan Roots, New American Lives*. Philadelphia: Temple University Press.

Marti, Gerardo. 2009. "Affinity, Identity, and Transcendence: The Experience of Religious Racial Integration in Diverse Congregations." *Journal for the Scientific Study of Religion* 48(1): 53–68.

Martinez, Isabel. 2019. *Becoming Transnational Youth Workers*. Camden, N.J.: Rutgers University Press.

Menjívar, Cecilia. 2000. *Fragmented Ties: Salvadoran Immigrant Networks in America*. Oakland: University of California Press.

Min, Pyong Gap. 1992. "The Structure and Social Functions of Korean Immigrant Churches in the United States." *International Migration Review* 26(4): 1370–94.

Montes, Verónica. 2013. "The Role of Emotions in the Construction of Masculinity: Guatemalan Migrant Men, Transnational Migration, and Family Relations." *Gender & Society* 27(4): 469–90.

Moya, Jose C. 2005. "Immigrants and Associations: A Global and Historical Perspective." *Journal of Ethnic and Migration Studies* 31(5): 833–64.

Popkin, Eric. 1999. "Guatemalan Mayan Migration to Los Angeles: Constructing Transnational Linkages in the Context of the Settlement Process." *Ethnic and Racial Studies* 22(2): 267–89.

Portes, Alejandro, and Min Zhou. 1993. "The New Second Generation: Segmented Assimilation and Its Variants." *Annals of the American Academy of Political and Social Sciences* 500: 74–96.

Ruehs, Emily M. 2016. "Adventures in El Norte: The Identities and Immigration of Unaccompanied Youth." *Men & Masculinities* 20(3): 364–84.

Schwaller, John Fredrick. 2011. *The History of the Catholic Church in Latin America.* New York: New York University Press.

Suarez-Orozco, Carola, Marcelo M. Suarez-Orozco, and Irina Todorova. 2010. *Learning a New Land: Immigrant Students in American Society.* Cambridge, Mass.: Belknap Press.

Treitler, Vilna Bashi. 2015. "Social Agency and White Supremacy in Immigration Studies," *Sociology of Race and Ethnicity* 1(1): 153–65.

U.S. Census Bureau. 2016. "Hispanic or Latino Origin by Specific Origin. American Community Survey 1-year Estimates." Washington, DC. www.census.gov.

Valdez, Zulema, and Tanya Golash-Boza. 2017. "U.S. Racial and Ethnic Relations in the Twenty-First Century." *Ethnic and Racial Studies* 40(13): 2181–209.

Vanthuyne, Karine. 2009. "Becoming Maya? The Politics and Pragmatics of 'Being Indigenous' in Postgenocide Guatemala." *Political and Legal Anthropology Review* 32(2): 195–217.

Wellmeier, Nancy. 1998. "Santa Eulalia's People in Exile: Maya Religion, Culture, and Identity in Los Angeles." In *Gatherings in Diaspora: Religious Communities and the New Immigration,* edited by R. Warner and J. Wittner, 97–122. Philadelphia: Temple University Press.

Wuthnow, Robert. 1994. *Sharing the Journey: Support Groups and America's New Quest for Community.* New York: Free Press.

Zelizer, Viviana. 1985. *Pricing the Priceless Child: Changing Social Values of Children.* Princeton: Princeton University Press.

Zhou, Min, and Carl Bankston. 1998. *Growing Up American: How Vietnamese Children Adapt to Life in the United States.* New York: Russell Sage Foundation.

CHAPTER 2

Resilience in the Time of a Pandemic

COVID-19, LGBTQ+ Latinx Activism, and the Politics of Belonging

NOLAN KLINE, ANDRÉS ACOSTA, CHRISTOPHER J. CUEVAS,
AND MARCO ANTONIO QUIROGA

Introduction

The March 2020 meeting of the Contigo Fund's Community Advisory Board was unlike past meetings.[1] Instead of gathering at the LGBTQ+ Center of Orlando—one of the city's most recognized LGBTQ+ social service organizations—members logged onto a virtual meeting hosted through video conferencing software and greeted one another through screens while sitting in their respective homes. "The hardest part of all of this is not being able to hug one another," one member lamented as others nodded in agreement. The shift to the online meeting for the Contigo Fund was one of necessity, rather than convenience, as cases of COVID-19 were increasing and recently issued guidelines from the U.S. Center for Disease Control and Prevention (CDC) suggested limiting groups of ten or more people in public spaces. "We have to remember that the work continues," co-author Marco Antonio Quiroga, the Executive Director of Contigo Fund, added. "These are going to be challenging times, but the movement keeps going."

The Contigo Fund is the largest LGBTQ+ philanthropic organization in the U.S. South, and it is the only philanthropic organization that funds matters focused on LGBTQ+ Latinx populations. The organization emerged after the June 12, 2016, Pulse Nightclub shooting, which at the time was the deadliest mass shooting in U.S. history and disproportionately impacted LGBTQ+

people of color. The violence occurred during Pulse's Latin night, and in the aftermath of the tragedy, a number of local activists called attention to the fact that there were deep inequalities in Orlando's LGBTQ+ population, which was reflected in the dearth of social services and support spaces for people with intersecting LGBTQ+ and Latinx identities. To address these inequalities, Contigo emerged as part of an ongoing social justice movement squarely focused on advancing the rights and representation in the leadership of LGBTQ+ Latinx individuals and all LGBTQ+ people of color. The 2020 COVID-19 pandemic and its concomitant challenges posed potential threats to this movement, but as we describe in this chapter, organizations that emerged after the Pulse tragedy continued their intersectional social justice aims. In this chapter, we show how two organizations that emerged after Pulse—the Contigo Fund and QLatinx—sustained their social justice work during the COVID-19 pandemic, demonstrating that despite a global public health crisis, these organizations worked to advance a politics of belonging for all LGBTQ+ people of color. Examining these organizations' work through scholarship on political efforts to assert Latinx immigrants' "undeservingness" to social services, we argue that Contigo Fund and QLatinx continue to build an oppositional politics of belonging during the pandemic.

Background: Intersectional Social Justice Organizing in Orlando

Social scientists attentive to Latinx resistance and resilience in the US have emphasized how Latinx social movements have worked to assert rights and entitlements for marginalized subsets of Latinx groups, particularly those with precarious immigration statuses (Lauby 2016; De la Torre and Germano 2014; Winders 2011; Pallares and Flores-González 2010). However, there is insufficient scholarship on Latinx social movements that focus on individuals with multiple intersecting identities (Terriquez 2015), such as those who are Latinx and LGBTQ+. As critical race scholar Kimberlé Crenshaw (1991, 1989) asserts, intersectionality is the way in which multiple identities and social structures converge to create unique forms of oppression and privilege. For example, Crenshaw (1989) underscores how for Black women in the United States, their social subjugation is rooted in sexism *and* racism, resulting in interlocking forms of marginalization. Such forms of oppression require scholarly attention that is attentive to the unique experiences of people at the intersection of multiple marginalized social locations. In this chapter, we focus on the social justice movement attentive to the intersectional identities of LGBTQ+ Latinx populations that emerged in Orlando after the Pulse shooting. We specifically focus on the COVID-19 emergency to not only demonstrate the need for an intersectional focus on Latinx resilience but also demonstrate how social justice organizations that emerged after the Pulse shooting have worked to advance their goals during a global health crisis.

The resilience we describe here during the COVID-19 pandemic is particularly noteworthy because of how health concerns have historically been used to frame political and legal exclusions of subsets of LGBTQ+ populations, such as individuals living with HIV, and Latinx populations, particularly Latinx immigrants. For example, U.S. immigration policies have historically restricted immigration into the country based on HIV status, a practice that has long codified discrimination against LGBTQ+ people under the guise of controlling a communicable disease epidemic (Institute of Medicine 2011). Further, the United States has a long history of conflating race, health, and immigration, and subsets of Latinx populations—specifically Latinx immigrants—have historically been excluded from various social programs based on their immigration status (Fairchild 2004). This has contributed to the widespread characterization of undocumented Latinx immigrants as being "undeserving" of social services (Willen 2012; Marrow 2012).

During the COVID-19 pandemic, lawmakers perpetuated notions of immigrants as undeserving of social benefits through creating particular "deservingness projects" (Kline 2019), or codifying the moral judgments of undeservingness into policy by creating explicit exclusions. These included prohibiting some immigrants from receiving economic relief intended to mitigate the consequences of COVID-19. The Contigo Fund and QLatinx combated these deservingness projects through engaging in an oppositional politics of deservingness and belonging, which specifically involved creating unique forms of COVID-19-related relief that prioritized populations with intersecting LGBTQ+ and Latinx identities.

Overall, efforts to combat deservingness projects and advance the intersectional aims of the LGBTQ+ Latinx movement in Orlando constitute what Yuval-Davis refers to as "political projects aimed at constructing belonging" (2006, 197). As Yuval-Davis explains, the politics of belonging include attention to specific social locations and contesting hegemonic power structures that reproduce boundaries of belonging meant to perpetuate an "us" or "them" binary (2006, 205). During the COVID-19 crisis, both QLatinx and the Contigo Fund specifically engaged in programs meant to advance an intersectional politics of belonging that combated forms of perpetuating divisions based on race, sex, gender expression or identity, sexual orientation, and immigration status. In doing so, the Contigo Fund and QLatinx not only responded to aggressive efforts to perpetuate notions of undeservingness to COVID-19 relief for some Latinx individuals, but also advanced their agendas of intersectional belonging by putting forward a politics of deservingness to pandemic-related relief. To do this, the organizations specifically emphasized the relationship between COVID-19 and political vulnerability linked to labor exploitation, immigration status, and governmental exclusions from pandemic-related relief efforts.

Orlando, Florida, Context

Orlando is the third most populated metropolitan area in Florida (U.S. Census Bureau, 2019a) and is known globally for its amusement parks. The area's economy hinges on labor in the hospitality, service, and tourism industries, and these jobs fail to sufficiently provide a living wage for workers. The area consistently tops lists of cities lacking affordable housing, ranking number one in the country in 2018 and number seven in 2020 (National Low Income Housing Association 2020). Low wages merge with the high cost of housing to create widespread economic precarity in the shadow of an amusement park colloquially known as the "happiest place on earth." This economic insecurity is particularly acute among some of the most marginalized populations in Orlando, particularly Latinx and LGBTQ+ individuals, and individuals at the intersection of those social locations.

Approximately 31 percent of Orlando's population identifies as Latinx (United States Census Bureau 2019b), and those residents represent a diversity of immigration statuses and life experiences. Central Florida's agricultural economy has historically played a role in Latinx migration to the region as migrant and seasonal farmworkers from Latin America moved to the Orlando area to engage in farmwork and continue to do so (Kline 2010). Additionally, the area's Puerto Rican population grew throughout the 1970s as a result of an economic downturn in Puerto Rico and the opening of Walt Disney World theme park, which inspired real estate investment and attractive retirement options for middle-class Puerto Ricans looking to relocate from the island or elsewhere on the mainland United States (Silver and Velez 2017; Duany and Rodriguez-Santos). Puerto Rican migration to Central Florida continued in the 1980s, and between 1990 and 2000, the Puerto Rican population in the area grew by 142 percent, resulting in Orlando having the largest number of Puerto Rican residents in Florida (Duany and Rodriguez 2006). Following Hurricanes Maria and Irma, the Puerto Rican population in Central Florida continued to increase, and the Orlando metropolitan area has become home to the second-largest Puerto Rican community in the United States (Cotto and Chen 2019).

In addition to a sizeable Latinx population, Orlando is also home to a considerable LGBTQ+ population and hosts a number of LGBTQ+ vacation festivals. The city ranks twentieth among municipalities with the largest percentage of LGBTQ+ residents (Newport and Gates 2015) and is the site of several LGBTQ+-themed events at Walt Disney World and Universal Studios, drawing international visitors annually. Despite the large Latinx and LGBTQ+ populations, Orlando's network of social service providers focused on LGBTQ+ and Latinx populations had historically overlooked the unique needs of individuals with intersecting LGBTQ+ Latinx identities (Kline 2020b). This omission from local organizations was particularly acute following the attack at the Pulse Nightclub.

At 2:02 a.m. on June 12, 2016, a shooter entered Pulse and killed 49 individuals and injured fifty-three others. In the aftermath of the shooting, the state's elected officials, including Governor Rick Scott and Attorney General Pam Bondi, failed to acknowledge that the shooting happened at a gay bar and on Latin night—a political moment of erasure and silencing of the unique identities among those most impacted (Kline and Cuevas 2018). Such silence among state government leaders reflected widespread community erasure of individuals with intersecting LGBTQ+ and Latinx identities that signaled to newly emerging social justice organizations, like QLatinx and the Contigo Fund, a sustained need to advocate for and advance the rights of LGBTQ+ people of color.

QLatinx is "a grassroots racial, social, and gender justice organization dedicated to the advancement and empowerment of Central Florida's LGBTQ+ Latinx community" (QLatinx 2020). Co-author Christopher J. Cuevas served as the Executive Director from the organization's founding until October of 2020, and oversaw the numerous initiatives and events that QLatinx organizes that are related to community-building, immigration advocacy, health equity, individual empowerment, and leadership training. Leaders from QLatinx host several community and organizational trainings on topics such as sexuality and gender diversity, social inequality, interpersonal and state violence, privilege, and intersectionality. QLatinx leadership routinely collaborates with local LGBTQ+ and Latinx-focused organizations to advance social, economic, and racial justice initiatives.

Like QLatinx, Contigo formed after the Pulse shooting and serves to "fund, strengthen and empower existing agencies and emerging ones working to improve the lives of LGBTQ and Latinx individuals, immigrants, and people of color in Central Florida" (Contigo Fund n.d.). Focusing on the root causes of oppression, Contigo works to eradicate all forms of discrimination based on race, sex, gender identity and expression, sexual orientation, religion, ability, and other socially-constructed notions of difference. With a focus on LGBTQ+ Latinx populations, the Contigo Fund works to support initiatives that can correct the consequences of systemic and institutionalized inequalities that disproportionately harm people with intersecting marginalized identities. Together, these two organizations represent leading efforts in Orlando to advance a politics of belonging that centers on the lives of all LGBTQ+ people of color. These populations were particularly vulnerable during the COVID-19 crisis, which at the time of this writing, continues to unfold.

COVID-19 Urgency

In December of 2019, health officials in China reported the first case of a novel coronavirus, severe acute respiratory syndrome coronavirus 2 (SARS-CoV-2), which causes COVID-19 (Burke et al 2020). The first case of COVID-19 in the United States was detected on January 19, 2020 (Holshue et al. 2020), and by March 11, the World Health Organization declared COVID-19 a pandemic (World Health Organization 2020). The U.S. response to the pandemic comprised a patchwork of federal, state, and local government actions. While some states issued specific public health measures aimed to reduce the spread of COVID-19, others took little action, resulting in conflicting approaches to containing the virus and different incidence rates across the country. Overall, the federal and state responses to COVID-19 were inconsistent and erratic, and efforts to control the virus's spread depended on specific state contexts.

As the pandemic progressed, economic consequences unfolded, including employers moving their work to remote settings and reducing their workforce. In response, congressional leaders passed legislation to provide monetary relief during the pandemic through the Coronavirus Aid, Relief, and Economic Security Act (CARES), which included an economic stimulus check of a maximum of $1,200 per person. The CARES Act included the first of three waves of stimulus checks sent out at the time of writing this chapter, and the legislation specifically excluded undocumented individuals and individuals living in households with undocumented family members (Peñaloza 2020). This exclusion from an economic relief is an extension of long-standing exclusions and a pandemic-related deservingness project.

In Florida, the deservingness projects and inconsistent responses to the pandemic at the national level were reproduced at a state level, resulting in policy tensions between the state and local governments. Counties and municipalities led the public health prevention efforts to reduce virus transmission while state leaders delayed action. For example, Orange County and the City of Orlando initiated curfews, ordered certain public spaces closed, and implemented mandatory social distancing policies before the state began taking needed precautions. News media, local elected officials, and activists attentive to the state's negligence during the pandemic drew attention to the questionable actions among state leaders, including the termination of the employee responsible for the state's publicly available map tracking COVID-19 infections (Wamsley 2020) and excessive delays and challenges in responding to unemployment claims (Iacurci 2020). Florida Governor Ron DeSantis lifted statewide restrictions on gathering in public spaces as a way to "reopen the economy" and new COVID-19 cases in Florida grew exponentially, making Florida an epicenter of U.S. infections by July of 2020. In 2021, the legislature passed and DeSantis signed into law preemption policies prohibiting local governments from enforcing local mask mandates. The political failings during the pandemic, however, extended beyond state negligence and refusal to protect public health in order to privilege economic interests. Indeed, the COVID-19 crisis further underscored long-standing social and health-related vulnerabilities among LGBTQ+ populations, people of color, and individuals at the intersection of those identities, and how such populations were subjected to a politics of undeservingness to relief.

LGBTQ+ individuals experience several social and health-related vulnerabilities that have been exacerbated by the COVID-19 pandemic. These vulnerabilities include economic inequality, housing insecurity, and discrimination, all of which were potentially aggravated during the COVID-19 pandemic (Institute of Medicine 2011; Kline 2020). Further, the COVID-19 pandemic began prior to the June 15, 2020, Supreme Court decision regarding Title VII workplace protections—the decision that effectively determined LGBTQ+ people could not be fired because of their sexual orientation, spotlighting the precarious employment situation for LGBTQ+ individuals. Notably, despite the Supreme Court's determination, the decision does not reach all LGBTQ+ populations since it only applies to employers with fifteen or more employees. This labor-related precarity was particularly acute during the COVID-19 pandemic as employers closed or reduced their staffing needs.

Similar to LGBTQ+ populations, Latinx and other people of color experience numerous social and health-related vulnerabilities that can be aggravated during the pandemic. Considerable scholarship has shown how social, political, and economic inequalities converge to directly shape health outcomes for people of color in the United States (Institute of Medicine 2003), and larger structural factors are often obfuscated by capitalist logics of self-sufficiency and individual responsibility (O'Daniel 2008; Morgen 2001). Existing social and political determinants of health worsened during COVID-19 as people of color are more likely than their white counterparts to engage in work that is considered essential or engage in work with limited work-at-home flexibility (Economic Policy Institute 2020), therefore increasing their likelihood of exposure to COVID-19. This is certainly the case in Central Florida, and perhaps most notably among Latinx migrant farmworkers, who are a particularly vulnerable subset of Latinx populations because of the occupational health hazards associated with agricultural labor and due to their precarious immigration statuses.

Like other immigrant groups, Latinx migrant and seasonal farmworkers are often excluded from a number of health programs because of their immigration status, lack of employer-provided insurance, and low wages that constrain their ability to purchase health insurance in the U.S. market-based medical system (Rylko-Bauer and Famer 2002). Moreover, Latinx farmworkers' health-related vulnerabilities are particularly exacerbated by the COVID-19 pandemic since agricultural work was considered an essential service and, therefore, continued during the pandemic without a temporary cessation. This meant that farmworker populations were continually working in settings where they were unable to socially distance, potentially increasing their risk of COVID-19 transmission. Agricultural labor, then, is a root cause of health inequality for Latinx farmworkers in the United States and Central Florida (Quesada, Hart, and Bourgois 2011). Political leaders, however, often frame Latinx immigrant and migrant groups, including migrant and seasonal farmworkers, as "drains" on health services, and immigrants are scapegoated for numerous health problems, including novel infectious diseases (Ransford, Carrillo, and Rivera 2010; Schoch-Spana et al. 2010; Eichelberger 2007). The COVID-19 pandemic was no exception to the ways in which immigrants have often been blamed for health concerns, as Florida Governor Ron DeSantis specifically blamed "Hispanic workers" for an increase in COVID-19 incidence following the state's economic reopening, which he championed (Luscombe 2020).

People who are both LGBTQ+ and Latinx experience especially heightened risks during COVID-19 because of their multiple social locations (Kline 2020b). For example, LGBTQ+ Latinx populations with precarious immigration statuses, such as those who are undocuqueer, encounter multiple forms of oppression based on their immigration status, race, ethnicity, and sexual orientation or gender expression. Moreover, undocumented immigrants, including undocumented students, have been excluded from federal relief efforts related to COVID-19, which may complicate already precarious employment for undocumented LGBTQ+ populations and further aggravate food insecurity, housing precarity, and the ability to adhere to medication regimens such as pre-exposure prophylaxis (PrEP; Kline 2020a). Such denials reflect ongoing exclusions from social services for undocumented immigrants that structure sweeping inequalities and perpetuate notions of undocumented immigrants as being "undeserving" of social services. These intersecting and potentially hidden vulnerabilities compelled QLatinx and Contigo Fund to create forms of relief for the most marginalized Latinx populations. In doing so, the organizations combated narratives of undeservingness and directly resisted COVID-19 related deservingness projects.

Resilience During a Pandemic
Financial Assistance and Subverting Bureaucratic Violence

As a result of the disproportionate impact of COVID-19 on people with intersecting LGBTQ+ Latinx identities, the Contigo Fund and QLatinx immediately organized a COVID-19 relief fund for LGBTQ+ Latinx populations. The fund was guided by an assessment with 228 respondents that QLatinx led; findings from the assessment revealed significant food insecurity and housing stability concerns, as 94 percent of respondents demonstrated some type of food insecurity indicator and 80 percent reported an inability to pay their rent or mortgage (Norman and Cuevas 2020). Once the fund launched, it raised over $30,000 in 82 days, and QLatinx and the Contigo Fund primarily oversaw the process for applying for and distributing funds. Moreover, the LGBTQ+ fund was available to all people who needed assistance regardless of immigration status. This was particularly important since undocumented immigrants are ineligible for public assistance programs like unemployment benefits, and Deferred Action for Childhood Arrivals (DACA) recipients and some authorized immigrants may fear using public benefits (Selyukh 2020). As part of the application process, Contigo and QLatinx leaders provided instructions in English, Spanish, Haitian Creole, Portuguese, and Vietnamese—languages that are most commonly spoken in Orlando and reflect the area's diverse immigrant population. The application itself was designed to be intentionally simple to complete as a way to reduce potential barriers to relief for applicants.

In addition to the relief fund, Contigo also set aside approximately $50,000 of its total $200,000 grantmaking budget in 2020 to be used as a rapid response grant to aid organizations during the COVID-19 pandemic. Further, the organization applied for—and secured—additional funds to directly disperse to individuals with the most need. The funds came from philanthropic foundations to which co-authors Acosta, Kline, and Quiroga collaboratively applied. These efforts directly responded to the exclusions that accompany state-created forms of relief, such as explicit limitations on eligibility, as in the case of stimulus checks, or unreliability, as demonstrated by the state of Florida's employment assistance failures.

Social scientists attentive to the mechanics of the state and its functions have used the term "legal violence" to describe the harms resulting from exclusionary policies that target a specific group (Menjívar and Abrego 2012; Abrego and Menjívar 2011). Anthropologist Carina Heckert has extended this idea through her concept of "bureaucratic violence" to describe how even if a policy does not target a group, bureaucratic practices can nevertheless create harm (2020, 34). This can occur through barriers that Heide Castañeda calls "bureaucratic disentitlement" (2019), including complicated paperwork in a language inaccessible to an applicant, obstinate or unhelpful staff, or a layer of policies and procedures that hinder successful completion for people who are precariously documented. As part of the LGBTQ+ relief fund and through rapid response grants, the Contigo Fund and QLatinx directly resisted the types of bureaucratic violence that the state perpetuated. More specifically, they created an oppositional politics of belonging through creating accessible forms of assistance that subverted typical processes associated with bureaucratic violence.

Advancing a Politics of Belonging by Supporting the Black Lives Matter Movement

As the pandemic continued, Contigo and QLatinx found ways to meaningfully move their programmatic efforts online. For example, co-author Christopher J. Cuevas has engaged in online discussions about transgender, gender nonconforming, and nonbinary acceptance, rights, and protections with Equality Florida—a statewide nonprofit organization that works to advance LGBTQ+ interests broadly. Further, QLatinx hosted an event to discuss the findings of the organization's gender equity survey and underscore needed efforts to improve gender equity in LGBTQ+ organizations throughout Central Florida. The report specifically highlighted particular attention to an ongoing need for welcoming and affirming spaces for LGBTQ+ people of color—particularly transgender women of color—and lack of representation of LGBTQ+ people of color in leadership positions among LGBTQ+ organizations in Central Florida. Documenting such needs is a critical aspect of QLatinx's work and informs specific advocacy, training, and organizational action. QLatinx also hosted mindfulness and wellness programs virtually, including yoga and meditation sessions, a digital storytelling project that featured how members cared for themselves during the pandemic, and email messages to promote mindfulness and meditative practice.

The Contigo Fund and QLatinx's efforts occurred alongside other local LGBTQ+ organizations shifting their work online during the pandemic. For example, the organization that runs the annual LGBTQ+ pride event hosted a series of "Stay in with Pride" virtual events, and one organization that focuses on LGBTQ+ and HIV advocacy hosted a number of online social events including Drag Queen Bingo. The unique focus on QLatinx and the Contigo Fund's efforts, however, was their emphasis on LGBTQ+ people of color. This emphasis continued during the Black Lives Matter marches and protests that mounted during the pandemic.

The 2020 Black Lives Matter protests that continue as of writing this chapter began shortly after a Minneapolis police officer murdered George Floyd, a Black man who was allegedly attempting to use a counterfeit $20 bill at a grocery store. Floyd's death resulted in global protests, and several social justice organizations—including the African American Policy Forum—emphasized that just two months prior, Louisville Metro Police Department officers had shot and killed Breonna Taylor, a Black woman, whose home officers illegally entered (Oppel and Taylor 2020). Earlier in the year, the death of Ahmaud Arbery, who, in February of 2020, was killed while jogging attracted national attention. Arbery's murderers, a white man and his son, chased the twenty-five-year-old from a pickup truck until finally gunning him down on a suburban road (Fausset 2021). As organizations like QLatinx and the Contigo Fund emphasized, Floyd, Taylor, and Arbery's deaths are part of an overall constellation of risk and murder for vulnerable Black populations, particularly Black LGBTQ+ populations. Nevertheless, murders of LGBTQ+ people of color may go without similar attention. For example, Tony McDade, a Black trans-masculine person who was killed by Tallahassee

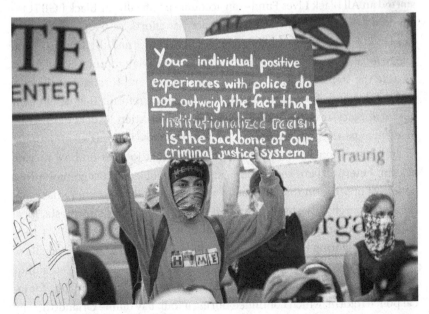

FIGURE 2.1   A protestor at a Black Lives Matter march in Orlando, Florida. Photo courtesy of J. D. Casto.

police on May 27, 2020, garnered considerably less national media attention than other murders that occurred in the same period of time, and a Mother Jones story on McDade's murder referred to his death as "the police killing you probably didn't hear about" (Thompson 2020).

In 2020, the Human Rights Campaign tracked the murder of forty-four transgender or gender nonconforming individuals, many of whom were people of color, noting that 2020 was the deadliest year since HRC began tracking transgender murders (Human Rights Campaign 2020). Indeed, LGBTQ+ people of color are more likely than any other population in the United States to be victims of hate crime violence (Park and Mykhyalyshyn 2016; Federal Bureau of Investigation 2015). Further, despite an increase in federal legal protections, hate crimes against LGBTQ+ people have increased in the past decade, and the most common type of violence perpetrated against LGBTQ populations is shooting (National Coalition of Anti-Violence Programs 2017). As part of their ongoing COVID-19 resistance efforts, QLatinx and the Contigo Fund specifically emphasized the unique vulnerabilities of LGBTQ+ people of color through fundraising efforts and public projects.

When the 2020 Black Lives Matter Protests began, the Contigo Fund started an All Black Lives Fund—an account specifically for Black LGBTQ+-led organizations designed to support activist efforts for people identifying as LGBTQ+ and Black. Further, leaders of QLatinx and the Contigo Fund joined local LGBTQ+ Black leaders at Black Lives Matter protests and rallies outside the steps of Orlando's City Hall building and throughout the city, making demands for police reform and economic reforms that would benefit local Black residents. Local LGBTQ+ organization leaders of QLatinx aided in organizing the rallies. This effort represented QLatinx's commitment to an intersectional social justice movement that focuses on how racism, sexism, heterosexism, xenophobia, and transphobia share a common root source of oppression that ultimately works to sustain white supremacy and heteropatriarchy. By showing up and aiding in leading the protests, local leaders demonstrated an overall politics of belonging for all LGBTQ+ people of color. During the protests, local officers assaulted LGBTQ+ people of color and dispersed tear gas into crowds, including crowds where co-author Christopher J. Cuevas was present. These actions amplified demands for local police reform, which continued during a four-day online Orlando Strong Symposium that the Contigo Fund organized.

The Orlando Strong Symposium

The Contigo Fund and QLatinx's commitment to a politics of belonging and amplifying the unique social locations of LGBTQ+ people of color was an integral component of the 2020 Orlando Strong Symposium. The symposium was a four-day event in June of 2020 that brought together local elected officials, nonprofit organization leaders and service providers, philanthropic organizations and small business leaders, and local community activists to discuss COVID-19 and racial inequality. All of the events were held online, and leaders from QLatinx and community board members of the Contigo Fund served as moderators who consistently referred back to addressing the needs of the most marginalized LGBTQ+ populations at the intersection of being LGBTQ+ and identifying as a person of color. For example, in a panel with local service providers, moderators asked for ways that cultural competency efforts could better understand the specific needs of Black LGBTQ+ individuals, particularly Black trans women. From this dialogue, leaders in local organizations described ways that they were making their organizations increasingly inclusive and responsive to the experiences of LGBTQ+ people of color. One leader of a nonprofit organization that works with LGBTQ+ youth specifically described ending a program in which law enforcement officers visit their organization for conversations with youth, recognizing "that not all the youth are comfortable with police," and noting the problematic nature of inviting law enforcement into what is designated to be a safe space for LGBTQ+ youth, including those who are also people of color.

Similarly, during conversations with elected officials and leaders in law enforcement, including local county sheriffs and chief of police, moderators asked for commitments to supporting LGBTQ+ people of color. Moderators challenged law enforcement agency leaders and Orlando Mayor Buddy Dyer by directly asking if they supported initiatives to reallocate funds from police to other services—an effort colloquially referred to as "defunding the police." Dyer invited the symposium attendees to express their interests at a local budget meeting, and as of writing this chapter, the Contigo Fund and QLatinx leaders continue to advocate for the reallocation of city funds. Further, moderators called on leaders in local law enforcement to better represent all LGBTQ+ people in their community liaison positions.

The City of Orlando Police Department and the Orange County Sheriff's Office have LGBTQ+ liaisons: officers who are intended to serve as intermediaries between law enforcement agencies and specific community groups. The City of Orlando also provides LGBTQ+ Safe Place training to local businesses—a program in which local businesses agree to assist LGBTQ+ people who are being victimized and display that commitment through a decal. These programs may be viewed as ways of breaking down anti-LGBTQ+ discrimination, but they do not respond to a history of racialized policing or ways in which police have antagonized LGBTQ+ individuals, undocumented immigrants, people of color, and individuals at the intersection of those identities. Accordingly, during the symposium, Contigo Fund moderators asked law enforcement agency leaders to be more inclusive of LGBTQ+ people of color, including the most marginalized and likely to be victimized: Black trans women. This call for greater representation of all of Orlando's LGBTQ+ community was particularly important as local law enforcement officers misgendered a twenty-seven-year-old transgender woman, Sasha Garden, who was murdered in 2018 (Wolf and Cordeiro, 2018). Officers seemed to deliberately misgender Garden by referring to her as a "man in a wig" when reporting the death, and to local leaders, her death underscored not only the disproportionate risk of violence faced by transgender people of color but the overall lack of respect from law enforcement. The symposium, therefore, provided an opportunity to emphasize that although local law enforcement agencies have established LGBTQ+ liaison positions, they have yet to fully and meaningfully respond to all of Orlando's LGBTQ+ populations.

Additionally, as part of the Orlando Strong symposium, a group of undocuqueer leaders, including co-author Marco Antonio Quiroga, came together as a panel to emphasize the unique vulnerabilities of people at the intersection of being undocumented, LGBTQ+, and a person of color. These multiple overlapping identities create unique forms of exclusion and oppression during COVID-19, particularly since undocumented immigrants were excluded from federal relief efforts. As the panel moderator succinctly put it when referring to essential workers with precarious immigration statuses, "they're the DACAmented doctors and nurses treating people with COVID; they're farmworkers, and they're the people excluded from federal aid." Moreover, as an undocuqueer panelist who works with LGBTQ+ farmworker groups noted, COVID-19 has complicated family relationships for some undocuqueer youth who are staying at home more as a result of COVID-19-related social distancing and may not feel able to be out to family members. As part of the panel, Quiroga noted the ironies of undocumented immigrants aiding in "reopening" the U.S. economy as workers in essential economic services and domestic labor, particularly under the Trump administration, which embraced notoriously hostile immigration policies. As Quiroga noted, "[Trump] is temporary; and our community is a strong and resilient community."

Challenges: The Staying Power of White Supremacy and a Currency of "Wokeness?"

Overall, the 2020 Orlando Strong symposium, which occurred during the COVID-19 pandemic and during a moment of heightened awareness of the disproportionate number of people of color who die from police officer violence, asserted a politics of belonging for LGBTQ+ people of color in Orlando and addressed continued forms of exclusion represented in law enforcement agencies. Nevertheless, there are challenges in doing this work. For example, in his efforts to assert the needs of LGBTQ+ people of color during the "dual pandemic" of COVID-19 and police brutality, co-author Marco Antonio Quiroga witnessed the staying power of white supremacy through some local LGBTQ+ leaders questioning the value of focusing on Black LGBTQ+ people, specifically during the symposium and fundraising efforts. For Quiroga, as a local leader with intersecting Latinx, Queer, and undocumented identities, such pushback demonstrated not only the power of white fragility, but also the necessity to do year-round education about collective liberation.

Similarly, co-author Cuevas witnessed a superficial commitment to racial justice in some Queer-organizing spaces, observing that leaders and organizations who never had a meaningful investment in racial equity suddenly made statements in support of Black lives. Rather than representing a transformative paradigmatic and political shift, such statements instead revealed how some organizations and leaders felt a need to show how they engaged in social justice matters by demonstrating an understanding of racial inequality and, more generally, an organizational "wokeness." This was reflected in part by some organizations being slow to respond with statements about the deaths of George Floyd, Breonna Taylor, Ahmaud Arbery, and Tony McDade, while others were noncommittal in using language unapologetically supporting Black lives. Hesitance and lack of commitment to language that condemns police violence against Black people indicates that some organizations fail to build a Queer social justice agenda from a Black, indigenous, and person of color (BIPOC) lens. Further, these factors suggest how some organizations operate within a larger social justice economy and that making statements about Black lives was a necessity to garner more social justice capital, or build what we call here "a currency of wokeness." In this respect, statements from some social justice organizations can be part and parcel of the residue of white supremacy in social justice organizing, much like other problematic efforts to advance inclusion in social justice spaces that may ultimately result in tokenizing identities. Superficial commitments may also create fissures between groups and undermine broader goals to advance an intersectional politics of belonging.

A Movement Doesn't Stop During a Pandemic

Overall, Contigo Fund's and QLatinx's work during COVID-19 responds to critical failures of the state that are perpetuated by systematic exclusions and deservingness projects. Their efforts constitute a specific political assertion of belonging by creating a fund accessible to all immigrants regardless of immigration status (a direct response to the formal exclusions created through the CARES Act) and broader efforts to assert how all LGBTQ+ people of color belong to the broader LGBTQ+ community in Orlando. The organizations' work during the pandemic demonstrates how despite a global public health crisis, both organizations continued sustained attention to advancing intersectional social justice.

COVID-19 exacerbated existing structural circumstances that contribute to inequalities among LGBTQ+ people of color. Overall, mobilizing financial resources, shifting programming online, and supporting the ongoing Black Lives Matter initiatives were ways to continue advancing an intersectional social justice movement in Orlando that focuses on LGBTQ+ Latinx individuals and all LGBTQ+ people of color. The examples we have provided here demonstrate how despite the COVID-19 pandemic, the ongoing intersectional social justice movement born out of the Pulse tragedy did not slow. Instead, it continued by combating deservingness projects related to COVID-19 that manifested in exclusions from specific types of federal relief and continuing to uplift and support efforts to advance social justice and racial equity, such as the Black Lives Matter movement.

The political projects of belonging that the Contigo Fund and QLatinx engage in highlight the everyday work of diverse groups of Latinx individuals to assert and negotiate belonging. The practices identified here demonstrate the sustained commitment these and other Orlando-based organizations have made to resist efforts to perpetuate notions of difference based on race, sex, gender identity or expression, sexual orientation, and immigration status.

Note

1.   This chapter is the result of ongoing ethnographic fieldwork supported by the National Science Foundation (Award Number 1918247).

References

Abrego, Leisy J., and Cecilia Menjívar. 2011. "Immigrant Latina Mothers as Targets of Legal Violence." *International Journal of Sociology of the Family* 37(1): 9–26.

Burke, Rachel M. 2020. "Active Monitoring of Persons Exposed to Patients with Confirmed COVID-19—United States, January–February 2020." *MMWR. Morbidity and Mortality Weekly Report* 69.

Castañeda, Heide. 2019. *Borders of Belonging: Struggle and Solidarity in Mixed-Status Immigrant Families.* Stanford: Stanford University Press.

Contigo Fund. n.d. "Who We Are." Accessed June 30, 2020. http://contigofund.org/en/who-we-are/.

Cotto, Ingrid, and Adelaide Chen 2019. "Census Bureau: 'Puerto Rican Population in Orange, Osceola Jumps 12.5% after Hurricane Maria.'" *Orlando Sentinel.* September 27, 2019. www.orlandosentinel.com/news/florida/os-ne-census-florida-puerto-rico-population-increase-20190927-lx3i6rxghzhehhf3md6x7hgfmu-story.html.

Crenshaw, Kimberlé. 1989. "Demarginalizing the Intersection of Race and Sex: A Black Feminist Critique of Antidiscrimination Doctrine, Feminist Theory and Antiracist Politics." *University of Chicago Legal Forum* 139.

———. 1991. "Mapping the Margins: Intersectionality, Identity Politics, and Violence Against Women of Color." *Stanford Law Review* 43: 1241.

De la Torre, Pedro, and Roy Germano. 2014. "Out of the Shadows: DREAMer Identity in the Immigrant Youth Movement." *Latino Studies* 12(3): 449–67.

Duany, Jorge, and Félix V. Matos Rodríguez. 2006. *Puerto Ricans in Orlando and Central Florida.* New York: Centro de Estudios Puertorriqueños, Hunter College.

Economic Policy Institute. 2020. "Not Everybody Can Work from Home: Black and Hispanic Workers Are Much Less Likely to Be Able to Telework." Accessed June 30, 2020. www.epi.org/blog/black-and-hispanic-workers-are-much-less-likely-to-be-able-to-work-from-home/.

Eichelberger, Laura. 2007. "SARS and New York's Chinatown: The Politics of Risk and Blame During an Epidemic of Fear." *Social Science & Medicine* 65(6): 1284–95.

Fairchild, Amy L. 2004. "Policies of Inclusion: Immigrants, Disease, Dependency, and American Immigration Policy at the Dawn and Dusk of the 20th Century." *American Journal of Public Health* 94(4): 528–39.

Fausset, Richard. 2021. "What We Know About the Shooting Death of Ahmaud Arbery." *New York Times.* July 13, 2021. www.nytimes.com/article/ahmaud-arbery -shooting-georgia.html.

Federal Bureau of Investigation. 2015. "Hate Crime Statistics." https://ucr.fbi.gov/hate -crime/2015/topic-pages/victims_final.

Holshue, Michelle L., Chas DeBolt, Scott Lindquist, Kathy H. Lofy, John Wiesman, Hollianne Bruce, and Christopher Spitters. 2020. "First Case of 2019 Novel Coronavirus in the United States." *New England Journal of Medicine* 382: 929–36.

Heckert, Carina. 2020. "The Bureaucratic Violence of the Health Care System for Pregnant Immigrants on the United States-Mexico Border." *Human Organization* 79(1): 33–42.

Iacurci, Greg. "Florida Unemployment Pay Drama Rages on as Residents Face Evictions." *CNBC.* May 12, 2020. www.cnbc.com/2020/05/12/florida-unemployment -benefits-delayed-as-residents-face-eviction.html.

Institute of Medicine. 2011. *The Health of Lesbian, Gay, Bisexual, and Transgender People: Building a Foundation for Better Understanding.* Washington, DC: National Academies Press.

Kline, Nolan. 2010. "Disparate Power and Disparate Resources: Collaboration Between Faith-Based and Activist Organizations for Central Florida Farmworkers." *Napa Bulletin* 33(1): 126–42.

———. 2019. "When Deservingness Policies Converge: U.S. Immigration Enforcement, Health Reform and Patient Dumping." *Anthropology & Medicine* 26(3): 280–95.

———. 2020a. "Rethinking COVID-19 Vulnerability: A Call for LGTBQ+ Im/migrant Health Equity in the United States During and After a Pandemic." *Health Equity* 4(1): 239–42.

———. 2020b. "Syndemic Statuses: Intersectionality and Mobilizing for LGBTQ+ Latinx Health Equity after the Pulse Shooting." *Social Science & Medicine* 113260.

Kline, Nolan, and Christopher Cuevas. 2018. "Resisting Identity Erasure After Pulse: Intersectional LGBTQ+ Latinx Activism in Orlando, FL." *Chiricú Journal: Latina/o Literatures, Arts, and Cultures* 2(2): 68–71.

Lauby, Fanny. 2016. "Leaving the 'Perfect DREAMer' Behind? Narratives and Mobilization in Immigration Reform." *Social Movement Studies* 15(4): 374–87.

Luscombe. Richard. 2020. "Republican Governors Blame Familiar Targets as Coronavirus Rates Soar." *The Guardian.* June 20, 2020. www.theguardian.com/world /2020/jun/20/coronavirus-republican-governors-blame-florida-texas-arizona.

Marrow, Helen B. 2012. "Deserving to a Point: Unauthorized Immigrants in San Francisco's Universal Access Healthcare Model." *Social Science & Medicine* 74(6): 846–54.

Menjívar, Cecilia, and Leisy Abrego. 2012. "Legal Violence: Immigration Law and the Lives of Central American Immigrants." *American Journal of Sociology* 117(5): 1380–421.

Morgen, Sandra. 2001. "The Agency of Welfare Workers: Negotiating Devolution, Privatization, and the Meaning of Self-Sufficiency." *American Anthropologist* 103(3): 747–61.

National Coalition of Anti-Violence Programs. 2017. "Lesbian, Gay, Bisexual, Transgender, Queer, and HIV-Affected Hate Violence in 2016." https://avp.org/wp-content/uploads/2017/06/NCAVP_2016HateViolence_REPORT.pdf.

National Low Income Housing Association. 2020. "The Gap: A Shortage of Affordable Homes." https://reports.nlihc.org/sites/default/files/gap/Gap-Report_2020.pdf.

Newport, Frank, and Gary J. Gates. 2015. "San Francisco Metro Area Ranks Highest in LGBT Percentage." Gallup. Accessed June 30, 2020. https://news.gallup.com/poll/182051/san-francisco-metro-area-ranks-highest-lgbt-percentage.aspx?utm_source=Social%20Issues&utm_medium=newsfeed&utm_campaign=tiles.

Norman, Amber R., and Christopher J. Cuevas. 2020. "Central Florida LGBTQ+ Relief Fund: Individual Needs Assessment." QLatinx. Accessed June 30, 2020. www.canva.com/design/DAD8jSjFDrE/002wrgB9U2KTHfQZ06vnqA/view#1.

O'Daniel, Alyson Anthony. 2008. "Pushing Poverty to the Periphery: HIV-Positive African American Women's Health Needs, the Ryan White Care Act, and a Political Economy of Service Provision." *Transforming Anthropology* 16(2): 112–27.

Oppel, Richard A., and Derrick Bryson Taylor. 2020. "Here's What You Need to Know About Breonna Taylor's Death." *New York Times*, April 26, 2020. www.nytimes.com/article/breonna-taylor-police.html.

Pallares, Amalia, and Nilda Flores-González. 2020. *¡Marcha!: Latino Chicago and the Immigrant Rights Movement.* Champaign: University of Illinois Press.

Park, Haeyoun, and Iaryna Mykhyalyshyn. 2016. "L.G.B.T. People Are More Likely to Be Targets of Hate Crimes Than Any Other Minority Group." *New York Times.* June 16, 2016. www.nytimes.com/interactive/2016/06/16/us/hate-crimes-against-lgbt.html.

Peñaloza, Marisa. 2020. "Lawsuit Alleges CARES Act Excludes U.S. Citizen Children of Undocumented Immigrants." *National Public Radio.* May 5, 2020. www.npr.org/2020/05/05/850770390/lawsuit-alleges-cares-act-excludes-u-s-citizen-children-of-undocumented-immigrants.

QLatinx. 2020. "Who We Are." Accessed June 30, 2020. www.qlatinx.org/who-we-are.

Quesada, James, Laurie Kain Hart, and Philippe Bourgois. 2011. "Structural Vulnerability and Health: Latino Migrant Laborers in the United States." *Medical Anthropology* 30(4): 339–62.

Ransford, H. Edward, Frank R. Carrillo, and Yessenia Rivera. 2010. "Health Care-Seeking Among Latino Immigrants: Blocked Access, Use of Traditional Medicine, and the Role of Religion." *Journal of Health Care for the Poor and Underserved* 21(3): 862–78.

Rylko-Bauer, Barbara, and Paul Farmer. 2002. "Managed Care or Managed Inequality? A Call for Critiques of Market-Based Medicine." *Medical Anthropology Quarterly* 16(4): 476–502.

Schoch-Spana, Monica, Nidhi Bouri, Kunal Rambhia, and Ann Norwood. 2010. "Stigma, Health Disparities, and the 2009 H1N1 Influenza Pandemic: Burdens on Latino Farmworkers in the US." *Biosecurity and Bioterrorism* 8(3): 243–54.

Silver, Patricia, and William Vélez. 2017. "'Let Me Go Check Out Florida': Rethinking Puerto Rican Diaspora." *Centro Journal* 29(3): 98–125.

Selyukh. Alina. 2020. "Will Filing For Unemployment Hurt My Green Card? Legal Immigrants Are Afraid." *National Public Radio.* May 11, 2020. www.npr.org/2020/05/11/851463729/will-filing-for-unemployment-hurt-my-green-card-legal-immigrants-are-afraid.

Terriquez, Veronica. 2015. "Intersectional Mobilization, Social Movement Spillover, and Queer Youth Leadership in the Immigrant Rights Movement." *Social Problems* 62(3): 343–62.

Thompson, Laura. 2020. "The Police Killing You Probably Didn't Hear About This Week." *Mother Jones.* May 29, 2020. www.motherjones.com/crime-justice/2020/05/tony-mcdade-tallahassee-florida-police-shooting-death/.

U.S. Census Bureau. 2019a. Annual Estimates of the Resident Population: April 1, 2010, to July 1, 2018. Accessed June 1, 2018. https://factfinder.census.gov/faces/tableservices/jsf/pages/productview.xhtml?src=bkmk#.

———. 2019b. QuickFacts Orlando City. Accessed June 30, 2020. www.census.gov/quickfacts/orlandocityflorida.

Wamsley, Laurel. 2020. "Fired Florida Data Scientist Launches a Coronavirus Dashboard of Her Own." *National Public Radio.* June 14, 2020. www.npr.org/2020/06/14/876584284/fired-florida-data-scientist-launches-a-coronavirus-dashboard-of-her-own.

Willen, Sarah S. 2012. "How Is Health-Related 'Deservingness' Reckoned? Perspectives from Unauthorized Im/migrants in Tel Aviv." *Social Science & Medicine* 74(6): 812–21.

Winders, Jamie. 2011. "Representing the Immigrant: Social Movements, Political Discourse, and Immigration in the US South." *Southeastern Geographer* 51(4): 596–614.

Wolf, Colin, and Monivette Cordeiro. 2018. "A Transgender Woman Died in Orlando Today, and How It Was Reported Was Awful." *Orlando Weekly.* July 19, 2018. www.orlandoweekly.com/Blogs/archives/2018/07/19/a-transgender-woman-died-in-orlando-today-and-how-it-was-reported-was-awful.

World Health Organization. 2020. "WHO Director-General's Opening Remarks at the Media Briefing on COVID-19—March 11, 2020." www.who.int/dg/speeches/detail/who-director-general-s-opening-remarks-at-the-media-briefing-on-covid-19--11-march-2020.

Yuval-Davis, Nira. 2006. "Belonging and the Politics of Belonging." *Patterns of Prejudice* 40(3): 197–214.

CHAPTER 3

No Choice but Unity

*Afro-Cuban Immigrants Building Community
in Los Angeles*

MONIKA GOSIN

> *One has to unite with others—there's no other choice.*
>
> —Pedro

Introduction

This chapter examines how Afro-Cubans[1] living in Los Angeles, California,
create social ties that foster a sense of community belonging in this ethnically
diverse gateway city where Cubans are but a small proportion of the population. While the majority of socio-scientific studies on Afro-Cuban immigrants importantly focus on their experiences of anti-Black racism, the focus
of the current research is on how Black Cubans nevertheless act as agents
in creating spaces to belong. Drawing on in-depth interviews, this research
highlights the face-to-face interactions by which they build connections with
people of various other ethnic/racial origins and the strategies with which
they daily transcend boundaries that define "us" and "them." In particular,
the research demonstrates how Black Cubans create social bonds based on
shared immigrant experiences or shared Latinx[2] identities while maintaining
their ethnic distinctiveness.

Traditionally, immigration scholarship has emphasized that successful
immigrant adaptation could be facilitated by ethnic enclaves where co-
ethnics can help newcomers find resources such as jobs and other forms of
social support (Portes 2012; Light and Gold 2000). However, this is not often
the case for Afro-Cubans, in part because of the bifurcation of the post-1959

Cuban migrant community by race (Portes and Armony 2018; Aja 2016). For instance, although Miami has the largest population of Cuban immigrants in the United States, this community is majority white, as few Black Cubans migrated in the first waves that arrived after Fidel Castro's rise to power in 1959. The Miami Cuban community has been less welcoming to Black Cubans, who have often chosen to settle elsewhere (Aja 2016). Black Cubans who live in spaces like Los Angeles, California (L.A.) encounter an environment where there is no single Cuban or Afro-Cuban enclave or neighborhood, and Latinx identity is primarily defined as "Mexican."[3] As there are also few other Afro-Latinxs of any national origin, Black Cubans find they may not be fully accepted by others because they do not fit prevailing ideas about what it means to be Black, Cuban, *or* Latinx (Thomas 2005). Hence, they must parse out the multiple layers of their identities to fit within a racial binary or oversimplified understanding of racial categories (Gosin 2017; Torres-Saillant 2010). The types of challenges faced by Afro-Cubans and other Afro-Latinxs, whose negotiation of the U.S. ethnic and racial terrain are complicated by their complex and multilayered identities and specifically by their blackness, are not often accounted for in traditional scholarly work on immigrant integration into the United States.

Given such challenges, in this chapter I bring together scholarly perspectives on immigration, constructions of belonging, and ethnic boundary-making to better understand how Afro-Cubans in L.A. foster a sense of community belonging. I contend that Afro-Cubans employ a strategy of unity—with people from disparate communities—as they work to approach full membership in the larger society. I highlight that Black Cubans often do not have the option to avoid some of the discomforts of boundary-crossing that privileged whites living in majority-white communities do, nor can they choose to retreat to areas filled with people of the same ethnic and racial configuration. Thus "no choice but unity" reflects a necessary adaptation. Yet by highlighting the strategic nature of *choosing* unity, I bring attention to more hopeful outcomes of Black Cuban social experience, and intervene in scholarship on Afro-Cuban immigrant experiences by taking a closer look at salient dimensions of Afro-Cuban immigrant experience related to blackness but also going beyond that of related stigma and rejection. Still, this "positive" focus is not intended to communicate the idea that simply "choosing unity" provides a utopian path to a post-racial society. Rather, even as I highlight Black Cuban agency, I also contend "no choice but unity" is an extra form of labor that some immigrants, such as Afro-Cubans, must engage in to establish belonging in their new homes. It is work that immigrants who do not fit neatly into preconceived categories choose to engage in to undermine oversimplified understanding of racial/ethnic identities, and is a dynamic process of place-finding that ultimately allows them room to express the multilayered self.

Background and Context
Post-1959 Afro-Cuban Immigration and Boundaries to Incorporation

Few studies focus on Cubans outside the Miami enclave, and until relatively recently, Black Cubans have been largely neglected in analyses of post-1959 Cuban immigrations (Gosin 2019, 2017; Prieto 2009; Aja 2016; Rothe and Pumariega 2008; Mirabal 2003).[4] While much of the research on "the" Cuban immigrant community has highlighted the success of the Miami enclave, there are deep disparities between Black and white Cubans in the city. For instance, Aja (2016) and Rothe and Pumariega (2008) found that Black Cubans fare worse than their white counterparts on various economic indicators. This, coupled with the rejection they sometimes experience from white Cubans in Miami, denies Afro-Cubans the type of benefits that other immigrants gain from settling into an ethnic enclave composed of people from their country of origin (Gosin 2019, 2017; Portes and Armony 2018; Aja 2016).[5]

Because of the low number of Afro-Cubans in Miami and the dispersal of Afro-Cubans across the country due to resettlement programs, an expanded focus outside Miami can provide much-needed insights. Existing studies show that those who live in spaces with large Latinx populations may, like other phenotypically Black Latinxs, encounter white or mestizo Latinxs who contest their "Latinx" identity, understanding blackness and Latinx-ness as incongruent (Gosin 2017; Jiménez Román and Flores 2010; Torres-Saillant 2002, 2003). For instance, in geographic areas where the Latinx population is primarily of Mexican origin, conflict occurs as some Mexicans disparage Afro-Cubans due to their blackness (Gosin 2019, 2017; Dowling and Newby 2010; Newby and Dowling 2007). Affinity with African Americans, who share a racial identity, is also not automatic. Studies show that Afro-Latinxs face rejection from some African Americans who do not regard them as "true Blacks" (Jiménez Román and Flores 2010; Torres-Saillant 2010). Taken together, such studies shed light on Afro-Cubans' unique positioning and the reasons that they may encounter obstacles in finding spaces for community belonging in the United States.

As a city that receives continual flows of new immigrants and where generations of post-1965 immigrants reside, Los Angeles is well suited for my research interest in analyzing how Afro-Cubans make inroads into spaces where there are few people who share their combination of ethnic and racial identifications. Despite the diverse representation of immigrants from all over the world, the L.A. Cuban population is quite small. According to the Pew Research Center, there are only about 55,000 Cubans in the area (or less than 1 percent of the population; Radford and Noe-Bustamante 2019). While Cubans have still made their mark in L.A. business and culture, published studies on Cubans in the area are scarce. Thus, by studying (Afro) Cubans in L.A., the current study fills a scholarly gap. Moreover, examining processes of incorporation by which Afro-Cubans form social relations with their mostly non-white neighbors in L.A., the study offers further challenge to traditional assimilation research models, revealing strategies that differ from those required in places where whites are the majority (Alba and Nee 2017, 50; Aranda et al. 2014; Okamoto 2014; Kasinitz et al. 2002).

Becoming Agents of Belonging

Immigration research has traditionally defined immigrant adaption with little attention to the mechanics and quality of interpersonal interactions at the local, face-to-face level (Stepick and Stepick 2009). Yet such interactive processes of building trust ultimately allow immigrants to feel integrated into their new communities (García and Schmalzbauer 2017; Aranda et al. 2014). Here I bring together scholarly perspectives on the ideas of "belonging" and of ethnic boundary making (and unmaking) to help fill these gaps in immigration scholarship and shed light on the dynamics involved in Afro-Cuban immigrant interactions with their new neighbors in a pursuit of spaces for community belonging in L.A.

The concept of "belonging" is multidimensional and conceptualized differently in various scholarly fields. Many scholars use the term "belonging" synonymously with collective identity or (legal) citizenship, paying less attention to the idea of belonging as it relates to an emotional feeling of being at home (Antonsich 2010). I bring to bear Probyn's (1996) definition of belonging, described by Antonsich (2010) as a "mode of affective community-making based on physical proximity, rather than common identity" (652). I examine how Afro-Cubans must become "agents of belonging," actively negotiating and *producing* a sense of being at home, rather than waiting for it to be conferred (Bickham Mendez and Deeb-Sosa 2020, 4; Yuval-Davis 2011; Aranda et al. 2014; Antonsich 2010). I focus on relational aspects that help people feel at home, affirming the labor of both building long-lasting stable relationships (Baumeister and Leary 1995) *and* creating the weaker ties that come through everyday encounters. As Antonsich notes, the belonging literature could benefit from more insight into how communities of belonging are produced within increasingly culturally diverse societies. In these sites, there is a need for explorations that capture how belonging differs relative to the strength or permeability of associated identity boundaries, and that take into account that belonging can go beyond solely working to consolidate collective racial/ethnic identity (Antosich 2010). I capture processes by which Afro-Cubans work to achieve belonging by both building community around a common "Cuban" identity, but also by creating social bonds based on several other types of commonalities that they share with their non-Cuban neighbors. In doing so, they affirm and make space for multiple dimensions of who they are as Cubans, Blacks, Latinxs, and immigrants.

Building relationships with strangers is ultimately about testing the permeability of boundaries (Shutika 2011, 15; Coll 2006). Sociologists have long focused attention on the existence and stability of ethnic boundaries, and their influence within specific groups of people (Wang et al. 2019). Scholarship on ethnic boundaries indicates that people show a preference for same-ethnicity friendships, even when there is opportunity to develop cross-racial relationships (Leszczensky and Pink 2019; Wimmer 2013). Members of smaller ethnic groups, however, may be more open to developing friendships across disparate groups, perhaps because of the lack of availability of co-ethnics (Leszczensky and Pink 2019). While my findings are consistent with this, I capture how "no choice but unity" across racial/ethnic boundaries is not a passive concession but an active and intentional strategy. Taking the central focus off the constraints that propel this choice, I instead focus on the simultaneous active creation, destruction, and recreation of ethnic boundaries (Wimmer 2013).

The study's specific focus on Afro-Cuban immigrants, who share an ethnic but not a racial identity with the majority Latinx group in the area also lends insight into processes through which the boundaries around the panethnic identity "Latinx" come to be (de)constructed. As Cristina Beltrán (2010) argues, the notion of an automatic collective political consciousness among those designated "Latinxs" is problematic. Instead, we should understand Latinx panethnicity as "a *process* of connections and interactions" that are at times "random" and "proliferating," a practice of becoming from which unexpected alliances may emerge which might not be overtly political (167). The current study lends insight into these processes and connections, revealing how Afro-Cuban immigrants construct unity in L.A. by creating bonds with other Latinxs and their diverse neighbors.

Methods

This research draws from in-depth interviews with twenty Afro-Cubans conducted in Los Angeles County in 2009. The thirteen men and seven women self-identified as "Black" or were often identified incorrectly by others as being of another Afro-descendent group. Their ages ranged from twenty-one to seventy-three. Five of the respondents have children in the United States. While the majority of the interviewees arrived as adults or older teens in 1980 or thereafter, two of the respondents had come to the United States in 1965 and 1971, respectively. The sample varied in the amount of time that individuals had lived in L.A.: the earliest arrival had been in the area for almost forty years, and the most recent had arrived two months prior to the interview. There was considerable variation in the occupations that respondents held, but they were generally educated, having completed high school level or greater in Cuba or the United States.

I first met many of the interviewees as we mutually enjoyed Cuban or Latin music events and danced at a nightclub I will call *Muévete*, which hosted popular Cuban Nights.[6] I maintained contact with folks by attending parties and gatherings in homes, taking Afro-Cuban dance classes, and meeting up to chat at a Cuban bakery based in Glendale. I was quite aware of the differences between myself and the interviewees (e.g., how my U.S. American identity and the fact that English is my first language provide me some comparative privilege in the United States). However, I found that several respondents treated me as somewhat of an insider because I am Black, and related to me because of my appearance. Like many of these respondents, I am often asked about my ethnicity because of what some perceived to be a "mixed" (race) look, and some interviewees remarked on our similar experience of being constantly questioned.[7] For those who agreed to be interviewed, these factors positioned me as a sympathetic interviewer and helped build rapport.

As I talked with the participants, I queried them about their journey to the United States, their experiences adjusting to life in a new country; the backgrounds of their friends, neighbors, and coworkers; and about the level of acceptance they felt from Cubans and other ethnic/racial groups in the United States. I began my interviews by asking respondents to tell me about what brought them to the United States and to Los Angeles more specifically. Some cited political reasons for their decision to leave Cuba, others indicated economic factors, while still others cited the desire to reunite with family members as primary reasons for deciding to come to the United States. The majority of them came through Miami when they first arrived, but some bypassed it altogether, traveling directly to the Los Angeles area. Two of the respondents, for instance, immigrated to the United States via Mexico by crossing the U.S.-Mexican border. I also asked participants about their identity, such as which identity they would choose when filling out forms; how others tended to identify them racially or ethnically; whether people ask them about their race/ethnicity/or national origins, and if so which ethnic groups are most likely to ask them the questions. In the course of the interview, respondents talked about their daily lives and how they relate to people of various racial/ethnic backgrounds as they navigated the social scene and created spaces of belonging in Los Angeles.[8]

Findings
Building Cuban Community in L.A.

While randomly running into other Cubans is a rare occurrence in L.A., all the respondents nevertheless actively sought to establish social bonds with other Cubans, creating a space for the expression of their cultural identity. Though Afro-Cubans living in Miami may not automatically bond with white Cubans, in L.A. respondents circulated in multi-racial Cuban groups, albeit with a very visible Afro-Cuban presence. Respondents explained that the makeup of their Cuban social circles portrayed a more familiar picture of the Cuba they left, where, despite the clear existence of racial tension, whites and Blacks commonly live and socialize together (Sawyer 2006). Indeed, the respondents acknowledged the existence of racial divisions among Cubans but also sought to preserve an expressly Cuban identity that is conceived of as being *inclusive* of racial difference. While race was not a major source of intra-Cuban division in L.A., respondents did indicate other intra-Cuban tensions based on generational, historical, political, or experiential differences. Yasiel, who arrived in the United States in the 2000s, argued that there is a "wall" between Cubans of his generation and "people that came here in the sixties . . . and seventies." This "wall" is often related to differential political orientations correlated to arrival in the United States soon after Fidel Castro came to power versus those who lived most of their lives in Castro's Cuba (Eckstein 2006). In spite of these "walls," however, various aspects of Cuban culture provide space to create an inclusive nexus.

Several respondents cited music as a unifier and L.A.'s Cuban music scene in particular as essential for community building. For instance, Juan, who arrived in the U.S. in 1980 during Mariel, was drawn to L.A. because of its Cuban music scene. He had spent several years in Seattle before moving permanently to L.A. "There was no music back there that I can relate to," he said about Seattle, "so I came to Los Angeles, and I see the music, the rumba, and I say, 'Oh, I'm going to stay here!'" Ernesto, who came to the United States in the 1990s as a *balsero*, notes, "It is hard sometimes to find, you know, a whole bunch of Cubans together in one place. Unless like you go on Sunday to MacArthur Park and you will find there's a whole bunch of Cubans from the 80s, but they are playing congas, the rumba, whatever." At these gatherings Cubans (and non-Cubans) would habitually come together to "hang out" and play music—anyone who wanted to drum and dance could join in. Through word-of-mouth, newly arrived Cubans would learn about local night spots that hosted Cuban music nights, such as *Muévete*, which would similarly function as spaces for Cubans to gather and meet. Another important musical event that helped newly arrived Cubans meet other co-ethnics was a free annual Cuban festival (held each May in Echo Park from 1993 until 2015).[9] The possibilities of engaging with Cuban culture through music not only worked to draw some Afro-Cubans to the L.A. area but helped facilitate the building of Cuban community by offering spaces of belonging and a springboard for them to build networks that could be utilized to help them integrate into their new society.

Other respondents spoke of making connections with other Cubans at Cuban-owned establishments. Elena explained, "Here in Los Angeles—and you see that Mexicans arrive, and talk about [finding] tortillas and 'bolillo' [a type of bread]. . . . So, we always begin to ask, 'Well, aren't there any Cuban stores here?' And, someone says, 'Oh yes, over there.' And, when you get there, someone else asks, 'So, where are you from? When did you arrive?' And . . . so you find out about another Cuban market or business and so on."

Other respondents frequented Cuban restaurants to make connections with both customers and the owners. Establishments such as the well-known Cuban bakery in Glendale and other restaurants were sites where newcomers to the area sought out familiar foods reminiscent of home and developed connections that often led to lasting bonds with other Cubans.

Meeting other Cubans on the job also enabled respondents to develop such social ties. As Lucy discovered, "When I began in my job [working in the department of public services] there was a lady that I met who was Cuban-American . . . and during a year or so—I met . . . three more [female] Cubans . . . at three in the afternoon we always get together to have Cuban coffee." Respondents also noted that the ties they developed with other Cubans could be instrumental in yielding job opportunities. Alejandro explained: "If there is a Cuban working in a job in which they have a good record, he/she might tell their boss that there is a Cuban in need of work. [The boss will] respond, 'Bring that Cuban 'round here.' So, that he can begin to work! . . . That's the way I got a job after being here for three months." As Lucy and Alejandro point out, despite the limited opportunities to meet other Cubans in L.A., when Cubans *did* get together, they quickly struck up new friendships and networks based on their national and cultural affinity. The efforts respondents make, crossing geographic, racial, and other boundaries to build Cuban community, captures the salience of the specific "national origin layer" among their multilayered identities. Their efforts to create spaces in L.A. where their (Afro) Cuban selves fit in highlights the duality of adaptation born of both necessity and desire.

Building Multiethnic Comm/unity

As there is no single Cuban neighborhood in L.A., Cubans are residentially spread out across the area, and thus are most likely to interact with non-Cubans in their day-to-day lives. Respondents often lived in neighborhoods that they described as "mostly Mexican," but some also lived in areas where no single group predominated. For instance, Regla positively described her neighborhood in Downey as having "Asians, a lot of Koreans, Taiwanese, Vietnamese, Indians, Africans from South Africa, Nigerians, [people from] Egypt, everything!" Others respondents emphasized, however, that "diversity" does not necessarily translate to social cohesion. Yasiel, for example, noted that when he first arrived in the United States, the tremendous diversity in L.A. was disorienting, especially because specific ethnic groups are often segregated from one another residentially. As he and others pointed out, navigating the geography of L.A. and making decisions about where to live, work, and so on was one of the first challenges that respondents described needing to overcome. Respondents described difficulties discerning where they belonged when people directly and indirectly insinuated that they, as Blacks *and* Cubans, could not truly belong.

Almost all the respondents had stories to tell about anti-Black racism they faced and others' confusion about the relationship between blackness and cultural markers of "Latinidad" like speaking Spanish (Gosin 2019, 2017). Regla's experiences encapsulate the type of negative experiences that Afro-Cubans faced: "One thing that happened to me. . . . I was in ESL classes for English, I had a [substitute] teacher come in . . . and he said, 'What are you doing in this class?' . . . And I said, 'I'm in this class because I hardly speak English,' and he said, 'Well, you not supposed to be in this class.' . . . Just because of my skin color, he thought I was African-American, and he wanted me to go to regular English class, when I couldn't, you know?"

For other respondents, the majority of whom came to the United States when they were adults, when interacting with Mexicans or other Spanish speakers, it was common to encounter people who were often surprised that a Black person could speak Spanish. As Ariane notes, "Sometimes I speak Spanish and they're like, hey, you speak very good Spanish, how do you learn Spanish?" Thus, for Black Cubans living in Los Angeles, there were frequent reminders that in the U.S. blackness was often viewed as incongruent with "Latinxness." To fully express the multiplicity of their identities, they would have to meet the challenge of those who would deny the legitimacy of their ethnicity and thereby block the road to full membership in U.S. society.

Despite such challenges, respondents also spoke about their ability to cross the boundaries that they encountered, which they attributed, in part, to an upbringing in Cuba where people from different racial groups are comparatively more integrated geographically and socially. Yasiel found it enjoyable to traverse boundaries that others seemed afraid to cross. He came to feel very adept at navigating L.A.'s diversity: "After that, all those experiences [feeling disoriented and out of place], you have to look for a standard way to communicate and to relate with everybody." As he pointed out, "One needs to learn the skill of how to understand every community, you know, where they come from. You know? Try to understand and respect that." Indeed, for the respondents, integrating themselves into their culturally diverse environment often included relationships built on cultural exchanges that yielded more paths to belonging. Thus, in contrast to study results on Cubans who migrated to L.A. before the 1970s, who had few Cuban to non-Cuban social interactions (Gil 1976), the majority of respondents reported that they had very diverse friendships. As Ernesto describes himself, "I became like an 'international Cuban,' I don't hang out just with Cubans, no."

For several of the respondents, conversations about material culture offered an avenue for cultural exchange and relationship building. For Lucy, Cuban coffee allowed her to make inroads with the Armenians in her diverse neighborhood. As she explains, both cultures prefer strong espresso-style coffee but prepare it differently. Elena recounts a humorous story, also related to drinking Cuban coffee, but with her Mexican friends. Cubans often use small cups to sip the strong coffee because, as Elena points out, just a small amount is enough. She explains, "The first time that I had my Mexican friends over for coffee I placed the cups and saucers and they looked at it strangely, because they were used to regular (American) coffee. 'Isn't this a tea set to play "house?"' they asked. 'I thought you were setting up so the kids could play.' . . . They thought that we were playing 'house.' Like kids!"

People of various cultural backgrounds often took interest in Cuban foods and other cultural aspects because they were simply very unfamiliar with Cuban culture. As Odalys explains regarding Cuban food, people would ask, "How is it made? Is it delicious? And what is that called? [I would explain,] 'This is *congrí*.'"[10] Deisy was surprised to learn that many Central Americans practiced the Cuban religious practice of *Santería*, and Fermín noted that Mexicans and many other Latinxs "*love* Cuban music." In places like Griffith Park, where Afro-Cubans and others assembled to dance and drum, Fermín and other Afro-Cubans forge friendships with non-Cubans through the enjoyment of a music style in which they took pride. For the respondents, explaining the preparation of foods and sharing other cherished aspects of their culture provided an opportunity to build trust with others who showed genuine interest in getting to know them. Through these exchanges, community belonging was not simply conferred to Afro-Cubans by local community members. Instead, while people of various cultural backgrounds demonstrated acceptance of the respondents by taking interest in Cuban culture, the respondents also inserted *themselves* into the cultural mix of L.A., affirming the value of what they have to offer, and proclaiming themselves legitimate inhabitants of the social space.

While highlighting their Cuban "difference" allowed Afro-Cubans inroads into their local communities, their interactions with Mexicans offer insight into the dynamics involved in the creation of a sense of *shared* identity, or "Latinidad" among local Latinxs. As previous research has indicated, tensions exist between Afro-Cubans and some Mexicans in the United States due to racial differences (Gosin 2019, 2017; Newby and Dowling 2007; Dowling and Newby 2010). Besides the issue of race, another documented source of tensions between Mexicans and Cubans relates to the historical disparity in U.S. treatment favoring Cubans versus other immigrants (Newby and Dowling 2007). In 1966, with the Cuban Adjustment Act, Congress promised the United States would take in and give legal status to those fleeing Cuba amid the Cold War. Cubans continued to have a significant advantage over most other immigrants until January 2017, when President Barack Obama ended the practice of allowing Cubans who came to the United States via dry land to have this privilege.[11] Yet, as Odalys points out, the long history of Cuban immigration to the United States makes Cuba a country where ". . . every home of every Cuban is touched with sadness. Because the one that has not lost a son has lost their mother to immigration." Such losses and the pain of family separations mean that despite the historically preferential treatment of Cubans in the United States, the immigrant experience for Cubans is not uniformly positive and can be very similar to that of other immigrants, including their Mexican neighbors. For instance, Yasiel talked about the "fish out of water" feeling that came from the need to learn a new language and adjust to cultural differences as an adult: "I was thirty years old [when I arrived in the United States]. For me [coming here] was like learning how to walk again." For Deisy, it was other cultural differences that she found difficult to adjust to: "The way it is in

Cuba is your neighbor next door is your friend and she's your neighbor. Here, you don't even see your neighbor. And sometimes today she's nice and tomorrow she's not nice. So, for me, there's no community in this country." Feelings of loss and longing for home and community prompted the respondents and other immigrants to develop social connections, particularly with other immigrants who could relate to such experiences and were in the same position of seeking community.

The respondents pointed out that often their Mexican neighbors were most instrumental in helping them adjust to life in the U.S. and overcome the alienation they experienced. For instance, Fermín captures how Afro-Cuban/Mexican relations can be more complex than the conflict narrative suggests. He reminisces, "When I came from Cuba, even though I had Cuban friends, I think a few of my best friends, they were Mexican. Because a lot of Mexican people, even though a lot of them, they got that mentality [that is anti-Black]. But there's this other group of Mexican people that are very nice. And they're . . . they like to communicate . . . and they like to help out." Elena also became close with a family of Mexican descent who were the first to help her become integrated into her new surroundings when she arrived in L.A. Of this family she said, "If I would have been able to pick who my family would be, I'd pick them—they were a great support when I arrived. One cannot close oneself off and say, 'Oh, only if they are Cubans, I will accept them.' No, no, their selflessness and help was a beautiful thing." As Elena expands, feelings of alienation prompted her into action when she came into contact with other immigrants, some of whom were Mexican, who had just arrived in the United States. She says, "Sometimes, they arrive without anything. And, we tell one another, 'Hey, here's a bed. Here's a fridge. I have a dining room set.' And so we begin to construct something significant. And this happens not only to Cubans but with all immigrants. Because we have been through *so much* we have become sensitive to others' needs and problems. And so we don't care anymore if they are Cuban. If someone asks, 'I need a bed.' Off we go to help them. You see?"

As one can see in the examples of these Afro-Cuban immigrants laboring to traverse boundaries by receiving help from and providing help to people of Mexican descent, the basis of intra-Latinx connections may be created based on cultivated empathy related to common immigrant experiences and sharing day-to-day cultural practices. Moreover, panethnic bonds and similar immigrant-related experiences can diminish what might otherwise have become unmitigated resentment due to the historically differential treatment of Mexicans and Cubans by the U.S. immigration system.

The common language of Spanish also provided a powerful basis for creating bonds with other Latinxs. Linguistic researchers have found that differences in Spanish dialects can be a source of division among Latinxs as some evaluate particular speech patterns and national varieties of Spanish to be "low class" or as indicators of marginalized status (Aranda et al. 2014; Zentella 2007). But though "national varieties of Spanish sometimes emphasize regional borders . . . those borders recede when the Spanish language is embraced as a common denominator" (Zentella 2007, 25). Zentella (2020) found that many Puerto Ricans in San Diego for instance, accommodate Mexicans by incorporating Mexican vocabulary into their speech and adopting some pronunciations. They, like other Latinxs, sought to retain their own way of speaking for cultural and/or nationalist reasons. But Puerto Ricans in San Diego also accommodated Mexicans through their speech patterns in conscious efforts to seek connection (Zentella, 2020). Similarly, Lucy became best friends with a Mexican woman at her job, and notes that through interactions with her and other Mexicans she worked with, as well as the Spanish-speaking Mexican clientele they served, she not only found the basis for fellowship but also began to use the Spanish language differently than she had in Cuba, picking up Mexican colloquialisms for instance. As she notes, "One starts to create a habit (pattern) of using certain words that one begins to use constantly, that I would not use in Cuba. Whether one likes it or not, the cultures begin to mix." Thus, as Lucy describes, part of building community for Spanish speakers in L.A. is actively adopting different forms of a language they already speak. Yet, given the daily frustrations that come from not being able to communicate well in English for some of the respondents, interactions with other Spanish speakers provided some relief and the comfort of being able to still speak their own language on a daily basis. As Dario explains, "You hear Spanish and get a familiar feeling." Elena adds that hearing spoken Spanish makes her feel happy and allows her to bond with her neighbors: "There are some that are looking at [differences in] nationalities, but no, the language unites us all." This feeling of belonging, of unity, is the motivation that extends interpersonal bonds into thriving panethnic relationships as Afro-Cubans form new communities wherein diverse forms of Spanish are spoken, at times blurring the lines between the disparate groups.

Discussion and Conclusions

This research has analyzed the efforts of Afro-Cuban immigrants to build community belonging in the Los Angeles community, a space where Cubans and Afro-Latinxs are few in number. It further disrupts the white Miami-Cuban exile model that is predominant in Cuban Studies and complements previous studies on Afro-Cuban experiences in the United States, which emphasize the negative impacts of the stigmatization of their blackness. As I have discussed in previous work, the issue of anti-Black stigma remains important (Gosin 2019, 2017). Yet in this chapter I shift our focus to highlight how Black people work as agents to strategically manage their complicated positioning, thus engaging in research that seeks to answer Karen Lacy's (2007) call for social scientific analyses of Black experiences that examine how Black people construct their identities across many different contexts. Hence, the current research reveals additional layers of social life, besides blackness, that are important to our understanding of what it means to be Black and Cuban in the United States. For instance, the study captures the salience of their national origin identity—even as the interviewees sought to integrate themselves into their new homes, they also actively sought out Cuban community, and worked to preserve their "Cubanness." For the respondents, this identity cannot be placed within a simple binary "Black" or "white" box; rather it is inclusive of racial diversity.

The small size of the population of Cubans in L.A., however, made it necessary to create connections with people from other national origins. By showing the face-to-face level processes by which Afro-Cubans create connections and friendships with their non-Cuban neighbors, the current research contributes to our understandings of how ethnic boundaries are broken, shifted, and created. Future research should examine the role gender plays in these network formations. In the current study, women were slightly more likely to talk about food and food preparation as being instrumental in forming networks, and men were more likely to discuss the music scene. A larger sample would allow further intersectional investigation into the extent to which the strategy of uniting with other disparate communities is structured by identities and social locations like gender and sexuality.

Nevertheless, in the current study we see that in a place such as Los Angeles where so many people are first-generation immigrants or their children or grandchildren, the formation of common "immigrant identities" may supersede national and cultural boundaries. As Afro-Cubans in this study find common ground with others who intimately know the experience of being an immigrant, they engage in boundary-breaking in mundane everyday interactions—over a meal, in the workplace, at music events—and so make space for the "immigrant" dimension of who they are. Moreover, the study lends further insight into how taken-for-granted categories like *Latinidad* emerge. In this case, common immigrant experiences and the bonds of the Spanish language helped Afro-Cubans build community with their non-Cuban Latinx neighbors despite the major cultural differences between these groups.

As Dina Okamoto (2014) argues in relation to her study on Asian American panethnicity in California, we see here that ethnicity and panethnicity are interdependent, functioning together. Immigrants can both hold fast to their national origins and build new bonds with other groups as participants explore not assimilation, but the construction of "layered and flexible" identities (Okamoto 2014). Thus, this research, focused on a multiethnic space like L.A., challenges assimilation research that conceives of America as a space with one core, white, culture and demonstrates that ethnic minorities can *resist* assimilation or challenge the dominant view of what assimilation means (Li 2009).

As the research indicates, the relationships that underpin "pan-Latinidad" can come more from circumstantial necessity than being driven by a particular political consciousness. I would argue, however, that the creation of such social bonds still holds political implications, not only in that they could be the basis for later advocacy, but in that they highlight the inequities that do not allow many people of color and immigrants a place to which they can retreat. Indeed, privileged whites can avoid crossing political/cultural boundaries, while for many in the United States, crossing boundaries is an extra labor—part of the work that they *must* do to integrate themselves into U.S. society.[12] Despite this challenging aspect of their new home, the Afro-Cubans in this study argue one must unite with others, even when they do not share the same ethnic/racial identity configurations. They proclaim "no choice but unity" not as a concession or affliction, but as a resolution and a declaration. When they say "no choice but unity" it is not in sadness about the scarcity of other Cubans alone, but in concurrent willingness to make the best of their current situation by unifying with others—a declaration that simultaneously conveys the folly of the alternative. This is not just "multiculturalism lite," that is, simply ignoring our differences or the realities of racial inequality in society. Rather, it is about how Afro-Cubans in this study work in their communities to expand boundaries and disrupt the processes wherein social groupings must be associated with inequality (Okamoto 2014). Emphasizing the agency involved in such community-building is not to deny that crises and political complications circle about them at all times, but to reveal the sanctuary they manage to create where they can express the multiplicity of their identities and find spaces to belong.

Notes

1. I use the term "Afro" according to U.S.-based scholarly convention. However, this term is not commonly used in Cuba, where the term "*negro*" is used instead, referring to phenotype.
2. While at the time of this study the identity label "Latino" was more resonant within the community in Los Angeles, I choose here to employ the more recent term Latinx in recognition of its growing conventional usage and to signal the disruption of the gender binary.
3. According to the Pew Research Center, the Latinx population in L.A. is 78 percent Mexican (Motel and Patten 2013).
4. For excellent studies on U.S.-based Afro-Cuban communities from earlier periods such as the late nineteenth to mid-twentieth centuries, see Greenbaum (2002), Abreu (2015), and Mirabal (2017).
5. The racial bifurcation of the Miami Cuban immigrant community into "black" and "white" is related to the racial and political climate of both Cuba and the United States, which encouraged primarily wealthier white Cubans to come to the United States after Fidel Castro came to power in 1959 and the U.S. government opposed his government during the Cold War.
6. The name of this restaurant and nightclub (now closed) has been changed.
7. African Americans and Latinxs are more likely than white, Anglo-Americans to express curiosity about my identity, having been more attentive to nuances in skin color and hair texture, and perceiving these nuances to be indicators of racial mixture.
8. Five of the interviews were conducted in Spanish. The interview transcripts were analyzed individually, then, utilizing a grounded theory approach, they were coded for common themes across interviews. All names are pseudonyms.
9. Here I am referring to the original L.A. Cuban festival, *La Presencia Cubana en Los Angeles*. This event was started in 1993 by Adolfo V. Nodal and Aurelio de la Vega and produced for many years by Marco Duval. The festival was held near the Jose Martí Plaza and monument in Echo Park (Adolfo Nodal, personal interview).
10. "Dirty rice."

11.   Cubans had arrived primarily by sea vessel until President Clinton's 1995 "Wet foot, Dry foot." This policy, ended by President Barack Obama, had made it no longer lawful to come to the United States by sea, but still allowed Cubans who made it to U.S. dry land to become legal permanent residents after one year.
12.   This white privilege bleeds into a white colonialist model of boundary crossing—by force (not choice).

References

Abreu, Christina. 2015. *Rhythms of Race: Cuban Musicians and the Making of Latino New York City and Miami, 1940–1960*. Chapel Hill: University of North Carolina Press.

Aja, Alan A. 2016. *Miami's Forgotten Cubans: Race, Racialization, and the Miami Afro-Cuban Experience*. New York: Palgrave Macmillan.

Antonsich, M. 2010. "Searching for Belonging—An Analytical Framework." *Geography Compass* 4(6): 644–59.

Aranda, Elizabeth M., Sallie Hughes, and Elena Sabogal. 2014. *Making a Life in Multiethnic Miami: Immigration and the Rise of a Global City*. Boulder: Rienner.

Alba, Richard D., and Victor G. Nee. 2017. "Rethinking Assimilation Theory for a New Era of Immigration." In *Beyond Black and White: A Reader on Contemporary Race Relations*, edited by Zulema Valdez, 44–70. Thousand Oaks, Calif.: Sage.

Baumeister, R. F., and M. R. Leary. 1995. "Need to Belong: Desire for Interpersonal Attachments as a Fundamental Human Motivation." *Psychological Bulletin* 117(3): 497–529.

Beltrán, Cristina. 2010. *The Trouble with Unity: Latino Politics and the Creation of Identity*. Oxford: Oxford University Press.

Coll, Kathleen. 2006. "Necesidades y Problemas: Immigrant Latina Vernaculars of Belonging, Coalition, and Citizenship in San Francisco, California." In *Latinos and Citizenship: The Dilemma of Belonging*, edited by Susan Oboler, 191–217. New York: Palgrave Macmillan.

Dowling, Julie A., and C. Alison Newby. 2010. "So Far From Miami: Afro-Cuban Encounters with Mexicans in the US Southwest." *Latino Studies* 8(2): 176–94.

Eckstein, Susan. 2006. "Cuban Émigrés and the American Dream." *Perspectives on Politics* 4(2): 297–307.

García, Angela S., and Leah Schmalzbauer. 2017. "Placing Assimilation Theory: Mexican Immigrants in Urban and Rural America." *Annals of the American Academy of Political and Social Science* 672(1): 64–82.

Gil, Vincent Edward. 1976. *The Personal Adjustment and Acculturation of Cuban Immigrants in Los Angeles*. PhD dissertation, University of California, Los Angeles.

Gosin, Monika. 2019. *The Racial Politics of Division: Interethnic Struggles for Legitimacy in Multicultural Miami*. Ithaca, N.Y.: Cornell University Press.

———. 2017. "'A Bitter Diversion': Afro-Cuban Immigrants, Race, and Everyday-Life Resistance." *Latino Studies* 15(1): 4–28.

Greenbaum, Susan. 2002. *More than Black: Afro-Cubans in Tampa*. Gainesville: University Press of Florida.

Kasinitz, Philip, John Mollenkopf, and Mary C. Waters. 2002. "Becoming American/ Becoming New Yorkers: Immigrant Incorporation in a Majority Minority City." *International Migration Review* 36(4): 1020–36.

Lacy, K. 2007. *Blue-Chip Black: Race, Class, and Status in the New Black Middle Class*. Oakland: University of California Press.

Leszczensky, Lars, and Sebastian Pink. 2019. "What Drives Ethnic Homophily? A Relational Approach on How Ethnic Identification Moderates Preferences for Same-Ethnic Friends." *American Sociological Review* 84(3): 394–419.

Li, Wei. 2009. *Ethnoburb: The New Ethnic Community in Urban America*. Honolulu: University of Hawai'i Press.

Light, Ivan, and Steven J. Gold. 2000. *Ethnic Economies*. Bingley, U.K.: Emerald Group.

Mendez, Jennifer Bickham, and Natalia Deeb-Sossa. 2020. "Creating Home, Claiming Place: Latina Immigrant Mothers and the Production of Belonging." *Latino Studies* 18(2): 174–94.

Mirabal, Nancy Raquel. 2003. "'*Ser de Aquí*': Beyond the Cuban Exile Model." *Latino Studies* 1: 366–82.

———. 2017. *Suspect Freedoms: The Racial and Sexual Politics of Cubanidad in New York, 1823–1957*. New York: New York University Press.

Motel, Seth, and Eileen Patten. 2013. "2011, Foreign-Born Population in the United States Statistical Portrait." *Pew Research Center*. January 29. www.pewresearch.org/hispanic /2013/01/29/2011-statistical-information-on-immigrants-in-united-states/.

Newby, C. Alison, and Julie Dowling. 2007. "Black and Hispanic: The Racial Identification of Afro-Cuban Immigrants in the Southwest." *Sociological Perspectives* 50(3): 343–66.

Okamoto, Dina G. 2014. *Redefining Race: Asian American Panethnicity and Shifting Ethnic Boundaries*. New York: Russell Sage Foundation.

Portes, Alejandro. 2012. "Tensions That Make a Difference: Institutions, Interests, and the Immigrant Drive." *Sociological Forum* 27(3): 563–78.

Portes, Alejandro, and Ariel C. Armony. 2018. *The Global Edge: Miami in the Twenty-First Century*. Oakland: University of California Press.

Prieto, Yolanda. 2009. *The Cubans of Union City: Immigrants and Exiles in a New Jersey Community*. Philadelphia: Temple University Press.

Probyn, E. 1996. *Outside Belonging*. London: Routledge.

Radford, Jynnah, and Luis Noe-Bustamante. 2019. "Facts on US Immigrants, 2017." *Pew Research Center*. June 3. www.pewresearch.org/hispanic/2019/06/03/facts -on-u-s-immigrants-2017-data/.

Román, Miriam Jiménez, and Juan Flores. 2010. *The Afro-Latin@ Reader: History and Culture in the United States*. Durham, N.C.: Duke University Press.

Rothe, Eugenio M., and Andres J. Pumariega. 2008. "The New Face of Cubans in the United States: Cultural Process and Generational Change in an Exile Community." *Journal of Immigrant and Refugee Studies* 6(2): 247–66.

Sawyer, Mark Q. 2006. *Racial Politics in Post-Revolutionary Cuba*. New York: Cambridge University Press.

Shutika, D. L. 2011. *Beyond the Borderlands: Migration and Belonging in the United States and Mexico*. Oakland: University of California Press.

Stepick, Alex, and Dutton Stepick, Carol. 2009. Diverse Contexts of Reception and Feelings of Belonging. *Forum Qualitative Sozialforschung / Forum: Qualitative Social Research* 10(3), Art. 15, http://nbn-resolving.de/urn:nbn:de:0114-fqs0903156.

Thomas, Anulkah. 2005. "Black Face, Latin Looks: Racial-Ethnic Identity Among Afro-Latinos in the Los Angeles Region." In *Latino Los Angeles: Transformations, Communities, and Activism*, edited by Enrique Ochoa and Gilda L. Ochoa, 197–221. Tucson: University of Arizona Press.

Torres-Saillant, Silvio. 2002. "Problematic Paradigms: Racial Diversity and Corporate Identity in the Latino Community." In *Latinos: Remaking America*, edited by Marcelo Suárez-Orozco, 435–55. Oakland: University of California Press.

———. 2003. "Inventing the Race: Latinos and the Ethnoracial Pentagon." *Latino Studies* 1: 123–51.

———. 2010. "Divisible Blackness: Reflections on Heterogeneity and Racial Identity." In *The Afro-Latin@ Reader: History and Culture in the United States*, edited by M. Jiménez Román and J. Flores, 453–65. Durham, N.C.: Duke University Press.

Yuval-Davis, N. 2011. *The Politics of Belonging: Intersectional Contestations*. Thousand Oaks, Calif.: Sage.

Wang, Dan J., Hayagreeva Rao, and Sarah A. Soule. 2019. "Crossing Categorical Boundaries: A Study of Diversification by Social Movement Organizations." *American Sociological Review* 84(3): 420–58.

Wimmer, Andreas. 2013. *Ethnic Boundary Making: Institutions, Power, Networks*. Oxford: Oxford University Press.

Zentella, Ana Celia, 2007. "Dime con quién hablas y te diré quién eres: Linguistic (In)security and Latino Unity." In *The Blackwell Companion to Latino Studies*, edited by Juan Flores and Renato Rosaldo, 25–39. Malden, Mass.: Blackwell.

———. 2020. "Aquí no se cogen las guaguas: Language and Puerto Rican Identity in San Diego." In *Dialects from Tropical Islands: Caribbean Spanish in the United States*, edited by Wilfredo Valentín-Márquez and Melvin González-Rivera, 184–200. New York: Routledge.

PART II

Finding Home and Claiming Place Through Familia

CHAPTER 4

Mujeres Luchadoras

Latina Immigrant Women's Homemaking Practices to Assert Belonging in a Philadelphia Suburb

VERÓNICA MONTES

Introduction

On a winter morning in 2016, a group of eight Mexican immigrant women, five children, four college students, and two college professors, myself included, swept the streets of a working-class neighborhood in a suburb of Philadelphia. The streets were empty perhaps because of the early hour, but more likely due to the cold. We swept the streets for nearly two hours, chatting all the while about our lives and what the neighborhood was like twenty years ago when no Mexican immigrants lived here. Once we finished our work, we were invited to a community lunch.

We arrived at a modest apartment, where we were welcomed by a woman in her mid-twenties, with a friendly smile, a sweet voice, and an eight-month-old baby girl in her arms. The familiarity of the women with each other was obvious as they easily, efficiently moved through the kitchen. In minutes, a spread of traditional Mexican dishes—*nopales* (cactus salad), beans, salsas, *barbacoa* (traditional lamb)—was set upon the dining table. Before enjoying the feast, Carmen, the leader of the group of women, asked everyone to introduce themselves and to name what they thought had been the most rewarding experience of the community activity we all had just finished. It soon became clear that the reflective exercise was not the first in which women had engaged as a group.

In time, I would learn that the women were part of *Mujeres Luchadoras* (Warrior Women), a grassroots organization dedicated to helping the community of Latino immigrants in Norristown, Pennsylvania. *Mujeres Luchadoras* later changed its name to *"Coalición Fortaleza Latina"* (Latina Strength Coalition), or CFL, as immigrant men began joining the organization. Drawing on open-ended interviews and participant observation, in this chapter, I analyze community-building activities developed by the CFL that have enabled Latino immigrants in Norristown, a suburb of Philadelphia, to cultivate a sense of belonging in the community. I discuss the spatial as well as organizational dimensions of those activities, their specific structures and meanings, and their roles as vehicles for the social recognition and visibility of Latino immigrants in the area.

I argue that the social practices by which Mexican immigrants in Norristown have developed a sense of belonging occur through a process of *haciendo familia* ("doing" family), through which immigrants deliberately create relationships that become as significant as their own families. Second, I examine how Carmen's house, which serves as *La Casa del Pueblo* (The People's House) during CFL meetings, became a space that has enabled Mexican immigrants in Norristown to develop creative, healing, and liberating practices of resistance, specifically, through a collective process of *conscientización* (conscious-raising). Third, my analysis demonstrates how *el Rancho Chiquito*, the community garden cultivated by the CFL, has functioned as a site of *convivencia* (coexistence), in which a "restorative space of belonging" (Hondagneu-Sotelo 2014) is imaginable. Ultimately, I conclude the chapter by articulating how through the engagement of each of these social practices CFL's members participate in what Argentinian anthropologist Segato has dubbed a *"proyecto histórico de los vínculos"* (historical project of bonds; Facultad Libre 2019), which have allowed these Latino immigrants to develop a sense of belonging in their new host society.

Homemaking, Belonging, and Migration

Studies on migration have revolved around a few key paradigms, including assimilation and transnationalism. While classical assimilation theory sees new immigrants following a "straight-line" convergence, becoming more similar over time in norms, values, behaviors, and characteristics to the host society; transnationalism, in its classical definition, is conceptualized as "the process by which immigrants forge and sustain multi-stranded social relations that link together their societies of origin and settlement" (Basch, Glick

Schiller, and Szanton Blanc 1994, 7). In recent years, however, a newer the-oretical approach to immigrants' experiences of settlement and integration has been unfolding in search of capturing how "immigrants practice place-making and invest meaning and effort into the project of making a new home" (Hondagneu-Sotelo 2017, 14). While most of this new theoretical approach has developed outside the United States (see Boccagni 2016; Duyvendak 2011; Ralph and Staeheli 2011), scholarly interest among U.S. social scientists has also begun to increase (see Castañeda 2018; Hondagneu-Sotelo 2017; Shutika 2011). Thus this newer body of scholarship theorizes the intersection between homemaking and belonging as part of the migration settlement process.

In the context of migration, what does home mean to immigrants? And how do immigrants feel at home? Italian sociologist Boccagni (2016) theo-rizes that the immigrants' home-making projects include both materiality and the realm of relationships, memories, and social imaginaries. Funda-mentally, this process involves the development of an attachment to a place as well as establishing a sense of security, familiarity, and autonomy within specific geographical, social, and temporal spaces (Lähdesmäki et al. 2016). Pechurina (2016) focuses on how material objects in the immigrant home produce routines and give meaning to relationships. In this context, home is conceptualized as an ongoing process "involving both the people we share home with but also the material objects therein" (Ralph and Staeheli 2011, 519). Thus, beyond conceptualizing home as a static place, some scholars (Gurney 1997; Jackson 1995) focus on the diverse ways people "do" and feel home. Home, therefore, is "experienced both as a location and a set of rela-tionships that shape identities and feeling of belonging" (Ralph and Staeheli 2011, 518; Yuval-Davis 2006).

This sense of belonging is constituted through shared meanings and a sense of social alliance between people and the places where they reside: it does not necessarily reference a geographic location but can include places that are physical, virtual, or imagined. As people develop a sense of belong-ing, "they enact cultural practices that enable them to establish and main-tain social, political, and economic relationships as well as social networks" (Shutika 2011, 15). Thus, a sense of belonging relates to the notion of home, and is constituted through human connections to the place one inhabits and shares with members of the same community.

The context of reception plays a determining role for immigrants' sense of belonging and feeling at home in their new host societies (Castañeda 2018).

In an adverse context of reception, such as that currently endured by immigrant communities of color in the United States where immigrants and their families have been criminalized and dehumanized, immigrants' level of integration and their sense of belonging in their new host societies have been destabilized. However, despite this adversity immigrant communities in general, and Mexican immigrant communities in particular, have begun to *echar raíces* (set down roots) in their new host societies, which allows them to experience a sense of feeling at home. To illustrate how immigrants in Norristown "do" home, in this chapter, I analyze how immigrants construct home-making processes through which they develop and claim a sense of belonging in the new society. Particularly, I examine shared meanings and social alliances between members of CFL and places and spaces in Norristown that allow them to achieve a sense of continuity, familiarity, and certainty, crucial ingredients in immigrants' search for home.

Research Context

In the late 1990s, the number of Mexican immigrants in Greater Philadelphia began to rise. By the mid-2000s, their presence prompted migration scholars such as Zuñiga and Hernández-León (2005) to refer to the area as a new immigrant destination. Although most of Greater Philadelphia's Mexican immigrants work and reside in the city proper, a significant number of them live in the suburbs where they can be closer to work. This is the case for the roughly ten thousand Mexican immigrants who reside in the working-class, former industrial town of Norristown (Vitiello et al. 2017), located approximately six miles northwest of Philadelphia. Before the arrival of Mexican immigrants, the town's demand for factory and mill laborers made Norristown a choice destination for Irish, Jewish, and Italian immigrants, as well as Black workers from the southern United States. Norristown's success as an industrial center began to decline after 1912, however, amid the exodus of mills and factories to the South (Vitiello et al. 2017). By the 1980s, when many of the town's stores closed their doors due to insurmountable competition with nearby shopping malls, Norristown's population dropped significantly.

However, by the late 1990s, the shift from a capital-intensive to a service-oriented economy revived the demand for two sources of immigrant labor in the area. One consisted mostly of South and Southeast Asians working in pharmaceutical research, financial services, and other fields, whereas the other, comprised mostly of Latinos, especially Mexicans, and some Africans were employed in the service sector (Singer et al. 2008).

The arrival of new immigrant communities has had a positive impact in the region both at the economic and social levels. For instance, in the early 2000s, Marshall Street, Norristown's chief commercial area, closely resembled a war zone nearly void of any sign of commercial life. Today, by contrast, the street contains numerous *panaderias* (bakeries), restaurants, grocery stores, beauty salons, clothing stores, and boutiques that specialize in items for use in traditional Mexican celebrations, including *quinceañeras* (fifteenth-birthday celebrations for girls), baptisms, and first communions. In a sense, the significant number of Mexican-owned businesses on Marshall Street has made the vicinity the commercial face of Norristown's "Little Mexico."

Despite the acknowledged importance of the Mexican immigrant population to the region's economy, in 2012 a series of ICE raids of immigrants' homes in the neighborhood unraveled the social fabric of Norristown's immigrant community. Many immigrant families were torn apart as a result, and a sense of fear permeated the town. In that context of social chaos, *Mujeres Luchadoras* was born.

The Origins of *Mujeres Luchadoras*

Mujeres Luchadoras would not exist without Carmen Guerrero. A petite woman with long black hair, expressive eyes, and an ever-friendly personality, Carmen has become a well-known community organizer, not only in Norristown but in greater Philadelphia. A proud descendant of indigenous parents who left their communities in the early 1960s, Carmen was born in Mexico City, where she lived before moving to Philadelphia. Like millions of immigrant women worldwide who leave their children behind upon traveling to work in other countries, Carmen came to the United States in 2000 while her three daughters—ages twelve, nine, and eight—remained in Mexico. After eighteen months of separation from her children, Carmen found a way to bring them to Philadelphia, and in October 2001, they were reunited.

Experienced in social justice organizing in Mexico, upon arriving in Norristown, Carmen turned her focus to improving the living and work conditions of Norristown's immigrant population. By 2003, with the support of her three daughters, she had managed to organize several groups, including ones for women, students, children, and even *jornaleros* (day laborers).

However, in 2012 Montgomery County, Pennsylvania, where Norristown is located, decided to implement 287(g), which later expanded into the Secure Communities Program (SCP). This program allows local police officers to access immigration databases of the Department of Homeland Security to arbitrarily verify the immigration status of anyone who might be pulled over by local police. Right after the implementation of SCP, a series of ICE home raids swept through Norristown. According to Carmen, as dozens of immigrants, mostly men, were arrested, detained, and deported, their families were effectively dismembered. As a result of these home raids, people were afraid to go out to the streets, to go to work, to take children to schools, and, above all, to participate in the groups Carmen had organized.

In response to the sense of desolation that these ICE raids left in the community, some Mexican immigrant women began to seek support among themselves. Immigrant women approached Amaya, Carmen's oldest daughter, who recognized the need to create a space where women could share information and discuss challenges in their personal lives, their families, and their community. This was how *Mujeres Luchadoras* was born as a space where women could gather to share information about resources available in their community.

Carmen also organized what she called "*la escuelita dominical*" (Sunday school), a series of classes for immigrants who could not attend the meetings on Tuesdays which she hosted in the parking lot of her workplace. Carmen invited immigration lawyers and people working in pro-immigrant organizations to inform attendees about their rights and about places where they might obtain assistance. Carmen fondly remembered that the "Sunday school was amazing because people started to see unity there. We began to see that more people were interested not only in learning but also in being leaders. That was what we were looking for since you can't do the work alone. It's very exhausting."

In 2016, Carmen met Elizabeth Sweet, an assistant professor at Temple University in the Department of Geography and Urban Studies, who offered to hold a workshop for *Mujeres Luchadoras* called "Body Mapping and Community Mapping" (see Sweet and Ortiz Escalante 2017), the focus of which, according to Carmen, was "to identify factors of violence in the community and how those factors came into households." After the workshop, Betsy and Carmen, along with two other faculty members at Temple University, co-wrote a grant proposal to fund a workshop on economic self-sufficiency that they submitted to an organization in Chicago. After many hours of work to finalize the proposal and a yearlong wait, they finally secured funding. In October 2016, thirty-five people registered for the workshop, co-taught by Carmen and Betsy, although only fifteen managed to complete it.

Workshop participants included not only women but also immigrant men, whose involvement prompted *Mujeres Luchadoras* to adopt a more inclusive name—the CFL—in February 2017. During the organization's brief lifetime to date, its members have accumulated experiences and knowledge that have prompted them to engage in a reflective process about themselves, their social circumstances, and their ability to find solutions to their challenges. With such experience and knowledge, members of the CFL initiated a series of community-oriented projects, including a community garden and a series of educational workshops for CFL members. Before delving into a discussion of the different projects developed by CFL in what follows, I detail the methodology used in this project.

Methods and Data

After a year of involvement with *Mujeres Luchadoras*, I talked to Carmen about my interest in documenting the different projects that the group was developing. Sensing that my work could preserve the institutional memory of the organization, Carmen enthusiastically agreed. In spring 2017, I submitted a research proposal to my college's Institutional Review Board to officially begin an ethnographic study consisting of face-to-face, open-ended interviews, participant observation, and informal interviews with CFL volunteers.

The data that I present in this chapter draw on many hours of participant observation that I conducted at activities organized by the CFL, including weekly meetings, workshops, family gatherings, and social, political, and cultural events. On average, the CFL's weekly meetings last at least two hours, and the number of members attending them varies from eight to twenty. In this chapter, I also draw on five interviews with Carmen, her daughters Amaya and Eva, and two other founding members of the CFL.

The interviews, which were audio recorded with the informant's permission and conducted in Spanish, lasted from one to two hours. In addition to the transcripts, I took field notes and drafted analytical memos. I also documented work performed by CFL members in dozens of photographs, which have since become the institutional memory of the organization. I also conducted a content analysis of eighteen journal entries written by members of the CFL who participated in the workshop on economic self-sufficiency.

One of the community activities that CFL has developed for its members is organizing workshops, which are regarded as a pivotal means of empowerment for its members. I attended four such workshops, which respectively addressed reproductive health, mental health, occupational therapy, and migration. In addition, I attended three social gatherings organized by CFL—in fall 2016 a community picnic at a farm in the countryside attended by about thirty people, in spring 2017 the celebration of the organization's third anniversary attended by about fifty people, and in summer 2017 the graduation ceremony for individuals who completed the workshop on economic self-sufficiency.

Last, I should mention that my epistemology as a feminist ethnographer defined the ways in which I conducted the research reported here. As in my previous research (Montes and Paris Pombo 2019), the study presented here was conducted within the framework of participatory research, in which participating as a volunteer with the CFL undoubtedly illuminated for me how its members make sense of what *home* means to them and, more importantly, how they foster that feeling of belonging in their activities. In that sense, participatory research is also emotional work, and the capacity of researchers who conduct such research to establish connections with social actors can be regarded as a resource for knowledge production (Arenas 2015; Van Wijnendaele 2014; Sharp 2009).

In what follows, I examine how the projects and activities developed by the CFL have served as important social mechanisms for creating a sense of community among its members, as well as for affirming their rights to claim space and belonging in their new society.

Haciendo Familia and Everyday Belonging

One Sunday morning in spring 2016, I started regularly attending the CFL's weekly meetings. As soon as I entered Carmen's house, where the meetings took place, I heard Carmen's voice and followed it down into the spacious finished basement, which contained a desk and a bookcase with books scattered on its shelves. Several campaign posters, one for "A Day Without Immigrants," and some newspaper clips of public events that Carmen had attended were hung on the walls.[1] Although a basement, two large windows provided enough daylight so that turning on the lights was unnecessary. In the center of the room, a dozen folding chairs had been arranged in a circle, and as attendees arrived, each quietly sat down in anticipation for the meeting to begin.

In all, eight people—six women and two men—attended the two and half-hour meeting that day. At its conclusion, Carmen invited us to go upstairs for lunch. Each attendee had brought a dish to share, and as I ascended the stairs, I heard people laughing and chatting joyfully in the kitchen while they warmed up the food. The small kitchen quickly filled with people who moved around each other as they prepared their dishes. Carmen grabbed food from the fridge, some people warmed up tortillas, another person made Mexican coffee (i.e., coffee with a pinch of cinnamon), and a couple of others brought the food into the dining room. Once the food was served, people started filling their plates and sat down around a midsize dining table spread with tostadas, beans, salsa, cheese, tortillas, tamales, and coffee. As I would soon discover, each meeting ended in the same way—with everybody eating in the dining room in a relaxed, intimate atmosphere permeated by laughter, jokes, and a sense of camaraderie. We all had the sense of being welcome at La Casa del Pueblo (the People's House), a name that one CFL member spontaneously began calling the group's meeting place. Immediately fond of the name, Carmen believed that *"La Casa del Pueblo"* perfectly captured what the space has meant to members of the CFL as a place where everyone is welcome and can feel at home.

Immigration scholars have documented how the existence of social and reciprocal networks within sites of immigrant settlement help immigrants to overcome challenges involved in settling in a new society (Flores-Yeffal 2013). For the members of CFL, *La Casa del Pueblo* became that place where social and networks of reciprocity materialize and a space where Mexican immigrants could foster new family-like ties based on relationships of *confianza* (trust), solidarity, empathy, and reciprocity—as the following quotes illustrate:

"It's a home for immigrants where we'll always have a big family." (thirty-six-year-old Dominican woman)

"It's like having a family, a place where you can find friends that you can trust." (fifty-six-year-old Mexican man)

"I like that I've found a home." (twenty-five-year-old Mexican woman)

These quotes were taken from journal entries written by several CFL members in the summer of 2017. These entries show how these immigrants actively engage in the process that I refer to as *haciendo familia* (doing family), whereby immigrants established meaningful relationships with others. These new links are vital in the social and emotional lives of these immigrants since it is these new interpersonal relationships that allow immigrants to find support in times of need. Such networks typically operate as surrogate families for immigrants that provide not only material support—shelter, job referrals, and loans, among other things—but also, and perhaps more importantly, emotional support and care during the process of *desarraigo* (uprooting) that immigrants experience upon leaving their countries of origin and resettling elsewhere.

Not only does *La Casa del Pueblo* provide its members the opportunity to engage in this process of *haciendo familia*, but it also fosters the space to create moments of *diversión* [playfulness] and laughter. According to Laguna (2017), the study of feelings such as anger, loss, pain, and suffering "has dominated academic conversation around minoritarian experience in the United States" and consequently distracted scholarly interest away from the distinct, ludic methods of diversion in such communities. For members of CFL, sharing these moments of diversion is translated to what they refer to as *sentirse a gusto* (feeling at ease). When members were asked what they liked about coming to the weekly meetings, most responses included the idea of *sentirse a gusto*, which I conceptualize as a subjective experience that one has regarding the space that one inhabits, particularly, feeling safe and joyful. Furthermore, this idea of *sentirse a gusto* evokes the possibility of creating a space for *convivencia* (coexistence) where members of CFL can perform longed-for cultural practices which allow them to experience a sense of freedom, and, most importantly, express themselves—as the following quotes shared by several CFL members reveal:

"I like how we get together at lunchtime." (twenty-two-year-old Mexican woman)

"I like how the members get together, how they learn, and how they get along." (forty-five-year-old Mexican woman)

"I feel free among my peers and in my community." (thirty-two-year-old Mexican woman)

"The CFL has helped me to not feel alone in the United States." (twenty-five-year-old Mexican woman)

"I like that we feel free and in community." (fifty-seven-year-old Mexican woman)

Playful *convivencia* in the CFL is clearly displayed during the potluck suppers where participants not only feast on traditional Mexican dishes, but also share lots of laughter, jokes, and a sense of *sentirse a gusto*. Often, contagious laughter erupts spontaneously after someone makes a silly comment. In those cases, laughter functions as what Dyrness (2011) has called "a source of healing"; by laughing, members of the CFL release some of the psychosocial tensions that they face daily as a result of the precarities that they face as (often) undocumented immigrants. Thus, in the context of a sociopolitical climate hostile to immigrants, playful *convivencia* can provide immigrants with the chance to "refigure the terms of their existence and transgress relations of inequality in their everyday lives" (Dyrness 2011, 154).

Thus, in the current U.S. political climate, where xenophobic discourses and the criminalization of Mexican immigrants prevail, the possibility of engaging in the process of *haciendo familia* in the new host society becomes crucial to cope with a hostile and aggressive environment. Perhaps more importantly, *La Casa del Pueblo* also becomes a site of emotional and spiritual restoration, where immigrants can feel as though they are beyond the threat of punitive U.S. immigration policy. Paraphrasing hooks (1990) in her analysis of the role of "homeplace," such spaces become crucial for the restoration of the dignity of communities of color within a society that strips them of their humanity.

Collective Process of *Conscientización*

Feminist scholars have documented the importance of intimate, safe spaces, where members of marginalized communities can support each other by giving voice to their experiences, questioning the structures that marginalize them, and nurturing their resilience (Dyrness 2011; Montes and Paris 2019). Indeed, spaces such as family kitchens became counter-spaces for resistance (Dyrness's 2011). In this regard, *La Casa del Pueblo* became a space that has enabled Mexican immigrants in Norristown to develop creative, healing, and liberating practices of resistance, specifically, through a collective process of *concientización* (conscious-raising).

Foundationally situated in the work of Paulo Freire's popular education model, the goal of *concientización* is to engage people to "transform unjust social, economic, and political conditions" (Choules 2007, 160). In this context, *concientización* recognizes human beings as active agents, which enables them "to take ownership of their own reality in order to modify it" (Boumlik and Schwartz 2016, 322). For the CFL members, a process of *concientización* began in 2012 when Carmen and her oldest daughter, Amaya, began organizing the weekly meetings of *Mujeres Luchadoras*. During those meetings, all participants engaged in the process of awareness of their realities and oppressions, as Carmen recalled: "We met every Tuesday, and we talked. We discussed what problems we had within the family and within the community and how we could solve them. We met, and sometimes there were ten and sometimes up to twenty people who showed up to talk about what our needs were."

Carmen's words vividly capture how, by sharing their personal stories, the *Mujeres Luchadoras* made sense of and recounted their lived experiences and the challenges that they endured as undocumented Mexican immigrant women in their own words and from their perspectives. Specifically, these weekly meetings allowed these women to identify their shared oppressions: lack of access to healthcare, education, employment, working rights, recreation, the transmission of sexual diseases, teenage pregnancy, drug addiction, alcoholism, domestic violence, and, of course, immigration. Thus, by listening to each other and realizing that they have shared many of the same problems, the women became less alienated. More importantly, as studies of other women-joined spaces have shown (Montes and Pombo 2019; Dyrness 2011), such spaces afford women the opportunity for self-reflection, which can lead to *concientización* over time.

Thus, for Carmen, CFL members' self-reflection on their own realities constitutes the first step in the process of *concientización*, which consequently might allow people to "begin to look objectively at the systems and causes of their oppression through dialogue and critical thinking and collectively embrace agency and action against the oppressive forces they are experiencing" (Boumlik and Schwartz, 2016, 322; see Birden 2004). As Carmen reflected, "Because when a person knows why she is here, she will start to defend herself, unlike a person who thinks that she is guilty of having come

FIGURE 4.1 Working with songs from the homeland: Carmen Guerrero and a member of CFL in June 2017. Photo by the author.

here and that the United States is doing us a favor here. No, when people start to know that there is an economic or global problem, then they start to say, 'Oh, I did not know.'"

For Carmen, as her words reveal, access to self-reflection becomes crucial in the processes of *conscientización*, which relies on the transformation of each individual's critical consciousness about his or her personal history and socioeconomic circumstances and their relationship with broader social structures.

If *Mujeres Luchadoras*' weekly meetings constituted a space where the awareness process began, CFL's workshops emerged as a space where this process was consolidated for participants. The first twelve-week workshop on economic self-sufficiency took place from October 2016 to February 2017. In Carmen's words, the workshop was a tool for "exploring the skills and knowledge that each one [CFL member] has and how through that knowledge one can generate resources to be self-sufficient economically." After the workshop participants shared their reflections about what they had learned:

"From the workshop, I learned how and where to save, how to generate income in case of an emergency—about how, if we unite, we can create a cooperative." (thirty-two-year-old Mexican man)

"From the workshop, I learned to organize my finances at home. I learned why we're here and why we migrate." (thirty-nine-year-old Mexican woman)

"I learned how to manage my money, create alternative sources of income, socialize, and create compananship." (Mexican man in his early thirties)

In addition to this first workshop, CFL members participated in a variety of workshops that included themes such as reproductive and mental health, "know your rights" workshops, stress management, and migration. At the time of this writing (2021), a group had begun monthly workshops on nutrition. CFL members chose the themes for the workshops, demonstrating the social agency of participants to identify first their learning interests and second members' commitment to educating themselves as a tool for social transformation. This commitment to education became apparent when CFL members were asked what they liked most about being part of this organization, and they responded:

"I have found a place where I have acquired a lot of knowledge thanks to the different workshops." (thirty-year-old Mexican man)

"I like that CFL acknowledges the importance of knowledge to get ahead." (thirty-five-year-old Mexican man)

FIGURE 4.2   CFL members attending a workshop at the organization's fifth anniversary, April 2018. Photo by author.

"I like CFL for everything we learn." (fifty-five-year-old Mexican woman)

"I like CFL because they give us tools based on knowledge to take away our fear." (twenty-two-year-old Mexican woman)

La Casa del Pueblo represents the first step for immigrants to engage in both an individual and a collective process of *concientización* that equips them with analytical tools to engage in critical reflection and dialogue which can lead to praxis, or what (Dyrness 2011) refers to as "public forms of resistance." Such resistance speaks to the ways in which the CFL's members may respond to structures of vulnerability that affect them and work to alter their circumstances. By so doing, members of the CFL can affirm their right to lay claim to space and forge a sense of belonging in their new society.

Rancho Chiquito: The Process of *Echar Raíces* through Participating in a Community Garden

In 2017, members of the CFL launched a new project—the cultivation of a community garden. In February of that year, without knowing the magnitude of the work and level of commitment that such a project would require of them, members began to germinate the first seeds of the vegetables that they had decided to plant in the garden once the cold winter came to an end. For most members, participating in the community garden project represented an opportunity, in one way or another, to re-create their homelands in the United States, hence the name "*Rancho Chiquito*" (Little Farm).

The project began when Carmen was invited to plant and harvest vegetables at the Edible Forest Urban Farm (EFUF). The invitation could not be better timed, for it came soon after members of the CFL had finished the workshop on economic self-sufficiency, in which they had learned some of the dynamics of the economy and the different ways through which they could attain financial independence. For Carmen, access to healthy, fresh, affordable food was at the core of any self-sufficiency, and she remembered thinking that "perhaps we, as a group, can get organized and open a community kitchen to feed our children and, above all, to make a change in our diets." When Carmen was invited to become part of the EFUF, she saw it as an opportunity to continue the work of the CFL workshops by promoting self-sufficiency within her community.

As a working-class, former industrial town in northwest Philadelphia, Norristown may not seem like a place where one might come across a verdant garden while strolling on a Sunday morning. However, on Forrest Avenue, a one-way side street, twin thirty-three-year-old brothers Joel and Caleb Derby began the EFUF in 2010 (Moye 2013). As part of the recent, robust community garden movement that since the mid-1990s has spread across U.S. cities, including Philadelphia (Saldivar-Tanaka and Krasny 2004), the EFUF has aimed to not only create spaces where people can access fresh, organic products but also incorporate aspects of community development and open space. As suggested in other studies on community gardens, those open spaces, mainly in inner cities, "have been hailed as safe havens that provide residents with a sense of nature, community, rootedness, and power" (Schmelzkopf 1995, 364). For immigrants who live in communities with high levels of social and legal vulnerability, such "gardens serve as restorative spaces of belonging and inclusion, encompassing both recreation and the re-creation of homeland practices and culture" (Hondagneu-Sotelo 2014, 120). In that sense, *Rancho Chiquito* has provided members of the CFL with another site of *convivencia*, where a "restorative space of belonging" (Hondagneu-Sotelo 2014) is imaginable alongside the possibility for the members to participate in what Segato has called a *"proyecto histórico de los vínculos"* (historical project of bonds) consisting of investing in the affective and emotional bonds of individuals to foster community relations of support and solidarity (Facultad Libre 2019).

Due to administrative complications, the maintenance of the garden at the EFUF had been neglected during the previous harvest season. Consequently, when members of the CFL were invited to develop the garden, much work remained to be done before the soil was ready to support plants. During the first month, the CFL's members spent several hours each Sunday cleaning the garden, removing weeds, disposing of gravel that had been used as a failed agricultural technique to moisten the soil, constructing new garden beds, and preparing the ground for planting. The number of members who showed up to work in the garden varied from week to week. At times, about thirty people worked in the garden at once, and not only members of the CFL, for often present were allies who believed in supporting the project.

As a space of *convivencia*, *Rancho Chiquito* is where men, women, children, and friends of the CFL come together to actively nourish and cultivate elements of homeland as well as social and material life that help immigrants in Norristown to re-create cultural practices for themselves and their families. One such aspect of the social life of the *terruño* (homeland) has been the sense of festivity that could be breathed in during each day of work in the garden. The delicious meals that followed the work emerged as some of the most visible manifestations of this sense of festivity. In the open space at *Rancho Chiquito*, members of CFL prepare homemade dishes such as hand-made tortillas, *sopes* (a thicker tortilla with pinched sides with vegetables and meat toppings), which recreate for many of these immigrants family gatherings they used to enjoy in their communities of origin.

Another less visible but more audible manifestation is the ever-present chatter as immigrants toil in the garden. Informal conversations while working in the garden addresses trivial matters such as the weather, recipes, and remedies for common illnesses; at other times, members of the CFL test their knowledge of U.S. and Mexican politics. Conversations vary along gender lines. While for immigrant men, conversations circulate around politics and work-related issues, for immigrant women, these conversations allow them to revisit some of their childhood memories, particularly for those with rural backgrounds. For example, on a hot summer afternoon in 2017, Carmen, along with two other women, Carmen and Maria, after working for a couple of hours in the garden, sat down to rest while drinking cold *horchata* (a traditional, sweet, rice-based drink flavored with cinnamon). They began talking about their childhood and their memories of the *campo* (countryside). Maria, a woman in her late fifties and with the onset of arthritis in her legs, remembered with some nostalgia her years as a *campesina* (peasant) planting tomatoes in her native Puebla, Mexico.

The garden also serves as a space where these immigrants become visible in the community through the execution of cultural celebrations such as the Day of the Dead. Over the last three years, these Latino immigrants have shared this tradition with the members of the community by inviting them to participate in the arrangement of the altars. By doing so, the members not only engage the local community to learn about their cultural traditions but also involve their children in these cultural practices, reinforcing healthy parent-child relationships, which in Carmen's terms sows the seeds for future community organizers who, from an early age, have participated in their parents' process of *echar raíces* in a new society.

In sum, *Rancho Chiquito* serves as another space of *convivencia* where not only the opportunity to participate in a community garden is possible, but more importantly it is a space where members of the CFL literally engage in a process of *echar raíces* in their new society. By engaging in the practice of gardening, these immigrants recreate cultural practices that resemble those of their homelands, such as their strong relationship with the land.

Final Remarks

The aim of this chapter has been to examine how members of CFL have developed a sense of home and belonging in their new host society by engaging in different social practices that include fostering new family-like ties with other Latino immigrants, developing a process of individual and communual *concientización,* and literally *echar raíces* in the new community through their participation in a community garden. Research with the CFL demonstrates how the group's projects and activities have served as pivotal social mechanisms for creating a sense of community, as well as to affirm members' rights as individuals to claim space and belong in their new society. By examining the interplay of belonging, homemaking, and migration, the chapter contributes to knowledge about Latino immigrant communities in the United States in three ways.

First, the efforts of the women and men of CFL to recreate a sense of home and belonging in their new host society reveal the importance of the establishment of relationships based on *confianza,* solidarity, empathy, and reciprocity, which have helped them to cope with a hostile sociopolitical climate. In search of feeling at home again, these immigrants instinctively turn to the practice of *haciendo familia,* which means that they deliberately choose friendships that, in many cases, end up becoming as significant as their own families. Thus, by recreating familial practices that many of the members once performed in their homelands, they have worked to foster family-like units in their new homes. These new relationships function as fictive kin in the absence of such since some members of CFL are alone in the new host society. Studies on solidarity networks have shown in the case of immigrants without this kind of community support, these chosen familial relationships become crucial to these immigrants' emotional and physical survival, especially in times of need, as has been the case during the current pandemic in which the Latino immigrant community has been among those most deeply affected. A few months after the pandemic began, Carmen, with the support of members of the community, myself included, began the delivery of *despensas* (boxes of fresh food products used in Latino cooking) not only to CFL members but also other Latino immigrants such as the *jornaleros* (day laborers). Thus not only do these chosen relationships help immigrants cope with the challenges of alienation but, more importantly, they do become crucial for developing a sense of belonging, as it is through these chosen family-like relations that these immigrants begin to jointly write their own history in the new host society.

Second, I see members of CFL not merely as subjects of suffering, but as agents who have demonstrated creative, healing, and liberating practices of resistance via distinct practices of *convivencia*. Such practices can be nourished only in a counter-space such as *La Casa del Pueblo*, which for Carmen, the group's founder, reflects her desire to help to create a space of home and safety in Norristown for each member of the CFL. In that regard, *La Casa del Pueblo* has become a space that belongs to *el pueblo* (the people), which seems to have created a sense of permanence and belonging within the physical space of Norristown for each member of the coalition. Moreover, as a space *"para el pueblo"* (for the people), *La Casa del Pueblo* represents the first step for the immigrants to engage in individual as well as collective processes of *concientización*, which has equipped them with analytical tools to comprehend their personal socioeconomic and historical circumstances and the relationship that those circumstances have with broader social structures. By so doing, CFL members may take ownership of their reality in order to change it, leading to a form of public resistance.

Finally, each one of these social practices examined in this chapter demonstrates the individual and collective activities that have allowed this immigrant community not merely to survive despite the complicated inequities that it has endured, but also to develop tremendous resourcefulness and resilience. By engaging in these practices these immigrants actively participate in their own *proyecto histórico de los vínculos* by cultivating affective and emotional bonds to develop community relations of support and solidarity. Through these activities and projects, members of the CFL not only make themselves visible in a society that has recklessly denied their presence, but also create practices through which they assert their belonging in their new society.

Note

1. The "Day Without Immigrants" was part of a series of protests that began in 2006 as a grassroot political response to xenophobic and nativist American migration policy against noncitizen immigrant workers in the United States (Heiskanen 2009).

References

Arenas, Iván. 2015. "The Mobile Politics of Emotions and Social Movement in Oaxaca, Mexico." *Antipode* 47(5): 1121–40.

Basch, Linda, Nina Glick Schiller, and Cristina Szanton Blanc. 1994. *Nations Unbound: Transnational Projects, Postcolonial Predicaments, and Deterritorialized Nation-States.* Amsterdam: Gordon and Breach.

Birden, Susan. 2004. "Theorizing a Coalition-Engendered Education: The Case of the Boston Women's Health Book Collective's Body Education." *Adult Education Quarterly* 54(4): 257–72.

Boccagni, Paolo. 2017. *Migration and the Search for Home: Mapping Domestic Space in Migrants' Everyday Lives.* New York: Palgrave MacMillan.

Boumlik, Habiba, and Joni Schwartz. 2016. "Conscientization and Third Space: A Case Study of Tunisian Activism." *Adult Education Quarterly* 66(4): 319–35.

Castañeda, Ernesto. 2018. *A Place to Call Home: Immigrant Exclusion and Urban Belonging in New York, Paris, and Barcelona.* Stanford: Stanford University Press.

Choules, Kathryn. 2007. "Social Change Education: Context Matters." *Adult Education Quarterly* 57(2): 159–76.

Duyvendak, Jan Willem. 2011. *The Politics of Home: Belonging and Nostalgia in Europe and the United States.* New York: Springer.

Dyrness, Andrea. 2011. *Mothers United: An Immigrant Struggle For Socially Just Education.* Minneapolis: University of Minnesota Press.

Facultad Libre. 2019. "Entrevista Pública con Rita Segato." Facultad Libre Channel. YouTube. www.youtube.com/watch?v=at46WYy0Xj4.

Flores-Yeffal, Nadia Yamel. 2013. *Migration-Trust Networks: Social Cohesion in Mexican US-Bound Emigration.* College Station: Texas A&M University Press.

Gurney, Craig M. 1997. "'. . . Half of Me Was Satisfied': Making Sense of Home Through Episodic Ethnographies." *Women's Studies International Forum* 20(3): 373–86.

Heiskanen, Benita. 2009. "A Day Without Immigrants." *European Journal of American Studies* 4(3). https://doi.org/10.4000/ejas.7717.

Hondagneu-Sotelo, Pierrette. 2014. *Paradise Transplanted: Migration and the Making of California Gardens.* Oakland: University of California Press.

———. 2017. "At Home in Inner-City Immigrant Community Gardens." *Journal of Housing and the Built Environment* 32(1): 13–28.

hooks, bell. 1990. *Yearning: Race, Gender and Cultural Politics.* Boston: South End Press.

Jackson, Michael. 1995. *At Home in the World.* Durham, N.C.: Duke University Press.

Laguna, Albert Sergio. 2017. *Diversión: Play and Popular Culture in Cuban America.* New York: New York University Press.

Lähdesmäki, Tuuli, Tuija Saresma, Saara Jäntti, Nina Sääskilahti, Antti Vallius, and Kaisa Ahvenjärvi. 2016. "Fluidity and Flexibility of 'Belonging': Uses of the Concept in Contemporary Research." *Acta Sociologica* 59(3): 1–15.

Montes, Verónica, and María Dolores Paris Pombo. 2019. "Ethics of Care, Emotional Work, and Collective Action of Solidarity: The Patronas in Mexico." *Gender, Place & Culture* 26(4): 559–80.

Moye, Jocelyne. 2013. "Brothers Turn a Norristown Street into an Urban Farm." *The Times Herald.* August 25. www.timesherald.com/news/brothers-turn-a-norristown -street-into-an-urban-farm/article_41078269-e879-575c-b460-5ff4f907d24b.html.

Pechurina, Anna. 2016. *Material Cultures, Migrations, and Identities: What the Eye Cannot See.* New York: Springer.

Ralph, David, and Lynn A. Staeheli. 2011. "Home and Migration: Mobilities, Belongings and Identities." *Geography Compass* 5(7): 517–30.

Saldivar-Tanaka, Laura, and Marianne E. Krasny. 2004. "Culturing Community Development, Neighborhood Open Space, and Civic Agriculture: The Case of Latino Community Gardens in New York City." *Agriculture and Human Values* 21: 399–412.

Schmelzkopf, Karen. 1995. "Urban Community Gardens as a Contested Space." *Geographical Review* 85(3): 364–81.

Sharp, Joanne. 2009. "Geography and Gender: What Belongs to Feminist Geography? Emotion, Power and Change." *Progress in Human Geography* 33(1): 74–80.

Shutika, Debra Lattanzi. 2011. *Beyond the Borderlands: Migration and Belonging in the United States and Mexico.* Oakland: University of California Press.

Singer, Audrey, Domenic Vitiello, Michael Katz, and David Park. 2008. *Recent Immigration to Philadelphia: Regional Change and Response.* Washington, D.C.: Brookings Institution.

Sweet, Elizabeth L., and Sara Ortiz Escalante. 2017. "Engaging Territorio Cuerpo-Tierra Through Body and Community Mapping: A Methodology for Making Communities Safer." *Gender, Place & Culture* 24(4): 594–606.

Van Wijnendaele, Barbara. 2014. "The Politics of Emotion in Participatory Processes of Empowerment and Change." *Antipode* 46(1): 266–82.

Vitiello, Domenic, Hilary P. Dick, Danielle DiVerde, and Veronica Willig. 2017. "Mexicans and Mexico." *The Encyclopedia of Greater Philadelphia.* Rutgers University. https://philadelphiaencyclopedia.org/archive/mexicans-and-mexico/.

Yuval-Davis, Nira. 2006. "Belonging and the Politics of Belonging." *Patterns of Prejudice* 40(3): 197–214.

Zuñiga, Víctor, and Rubén Hernández-León, eds. 2005. *New Destinations: Mexican Immigration in the United States.* New York: Russell Sage Foundation.

CHAPTER 5

Creating Home, Claiming Place

Latina Immigrant Mothers and the
Production of Belonging

JENNIFER BICKHAM MENDEZ AND NATALIA DEEB-SOSSA

In this chapter,[1] we draw on extensive ethnographic research with Latina immigrant women in two sites on opposite sides of the United States—"Squire Town" (ST), a community in Northern California with a long history of Latina/o farmworker settlement, and Williamsburg, Virginia, a much more recent destination for immigrants from Latin America, located in the historic colonial capital of this southeastern state.[2] We bring these two cases together within a comparative framework to analyze how Latina immigrant mothers, in distinct contexts, though excluded from full social membership, have made significant claims to place and belonging through their sustained individual and collective efforts to ensure the well-being of their families.[3]

Latinas/os have recently gained a national presence in the US, and in settlement communities across the country, they face multiple hardships in their daily lives due in large part to the intensification of state surveillance and policing of immigrant and minority populations (Foner and Simon 2015). For immigrant women, in particular, profound social disinvestment in low-income, minority communities combined with restrictionist immigration policies have severely affected their ability to meet their gendered obligations as caretakers of the family (Abrego and Menjívar 2011). Nonetheless, Latina women continue the daily work of survival, which requires them "to navigate and adapt within pathological social structures even when faced with limited options, prohibitive barriers, and dangerous potential consequences" (Farfán-Santos 2019, 70).

Consistent with other research on low-income Latina immigrants, in our field sites mothers played a primary role in the procurement of community resources to sustain their families (Menjívar 2000; Hondagneu-Sotelo 1994). Meeting their families' educational, health care, housing, and other needs meant that women had to learn to navigate unfamiliar institutional, geographic, and even political spaces. Through these public activities, these women established attachments to place and constructed feelings of "being at home"—what researchers have termed a "sense of belonging" (Antonsich 2010; Yuval-Davis 2006). However, our comparative analysis also reveals varied and place-specific pathways to belonging, adding empirical depth to understandings of how immigrants actively negotiate distinct social landscapes and weave themselves into community life (García and Schmalzbauer 2017; Schmalzbauer 2014).

In Williamsburg, a suburban area with a relatively small Latina/o presence, when mothers interacted with local institutions they risked standing out as an "'unbelonging' presence" and "be[ing] the subject of surveillance and policeability" (Licona and Maldonado 2014, 4). In this site where kinship and co-ethnic networks were sparse, women produced a sense of belonging and connection to place primarily through individualized means—by overcoming fear of the authorities in order to access life-sustaining services, hold their families together, and procure much-needed resources—often in the absence of male partners who had been deported. In so doing, they built and expanded their own support networks and persevered in the face of exclusion. Through such resilience they have been instrumental in maintaining a Latina/o presence in the Williamsburg area, establishing a foothold in the community that has enabled Central American families to send for children and other kin who now constitute a second wave of immigration to this historic place.

In contrast, in ST, California, where a Latina/o farmworker community has existed for generations, mothers organized collectively to challenge the depletion of health-care, recreational, and educational resources in their community. They actively claimed belonging through collective advocacy efforts, through which they contested the parameters of their social exclusion—a process that scholars call "the politics of belonging" (Antonsich 2010). By articulating collective, politicized demands for services and resources, they made claims to inclusion as deserving and legitimate members of the community, while simultaneously creating a sense of *comunidad* and *empoderamiento.*

In both sites, mothers' development of support networks and the relationships that they involved were central to their production of belonging and claims to place (Shutika 2011, 5). Mothers in ST and Williamsburg cultivated immigrant networks, as well as activated cross-class ties with professionals, university students, and other advocates from outside their community (Del Castillo 2007; Chavira del Prado 1992). Support networks assisted mothers in navigating new geographic surroundings (in the case of Williamsburg), as well as unfamiliar institutional and political spaces that enabled them to secure services and resources. Expanded support networks also facilitated ST mothers' pushing back against exclusionary discourses and practices to claim entitlement to educational and health-care services.

In the current moment, comparing Latina immigrants' efforts to carve out a place for themselves in different sites yields significant insights into the diverse and varied forms that integration and belonging take within specific contexts of immigrant reception as well as the gendered dimensions of these processes (Hondagneu-Sotelo 2017; Schmalzbauer 2014). Framing Latina immigrant mothers' struggles to meet their families' reproductive needs and fulfill their gendered role as caretakers as constitutive of place-making and integration recasts these women not merely as subjects of exclusion but also as agents of belonging. By centering our theoretical gaze on women's agency and resilience, we seek to expand scholarly attention beyond the deportability and fear that frame—but do not define—Latina/o immigrants' lives. In the discussion that follows, we review the relevant scholarship on immigrant women and belonging and then turn to the analysis of how Latina immigrant mothers' struggles to meet the needs of their families produced distinct forms of belonging in ST and Williamsburg.

Latina/o Immigrants and Belonging

Given its potential for capturing the nuances of social integration, particularly for immigrant groups, recent scholarship has sought to bring theoretical specificity to analytical dimensions of belonging, which is broadly understood as an emotional connection to place and a sense of feeling "at home" (hooks 2009; Yuval-Davis 2006). Geographers have theorized the significance of belonging as a key aspect of place-making—the process of establishing affinity with specific geographic places—which produces a sense of socially recognized membership (Nelson and Hiemstra 2008; Trudeau 2006). Notably, belonging is not a "reified fixity," but an ongoing, dynamic process that involves everyday practices reflective of "the desire for some sort of attachment, be it to other people, places, or modes of being" (Probyn 1996, 19). Thus belonging is actively negotiated and produced, not merely granted (Yuval-Davis 2011, 11; see also Fenster 2004), and is dependent on the types and quality of relationships that people build within specific places (Shutika 2011, 15; Coll 2006).

Theorists have argued that, beyond a "sense of belonging" or a subjective feeling of rootedness, another salient dimension of belonging involves the construction, redrawing, and contestation of social boundaries (Antonsich 2010). Under conditions of globalization, diverse modalities of social membership beyond legally defined citizenship have emerged, engendering new forms of exclusion and abandonments of vulnerable groups, but also new spaces and possibilities for claims to inclusion (Yuval-Davis 2011; Christensen 2009). "The politics of belonging" captures such contestatory claims to social membership in the face of politicized exclusion (Antonsich 2010).

Immigration scholarship has long underscored the importance of the "context of reception" for immigrant integration, opportunities for upward mobility, and experiences of belonging (see Castañeda 2018, 8). And feminist scholars have argued that immigrants' experiences of settlement and incorporation are deeply contoured by the effects of intersecting social locations of gender, race, ethnicity, and immigration status as they take shape within specific geographic places (Hondagneu-Sotelo 2017; Mahler and Pessar 2001). Thus women's experiences will vary across immigrant destinations "because there are multiple borders of belonging and exclusion within each site that may be experienced differently depending on women's social location" (Dreby and Schmalzbauer 2013, 4).

The contested boundaries of social membership in the United States have taken on increasing importance as immigration enforcement has expanded beyond the border with Mexico into the interior (Coleman 2007). The collaboration between Immigration and Customs Enforcement (ICE) and local law enforcement has expanded the reach of immigration policing, permeating the everyday lives of immigrants with risk and intensifying fear and anxiety within Latina/o communities (Golash-Boza 2015; Menjívar and Kanstroom 2013). Heightened enforcement along with restrictive immigration laws have destabilized Latinas/os' claims to belonging. Latinas/os of any citizenship status may be racially stigmatized as "not of this place" because of how their physical features mark them as "other"—particularly in small towns where few Latinas/os reside and where they become hypervisible within over-whelmingly white or black-and-white ethnic landscapes (Licona and Maldonado 2014).

Despite considerable cultural variation within and across communities, Latina mothers are largely charged with acting as the main caregivers of their families and unconditionally supporting their children emotionally and economically (Abrego and Menjívar 2011). Latina immigrant mothers fulfill their socially prescribed, gendered role by taking responsibility for health care and educational decision-making and procuring the necessary resources to ensure the well-being of their families (Chavira del Prado 1992). As other research has shown, in order to engage in these activities, women must interface with local institutions like social services, clinics, and schools (Hondagneu-Sotelo 1994; Chavira del Prado 1992).

In the United States, Latina immigrant women's abilities to provide for their families have been greatly inhibited. On one hand, neoliberal policies have eroded public safety nets and educational services, particularly in poor communities. On the other hand, restrictive immigration laws and the ever-present threat of deportation prompt mothers to avoid contact with health-care and social service providers out of fear of detection of their immigration status (Park et al. 2011; Yoshikawa 2011). Such "legal violence" intimidates immigrant mothers by threatening entrapment, inhibiting their access to services for which they or their children are eligible (Abrego and Menjívar 2011, 16).

Despite elevated fear and exclusionary conditions, the routines of daily life persist in Latina/o communities. By continuing the work of raising and caring for their families, mothers play a leading role in carrying out social reproduction—the structured practices that "sustai[n] production and so-cial life in all its variations," which, importantly for our analysis, necessi-tates material and social investments in place, crucial for the production of belonging (Katz 2008; Smith and Winders 2007). At the same time, as Farfán-Santos (2019) has aptly demonstrated in the case of undocumented Mexican women, "maternal sentiment becomes a space for advocacy—one in which women feel that they can, and in fact, must play a role in protecting the future of their children despite illegality" (70). For the Latina women in

ST and Williamsburg, motherhood became both a source of resilience that compelled them to move beyond fear to procure resources for their families and a force that galvanized collective claims to belonging.

In our research sites, social networks served women as a significant mechanism for providing for their families and as sources of support and assistance. For immigrant and other minority mothers, reliance on kinship and friendship networks can represent an important carework strategy, providing transportation assistance and child care as well as material resources like small loans, clothing, and food (Weigt 2018; Seccombe 2011; Domínguez and Watkins 2003). And, particularly for undocumented immigrant women who contend with the effects of illegality and associated barriers to health care, informal networks become a crucial means for procuring medical resources (Menjívar 2002).

As Menjívar's (2000, 157–93) landmark study of Salvadoran immigrants in Los Angeles has shown, gender shapes the processes through which immigrants forge informal networks of exchange. While poor immigrant women may have fewer material resources than men, they nonetheless create beneficial reciprocal ties with other women on which they rely for crucial material and emotional support. And women's more frequent engagements with community organizations and local institutions also provide opportunities for the expansion of such networks.

However, informal immigrant networks also have a downside, as they can reproduce and exacerbate unequal power relations and even act as sources of social control and abuse (Portes 1998; Hondagneu-Sotelo 2007). Intimate ties that enable survival for low-income minority women can also prevent them from learning of opportunities for advancement (Domínguez and Watkins 2003). And, in a context of economic scarcity, support networks based on family and friends can result in tensions and draining, conflictive relationships that limit opportunities for social mobility (Menjívar 2000; Domínguez and Watkins 2003).

The most beneficial networks tend to be heterogeneous and based on "weak ties" that transcend class lines, thereby providing diverse sources of information about opportunities (Dominguez and Watkins 2003; Granovetter 1973). In ST and Williamsburg, Latina immigrant women activated social ties both with co-ethnics and across lines of race-ethnicity and class. And for the mothers of ST, these latter connections and resulting relationships of *acompañamiento* were particularly important for their collective organizing efforts. Although the literature on immigrant support networks tends to frame them in terms of social capital (Portes 1998), we argue that the cultivation of social ties both within and outside Latina/o immigrant communities also represents a significant mechanism for place-making and belonging. In both ST and Williamsburg, developing support networks not only facilitated the procurement of resources, but also assisted Latina immigrant mothers in gaining institutional knowledge and navigating unfamiliar institutional and political terrain.

Our comparison of the experiences of Latina immigrant women in a traditional and "new" destination illuminates how social, demographic, and geographical contexts matter for the modes of belonging that emerge among immigrant mothers (García and Schmalzbauer 2017). As in other new immigrant destinations, women's networks were much weaker in Williamsburg, where immigrant women had to overcome social isolation fostered by a lack of public transportation; the dispersed, low-density geography of Williamsburg; and the relative absence of extended family and other co-ethnics. Despite the "otherness" brought on by residing in a locality with few other Latinas/os, they developed a "sense of belonging" through individualized practices of overcoming fear, learning to drive, and orienting themselves within new physical and social surroundings, and they slowly built support networks to assist them in meeting their families' needs. In contrast, the mothers of ST, a community located in an area with a long-standing Latina/o presence, were able to build and expand already existent networks with co-ethnics and political allies, which served to support their politicized claims to belonging and inclusion.

Methods: Politically Engaged Comparative Research

We draw from separately conducted, independently designed ethnographic research projects with Latinas/os and their families in Williamsburg and ST and bring our data together to analyze the place-specific and gendered dimensions of the production of belonging. The benefit of merging data sets gathered through extensive fieldwork in two research sites lies in enabling the delineation of points of comparison that extend beyond an individual case, while retaining the richness and depth of ethnographic analysis. Our work has been grounded in our relationships and political alignments with Latina/o immigrant communities. Both research projects have involved fusing advocacy work with research endeavors as well as engagement in collaborations with community organizations.

Jennifer has conducted extensive ethnographic research with Mexican and Central American immigrants and their families in Williamsburg, Virginia. In the early 2000s, her collaborations with a network of service-providing organizations brought her into the lives of immigrant families, setting the stage for ten years of participant observation in various spheres of daily life. Between 2003 and 2013, she visited families in their homes, attending family celebrations like birthday parties and baby showers as well as cultural activities and religious events. From 2003 to 2006, she collaborated with the Program in Integral Children's Health (PICH), an early childhood services organization that served low-income families, to organize and facilitate a monthly parent-support group for Spanish-speaking immigrant families. Between 2003 and 2008, she and a group of student research assistants also conducted semistructured intensive interviews with twenty-nine immigrants from Central America and Mexico. Since 2013, she has maintained sustained contact with three families and has conducted informal follow-up interviews with family members. In addition, between 2017 and 2018 she spent seven months undertaking classroom observations in an English as a second language (ESL) classroom and conducted in-depth interviews with recently arrived Central American high school students.

In 2008, Natalia began her politically engaged research, advocacy, and support activities with ST's farm-working community, which continues to date. She collected women's *testimonios* from twenty-four *pláticas* (heart-to-heart talks) conducted from 2008 to 2010 with farmworker women, ST community members, and student and local activists who supported the farmworker mothers' organizing efforts, as well as teachers and school officials at Pitbull Elementary School, which the school district closed in 2008. Natalia conducted observations at multiple meetings and community events that the mothers convened during the year following the school's closure. These included mothers' weekly meetings, in which they discussed their struggles and joys and shared *consejos* (advice) about problems they encountered in daily life.

Our shared methodological approaches led us to identify a set of common themes that enabled us to draw connections across case studies. To build a comparative analysis, we then selected ethnographic narratives, quotations, and testimonies from our field notes and interviews that elucidated and typified these themes. In the next sections we examine how Latina immigrant mothers in these different sites of immigrant reception struggled individually to procure services and other resources for their families and/or organized collectively to demand them and how, through these activities, they enacted varied forms of belonging.

Squire Town, California

ST is a rural community located in Northern California's agricultural heartland. Its population of 1,200 is composed of 64 percent Latina/o-origin families, with 31 percent of the population identifying as white (U.S. Census Bureau 2010). ST relies economically on agriculture, with several industrial canneries and casinos located nearby also serving as sources of employment. Most residents are employed in seasonal agricultural work, having migrated to California from the state of Michoacán, Mexico. As a group, farmworkers have the lowest annual family incomes of all U.S. wage and salary workers (Larson 2000). In 2015, 18 percent of ST residents lived below the federal poverty level, while only roughly 7 percent held a bachelor's degree (US Census Bureau 2015). In the majority of Latina/o farm-working families in ST, at least one member lacks authorized immigration status. In a reflection of the precarities confronting "mixed-status" families in the current moment, several parents have recently asked the elementary school principal to be the designated guardian of their children in the event of their deportation.

In the early 2000s, around ten farmworker women gathered to form a women's group that they dubbed "*Charlas de Café*." These women used this informal group to plan activities at the church and school, share meals, and socialize over coffee. In the years that followed, the group began to take on new purpose, changing its name to *El Grupo de Mujeres* (EGM), and emerging as "an advocacy group."

Four women—Pilar, Ofelia, Julieta, and Clara—became key leaders of EGM. At the time of Natalia's research, they had resided in ST for an average of twenty-five years, and like most residents of ST, they all hailed from Michoacán, Mexico. Married and in their thirties and forties, with between two and five children each, these leaders were heavily involved in the school system and regularly attended meetings at the school. In addition, over the years of their involvement with EGM, they developed close ties with community organizations, like the California Rural Legal Assistance Foundation (CRLAF), an organization that provides advocacy, educational services, and support to farmworker communities. Indeed, as EGM became more deeply involved in advocacy activities, the group formed a close relationship with Juliana, a community organizer with CRLAF, who was originally from Texas and had spent many years involved in the Chicano movement.

One of EGM's first actions was to establish a child-care center, which they managed to maintain in operation through continued volunteer and advocacy efforts. As Pilar recalled, "Many of us needed child care. We did not have our families nearby.... [They] were all back in Michoacán. We had to create a new community here, and we did. The evidence is that the child-care center has been a success, as it is the only child-care center in ST. It has been open for more than fifteen years."

Despite this successful addition to the community, beginning in the mid-2000s ST began to witness the depletion of resources vital to its well-being, increasing the burden of care work and reproductive duties for farm-working mothers. Citing "financial problems," the county closed the migrant community clinic, followed by the teen center and the town's public park (Deeb-Sossa and Manzo 2018; Deeb-Sossa and Moreno 2016). The final blow came in 2009 with the closure of Pitbull Elementary, which had served as a central gathering place for families—"the heart of the community" in Ofelia's words. As Clara put it, "They [county officials] have slowly cut all the oxygen and blood supply to our town!"

In 2009, the mothers invited Natalia to their community to help them organize against the school board's decision to close the school. In one of the first meetings, Pilar recalled how school administrators seemed completely uninterested in seeking community input, a clear sign to her and the other members of EGM that the administration devalued them: "They never asked for our opinion. They didn't even talk to us directly. We learned about their plan through rumors." After the school's closure, students—the vast majority of whom were children of farmworkers—were bused sixteen miles away to a neighboring elementary school located in the town of Timberland (Deeb-Sossa and Manzo 2018; Deeb-Sossa and Moreno 2016). While the school district cited a financial deficit as the rationale for closing the school, they had approved the construction of another elementary school in a wealthier nearby neighborhood. Learning this drew EGM's attention to issues of justice and equity within the school district. Julieta asked, "Why is it always the poor who get affected? It was our school that got closed, not the ones in wealthier communities."

In the months that followed, farmworker mothers from EGM began to mobilize their community. They gathered information about similar school closures and their children's educational rights and investigated the possibility of opening a charter school. While they were unable to reverse the school board's decision, they successfully advocated for their children to be rezoned to a charter school in a neighboring county (Deeb-Sossa and Manzo 2018; Deeb-Sossa and Moreno 2016). After this experience, the women felt empowered to tackle other issues in the community and to continue to fight for inclusion. They organized a town hall meeting in which residents were invited to voice their concerns. The issue of access to health-care services emerged as a central concern in this meeting and became the new focus for the women's organizing efforts.

Williamsburg, Virginia

Like many small towns, cities, and suburbs in the Southeast in the 1980s and 1990s, Greater Williamsburg (with a population of ~155,000) began to experience rapid growth and development, largely tied to the "rebranding" of the area as an upscale retirement destination (Bickham Mendez and Nelson 2016). The influx of wealthy retirees from northern states helped galvanize a construction boom in the 2000s and an increasing numbers of jobs in the hospitality, food-service, and construction sectors, which drew Latina/o immigrants to the area in unprecedented numbers (700 percent growth of "Hispanics" between 1990 and 2010, to reach roughly 5 percent of the population; U.S. Census Bureau 2013). By the early 2000s, for the first time, Spanish-speaking immigrants, mostly from Mexico and the Northern Triangle of Central America, had achieved a noticeable presence in the area.

While immigrants were readily incorporated into seasonal, highly flexible jobs in hotels, construction, landscaping, and restaurants, they faced considerable barriers in the arena of social reproduction—housing, child care, and health and human services. Car dependency and limited affordable housing options in the low-density and dispersed residential space in Williamsburg presented significant difficulties, especially given undocumented immigrants' ineligibility for driver's licenses (Bickham Mendez and Nelson 2016).

In the early 2000s, increasing numbers of women began to arrive in Williamsburg, often leaving their children in the care of mothers, aunts, and sisters to join their husbands and families who had settled in the area. When these women became pregnant, they faced new challenges as they confronted the need for prenatal and infant health-care and other services for themselves and their children. Given the paucity of reliable and low-cost child care and the general absence of extended family, most had to exit the labor market to care for young children. They expressed intense feelings of being pulled between the care and well-being of their US-born children and those they left behind—especially since they could not send as much money to their home countries as they had in the past.

They also recognized that if they were to return to their home countries, their U.S.-born children "would lose a lot." Daniela, who left her four children in rural Santa Ana, El Salvador, to come to Williamsburg and later gave birth to two more children in the early 2000s, described her longing to return to see her children, but also her recognition that in her *cantón* (hamlet) she would likely earn only the equivalent of three or four U.S. dollars per day. She was haunted by dreams of returning to her home country with her baby daughter and lacking money to buy her milk. Mothers like Daniela spent long periods of time isolated in the home, as they often did not drive or have access to a car. They became heavily dependent on their male partners, which combined with the effects of illegality to accentuate the vulnerabilities they faced at home, including being susceptible to domestic violence (Deeb-Sossa and Bickham Mendez 2008).

However, as time passed, immigrant women's culturally assigned care-taking activities (along with economic need) helped propel them out of the home as they ventured into new, uncharted institutional spaces in order to meet the needs of their families. Women increasingly took the lead in interfacing and negotiating with health-care and other service providers; landlords, teachers, health-care, and social workers; and even lawyers and jail officials. And these efforts paved the way for a process of continued immigrant settlement that unfolded over the course of the next ten years, as family members from Central America continued to arrive.

Mirroring national trends (Radford 2019), by 2011 Mexican immigration had tapered off, and the immigration of women, adolescents, and children from Central America had increased, as immigrants sent for family members to escape escalating levels of state and gang-related violence. One of the most significant areas in which the impact of this new wave of Central American migration was felt was in the public schools, where the number English-language learners more than tripled from the 2009–10 school year to 2017–18, to reach 5 percent of the student population (Williamsburg-James City County School Division Administrative Staff 2019).

Not surprisingly, mothers from early cohorts of immigrants who had now lived in the area for more than a decade began to describe a shift in their identification with the place. For example, Marta reflected, after raising her three children (now teens and young adults) in Williamsburg, that she feels "*dividida*" (divided): "Sometimes I think about Mexico, but I believe I would miss everything here if I were there. I feel that my home is here because my family is here, even though we are not all together because Manuel (her husband who had been recently deported) is not with us, but still, my kids are here. I even feel at times that this is my town after all these years of having lived here."

In the next sections, we discuss two diverse sets of practices through which Latina mothers in Williamsburg and ST procured resources for their families, accessed services, and (in the case of ST) advocated politically for resources and services in their community. By (1) learning to navigate new institutional, geographic, and political spaces, and (2) building and expanding social networks, immigrant mothers produced belonging through survival and resistance.

Navigating Unfamiliar Geographic and Institutional Spaces

In their capacity as caretakers of their families, mothers learned to navigate new and unfamiliar institutional and (in the case of Williamsburg) physical terrains in their community. For mothers in Williamsburg, navigating their physical surroundings meant learning to drive, despite being ineligible for driver's licenses and lacking driving experience in their home countries. Women like Marta, Maria Teresa, and Rosario took on the challenge of driving "*por necesidad*" in order to go about the routines of daily life.

After several years, Rosario was able to bring to Williamsburg her younger sister Juana, who soon had children of her own with a man who subsequently left her to return to El Salvador (though he later returned). Rosario schooled Juana on overcoming her fear of driving—"Because this is the way it is here. And you have to take care of your kids. No one else is going to do it for you.

Look at me. I was afraid and never drove before. No one helped me. I had to move forward and find the strength where there was none." Despite the fear and the risks that driving without a license entailed, these women learned to navigate the dispersed suburban landscape in order to commute to work and, perhaps more significantly, to take their children to medical appointments and to attend parent-teacher meetings, religious services, and school activities—all of which took them beyond the home-to-work circuit.

In so doing, the mothers in Williamsburg confronted the daily fear that they could come into contact with the police—which could result in their detention and separation from their children. Leticia described how she coped with the fear she felt. "Something I think about [. . .] what would happen. . . . Because I go around in my car because I have to get to work but I don't have a license or papers or anything. And if I get stopped by the police? And then I think . . . well *ni modo* [there is no other way] God willing and in the name of God."

More recently, women have started to employ social media and GPS technology to assist them in navigating geographic space and to share information like school bus arrival times and delays. Reina, a nineteen-year-old high school student, told Jennifer about her older sister, who came to Williamsburg four years ago and now uses Uber to commute to her job at a commercial laundry facility. Reina, who lives with her two sisters and whose parents remain in El Salvador, described how a member of their church helped her sister load the application on her phone and explained to her that it was a safe way to commute.

In the event that their partners, brothers, and sons were deported, jailed, or detained, women mobilized the social and economic resources necessary to pick up the pieces and keep their families intact. Through this process, they also learned to navigate the court and criminal justice system. Despite the terrifying prospect that police contact held for Marta, who feared more than anything being separated from her children, she continually and unflaggingly mobilized resources in support of her teenage son—who lacked authorized immigration status—when he repeatedly became entangled with police over underage drinking, petty theft, and drug use. When he was taken into police custody for possession of alcohol, she mustered her courage and went to retrieve him from jail. She contacted two former law students who had attended her church to refer her to an attorney, who eventually was successful in applying for Deferred Action for Childhood Arrivals (DACA) status for her son after defending him against the misdemeanor charges.

When her husband was jailed after being convicted of criminal charges (which he and his family vehemently denied), Marta coordinated information-sharing with family members and pooled resources from extended family for his defense and many appeals. Despite her fears of contact with the authorities, she brought her children to visiting hours at the jail every week. She handled all interactions with the attorney, who did not speak Spanish. She sought assistance from members of her church, and through networks of supporters she had met when she received services from family assistance programs, and was able to obtain free counseling services for her daughter. She hosted family members who came from New York and Pennsylvania to attend her husband's sentencing and trial. Marta struggled successfully to support her two teenagers on her income after her spouse's incarceration and eventual deportation.

Through care-taking activities of daily life and efforts to keep their families intact, Latina immigrant women in Williamsburg have confronted and even mastered the fear instilled by forms of immigration enforcement that police the geographies of social reproduction—and in so doing have made "home" possible for their families (Schmalzbauer 2014). Marta's repeated refrain when Jennifer would greet her and ask how she was doing, "Well, we're still here," resonates in the current moment of intensified immigration enforcement. It is through the continued survival work involved in raising their children that immigrant Latina women in Williamsburg have actively woven themselves and their families into the community, producing a sense of belonging in the face of exclusion.

In the community of ST, mothers learned to navigate new institutional settings and local political spaces in the pursuit of community health-care services and educational resources for their children. During their struggles to contest the closure of Pitbull Elementary School, the mothers of EGM directly confronted exclusionary practices, but also learned how to advocate collectively for the educational rights of their children, including how to effectively petition the school district and make their demands heard.

During the *pláticas* with Natalia, the mothers recalled "being ridiculed" by the school board, and other actions that they found "intimidating" and "insulting." For example, when some mothers had to leave the meetings early in order to return home to prepare dinner for their families (as they had come directly from fields), school board members publicly reprimanded them. Ofelia also described having to learn proper procedures for addressing the school board so that their concerns would register: "At our first school board, fifteen parents went. We had chosen two as our spokespeople. But the board, they were very sly and did what only a very devious person would do, they went and told the press that only two parents were concerned about the closure of the school. They told the newspapers that only two parents went to the school board meeting, and they never mentioned the other fifteen parents because they only counted the two that went up to the mic."

After this experience and aided by Juliana, the community organizer from CRLAF, the farmworker mothers strategized about how to ensure that their voices were heard. As Juliana recalled in an interview, "We had to find a way to maximize our presence and make our voice count. All, parents and children, everybody, must go up to the mic and, even if you blank out, and even if you just say, 'I agree with the parent that spoke in front of me,' then that is all you have to say with your name and you will be counted."

By the second board meeting, organizers felt more prepared. Regardless of their English-language abilities, all parents who attended—more than fifty-five by Clara's count—went to the microphone, gave their name, and made sure they were counted. Ofelia relayed, "This time we were prepared to meet the board. The board was all white, but we did not stop. Although we are Mexicans, we told them, 'You want to decide for our children. We want the welfare of our children. Therefore, we, not you, have to decide.'"

Through such public participation in community life, the farmworker mothers challenged classist and racist exclusion, as well as a deficit perspective regarding their children's academic achievement (Valencia and Solórzano 1997). Undeterred by intense discrimination and equipped with the knowledge and skills they had acquired, they continued challenging the educational inequities that their children faced (Deeb-Sossa and Manzo 2018; Deeb-Sossa and Moreno 2016). Through engaging in a "politics of belonging," they also made claims to rights and services as deserving members of both the community and US society.

In the end, the mothers were unable to reverse the decision to close the elementary school. However, during a community *plática* with Natalia, they agreed that their mobilizing efforts had been "worth it." They recognized that they had gained important institutional knowledge about the inner workings of local educational and political systems, and they saw firsthand how their advocacy efforts improved their children's educational opportunities when they resulted in their transfer to a charter school. Finally, through their struggles with the school district, they cultivated relationships with long-term allies, which became a key resource in their successful efforts to establish a community health clinic in ST three years later.

Building and Expanding Social Networks

In both Williamsburg and ST, mothers cultivated support networks with other co-ethnics and also expanded their networks across race and class lines, which became central to their efforts to procure and, in the case of ST, demand resources and services for their families. The process of network development and expansion, however, unfolded both in highly gendered and place-specific ways in these distinct social and geographic contexts.

Like other "new immigrant destinations," in Williamsburg low-density, dispersed public space and lack of reliable public transportation inhibited the development of networks of assistance among early cohorts of Latina/o immigrants (Schmalzbauer 2014). Despite these barriers, over the course of the next decade, immigrant mothers began to slowly forge support networks that enabled them to pool resources and share information. A support group for immigrant parents, organized by an early childhood program serving "at-risk" families, was one early space in which social networks among immigrant women were built and strengthened. Immigrant mothers who met each other at the support group began to share childcare, so that they could rejoin the paid labor force. Those who drove offered others rides to support group meetings, work, and health-care and social service appointments.

In addition, mothers also used family and workplace and religious-based networks to circulate information about available services for children, such as those offered by Early Headstart as well as other community and faith-based organizations that provided food assistance, school supplies, and donated Christmas gifts for children without requiring state-issued forms of identification. They shared information about weather-related school closures, bus schedules, and kindergarten registration, as well as about service-providing agencies and offices that employed bilingual staff or where staff was more welcoming. They also found ways to circumvent the expensive and difficult-to-navigate health-care system by contacting family members, pharmacists, and physicians in their home countries to obtain prescription medications as well as traditional medicines and to receive diagnoses for family members' illnesses over the phone. They even located and spread the word about *curanderos* (folk healers) who lived in nearby cities.

Mothers in Williamsburg also expanded their support networks by activating "weak ties" with those outside their circles of family and co-ethnic friends and acquaintances. They used contacts with sympathetic social workers and outreach workers, such as those from early childhood services agencies, as well as co-workers and supervisors from work and professionals they met through social services or church to enlist their assistance in navigating local institutions. These supporters accompanied them—often as interpreters—to appointments at the safety net clinic, social services, and the Department of Motor Vehicles, and meetings at local schools.

External networks were also an important source of support for mothers' efforts to secure housing. For example, Rosario, a thirty-two-year-old mother of two preschoolers, enlisted Jennifer's help in translating and drafting correspondences and notices from the property management company that managed the apartment where she, her husband and children, and her sister's family resided. When the company notified the family that the apartment would be sold and the lease terminated, the four adults and four children had six weeks to find a new residence in an extremely tight and expensive rental market—made more challenging for undocumented immigrants because of credit checks and identification requirements. Rosario had to negotiate with landlords who not only spoke no Spanish, but also were reluctant to rent to both "illegals" and families with small children. After a desperate search, Rosario's supervisor at the restaurant where she

FIGURE 5.1   Accompanied by an English-speaking, native-born supporter, a mother from El Salvador attends kindergarten registration at an elementary school in Williamsburg, Virginia. Photo by Bickham Mendez.

worked helped her locate a small rental house. The property owner, a friend of the supervisor, did not require credit checks or other documentation.

As women in Williamsburg both developed and expanded their networks, they gained confidence and overcame to some degree their hesitation and fear about contact with service providers and agencies. In Hayda's words, "I used to think that they would put my name in the computer . . . and then they could find my address. But now I am not so afraid." At a support group meeting, Sofia marveled at her newfound independence: "I had always lived with my parents. Over there [in Mexico], sons and daughters live with their parents until they are married. I learned that I am capable of doing many things on my own."

In contrast, in ST, a site with a long history of seasonal migration and Latina/o immigrant settlement, farmworker mothers' process of network-building unfolded over a much longer span of time. Through their continued organizing efforts, they strengthened long-standing community and family support networks and also expanded their networks by activating ties with allies from outside the farm-working community. Network-building was central to the eighteen-month process of outreach and advocacy that resulted in the reopening of a community clinic, which had been closed several years prior.

In early 2011, the mothers of EGM used their ties with a local university professor to put them in contact with a group of medical students who co-directed a student-run clinic in the nearby city of Sacramento that offered services in Spanish—largely serving the indigent population. That summer, EGM, accompanied by the university professor, organized several meetings with the medical students as well as staffers at the Service and Volunteer Center (SVC) and the school district, community organizers from CRLAF, and other local partners to advocate for reopening the community clinic.

At these meetings, the mothers clearly identified their community's most pressing need as affordable, accessible, and culturally sensitive health care (Deeb-Sossa and Manzo 2018; Deeb-Sossa and Moreno 2016). They insisted, however, on the need for a primary care center—not monthly health fairs—to offer regular care in the community, especially for pregnant mothers and the elderly. At the meeting, Ofelia explained, "We need to have a relationship with the doctors. . . . Otherwise, how are they going to know what is wrong with me or my children." Clara chimed in: "We need doctors in the community. I cannot travel half an hour to an hour to see a doctor.

Who has that kind of time when they work, have small children and have to care for elderly parents?"

By 2012 their advocacy efforts began to bear fruit, resulting in the establishment of a student-run clinic in ST, funded by the nearby university and housed (with permission from the school district) in the former site of the old clinic. The establishment of the clinic took place through a community-driven process involving the building of relationships and networks within the farm-working community and between the community and outside supporters (Deeb-Sossa and Manzo 2018; Deeb-Sossa and Moreno 2016).

The farm-working mothers' development of external ties with key allies— like the university professor and Juliana, the community organizer at CRLAF— crossed lines of power and privilege, providing access to decision-makers and key resources through *acompañamiento*—"the cultural, improvisational practices of relationship and community building performed . . . at the interstices, or in-between spaces . . . of cultural and institutional life" with the aim of "creat[ing] a sense of belonging, a cultural citizenry" (Sepúlveda 2011, 559).

Supporters engaged in *acompañamiento* through the process of petitioning the school district for the use of the building that the former clinic had occupied. Together the mothers and their allies strategized about how to build a case for leasing the space for the proposed clinic free of charge.

FIGURE 5.2   Opening ceremony for student-run clinic at Squire Town. Photo courtesy of Brenden Tu.

To support their petition, EGM solicited letters from business owners, agricultural producers, and representatives from the local medical school to demonstrate that the initiative fulfilled a community need and was sustainable. For the mothers of ST, the successful outcome of their efforts to open the free community clinic reflected health-care service accountability to their community, and this victory further strengthened social bonds within the ST community.

Creating *Comunidad* in Squire Town

For the mothers of ST, the struggle to open the clinic and advocate for other services in their community produced a renewed sense of *comunidad* in which they felt *apoyadas/os* (supported). As Ofelia said during the clinic's opening ceremony, "Our coming together as one to open the clinic shows we can be a close-knit community that can relate and care for each other." Pilar nodded in agreement and added that the addition of the clinic provided a sense of *consuelo* (comfort), *estabilidad* (stability), and *pertenencia* (belonging). It was common for the mothers to exclaim that they "were working for something bigger than ourselves." At one meeting Clara reminded the group, "We must always remember that we are not alone. . . . We are *un pueblo* (one people) and we will fight for what is best for our children—for mine and for yours" (pointing to each woman at the meeting).

The mothers reminded each other how they and their children belong to the United States and to ST, and they linked this to an understanding of social rights and deservingness. As Julieta exclaimed, "We need to know who we are, where we come from, and where we belong. We belong here because we are from here and we live here, and even if we don't speak English or are white, we have the same rights as others. We have a right to healthcare and to good doctors." Juliana raised her fist in the air and declared: "Being Mexican is being American. We are the real Americans. . . . Didn't their ancestors migrate here? They are the immigrants, we are not!"

The farmworker women's advocacy and organizing revealed to them the power they had to make a difference in their lives and in their community— they came to recognize their empowerment (*empoderamiento*). The members of EGM defined "*empoderamiento*" as having decision-making power and options; understanding that they have rights; having access to information and resources as well as learning skills that are important to them; and feeling capable of challenging deficit perceptions and stereotypes about their community. By constructing themselves as a *comunidad*, deserving of inclusion, these women challenged and contested boundaries of social membership through the politics of belonging.

Concluding Reflections: Gender, Belonging, and Resilience

Latina immigrant mothers in ST and Williamsburg faced considerable obstacles in carving out a place for themselves within these localities. Their claims to place and belonging were greatly impinged on by the exclusionary practices enacted by those in positions of institutional authority in education, the criminal justice system, and health-care and social services. However, like other groups of women of color at the margins, these mothers used their lived experience at the intersections of racism, sexism, and classism to cope, survive (Calderón and Saldívar 1991, 4; Collins 2000; Hurtado 2003), and also resist (Sandoval 2000; Moraga 1981, 23).

This analysis reveals how gender, as it intersects with other vectors of power and difference, shapes the ways that belonging is produced. In both sites, Latina immigrant mothers created belonging and community as they engaged in the gendered activities associated with providing for their families. Social reproduction is an arena through which poor immigrant women are policed and regulated, but it is also through these activities of daily life that women emerge as agents who establish connections to place. And while some of these seemingly banal activities may not purposefully challenge politicized exclusion, we argue, like Vega (2015), that they nonetheless represent significant forms of belonging.

A comparative analysis of immigrant women in ST and Williamsburg reveals the importance of place-associated factors for producing different pathways to belonging. In the case of EGM in ST, mothers' role as caretakers became a politicizing force, galvanizing collective claims to belonging. By using acquired knowledge and skills to agitate against the depletion of educational and other services in their communities and the unequal educational opportunities available to their children, farmworker mothers articulated collective demands for inclusion within the U.S. polity. Through the development of networks that helped establish partnerships with allies, these mothers contested their and their families' exclusion from access to affordable and quality health care. Through the "politics of belonging," farmworking mothers made claims to membership, inclusion, and *comunidad*.

In Williamsburg, immigrant women arrived in the late 1990s and early 2000s in a very different context—a new immigrant destination where support networks were scarce and the limited presence of other Latinas/os caused them to stand out as "foreign" and "other." Despite the fear and increased insecurity produced by a punitive immigration regime, immigrant women in Williamsburg have developed survival tactics that integrate them into the community. Their case suggests that confronting and overcoming fear—a critical element of social exclusion—represents a necessary ingredient for cultivating "a sense belonging" by making "home" possible. In the contemporary context of increasingly restrictive policies that limit access to health care and human services and target the very arena of social life through which immigrant women fulfill cultural expectations of motherhood, Latina mothers' network-building takes on heightened significance as a means for making claims to place and belonging.

Placing these cases within the same analytical framework and using belonging as an axis of comparison demonstrates that these immigrant women do not passively accept the conditions of their exclusion and, through confronting their fears and continuing the work of daily life, make valuable contributions to their families and communities. Taken together, these cases demonstrate that in diverse immigrant communities, despite experiences of profound marginalization, women enact resistance, resilience, and creative forms of agency.

Notes

1. This chapter is reprinted (with some modifications) from a 2020 article that appeared in *Latino Studies* 18(2), 174-194.

2. We use "Latina/o" to refer to people who reside in the United States and trace their roots to Latin American social and cultural worlds. In this chapter, we do not employ the more recent term "Latinx," as it was not used by our respondents at the time that this research was conducted.

3. Issues of confidentiality and ethics played out differently in our separately conducted studies. To protect confidentiality, the names of individuals and organizations have been changed throughout the chapter. Additionally, Natalia uses pseudonyms to refer to her field site and nearby communities. Quotes that lack citations are taken from our interviews and field notes.

References

Abrego, Leisy J., and Cecilia Menjívar. 2011. "Immigrant Latina Mothers as Targets of Legal Violence." *International Journal of Sociology of the Family* 37(1): 9–26.

Antonsich, Marco. 2010. "Searching for Belonging—An Analytical Framework." *Geography Compass* 4(6): 644–59.

Bickham Mendez, Jennifer, and Lise Nelson. 2016. "Producing 'Quality of Life' in the 'Nuevo South': The Spatial Dynamics of Latinos' Social Reproduction in Southern Amenity Destinations." *City and Society* 28(2):129–51.

Calderón, Héctor, and José David Saldívar. 1991. "Introduction." In *Criticism in the Borderlands: Studies in Chicano Literature, Culture and Ideology*, edited by Héctor Calderón, Ramón R. Saldívar, and José David Saldívar, 1–7. Durham, N.C.: Duke University Press.

Castañeda, Ernesto. 2018. *A Place to Call Home: Immigrant Exclusion and Urban Belonging in New York, Paris and Barcelona.* Stanford: Stanford University Press.

Chavira del Prado, Alicia. 1992. "Work, Health, and the Family: Gender Structure and Women's Status in an Undocumented Migrant Population." *Human Organization* 51(1): 53–64.

Christensen, Ann-Dorte. 2009. "Belonging and Unbelonging from an Intersectional Perspective." *Gender, Technology and Development* 13(1): 21–41.

Coleman, Mathew. 2007. "A Geopolitics of Engagement: Neoliberalism, The War on Terrorism, and the Reconfiguration of U.S. Immigration Enforcement." *Geopolitics* 12(4): 607–34.

Coll, Kathleen. 2006. "Necesidades y Problemas: Immigrant Latina Vernaculars of Belonging, Coalition, and Citizenship in San Francisco, California." In *Latinos and Citizenship: The Dilemma of Belonging*, edited by Susan Oboler, 191–217. New York: Palgrave Macmillan.

Collins, Patricia Hill. 2000. "Gender, Black Feminism, and Black Political Economy." *Annals of the American Academy of Political and Social Science* 568(1): 41–53.

Deeb-Sossa, Natalia, and Jennifer Bickham Mendez. 2008. "Enforcing Borders in the *Nuevo* South: Gender and Migration in Williamsburg, VA and the Research Triangle, NC." *Gender and Society* 22(5): 613–638.

Deeb-Sossa, Natalia, and Rosa Manzo. 2018. "Community-Driven Leadership: Mexican-Origin Farmworking Mothers Resisting Deficit Practices by a School Board in California." *Journal of Latinos and Education* 17(1): 1–17.

Deeb-Sossa, Natalia, and Melissa Moreno. 2016. "No Cierren Nuestra Escuela!: Farm Worker Mothers as Cultural Citizens in an Educational Community Mobilization Effort." *Journal of Latinos and Education* 5(1): 39–57.

Del Castillo, Adelaida R. 2007. "Illegal Status and Social Citizenship: Thoughts on Mexican Immigrants in a Postnational World." In *Women and Migration in the U.S.-Mexico Borderlands: A Reader*, edited by Denise A. Segura and Patricia Zavella, 92–105. Durham, N.C.: Duke University Press.

Domínguez, Silvia, and Celeste Watkins. 2003. "Creating Networks for Survival and Mobility: Social Capital Among African-American and Latin-American Low-Income Mothers." *Social Problems* 50(1): 111–35.

Dreby, Joanna, and Leah Schmalzbauer. 2013. "The Relational Contexts of Migration: Mexican Women in New Destination Sites." *Sociological Forum* 28(1): 1–24.

Farfán-Santos, Elizabeth. 2019. "The Politics of Resilience and Resistance: Health Care Access and Undocumented Mexican Motherhood in the United States." *Latino Studies* 17(1): 67–85.

Fenster, Tovi. 2004. "Belonging, Memory and the Politics of Planning in Israel." *Social and Cultural Geography* 5(3): 403–17.

Foner, Nancy, and Patrick Simon, eds. 2015. *Fear, Anxiety, and National Identity: Immigration and Belonging in North America and Western Europe*. New York: Russell Sage.

García, Angela S., and Leah Schmalzbauer. 2017. "Placing Assimilation Theory: Mexican Immigrants in Urban and Rural America." *Annals of the American Academy of Political and Social Science* 672(1): 64–82.

Golash-Boza, Tanya Maria. 2015. *Deported: Immigrant Policing, Disposable Labor and Global Capitalism*. New York: New York University Press.

Granovetter, Mark S. 1973. "The Strength of Weak Ties." *American Journal of Sociology* 78: 1360–80.

Hondagneu-Sotelo, Pierrette. 1994. *Gendered Transitions: Mexican Experiences of Immigration*. Berkeley: University of California Press.

———. 2007. *Doméstica: Immigrant Workers Cleaning and Caring in the Shadows of Affluence*. Oakland: University of California Press.

———. 2017. "Place, Nature and Masculinity on Immigrant Integration: Latino Immigrant Men in Inner-City Parks and Community Gardens." *NORMA* 12(2): 112–26.

hooks, bell. 2009. *Belonging: A Culture of Place*. New York: Routledge.

Hurtado, Aida. 2003. *Voicing Chicana Feminisms: Young Women Speak Out on Sexuality and Identity*. New York: New York University Press.

Katz, Cindi. 2008. "Bad Elements: Katrina and the Scoured Landscape of Social Reproduction." *Gender, Place and Culture* 15(1): 15–29.

Larson, Alice C. 2000. "Migrant and Seasonal Farmworker Enumeration Profiles Study." *California Health Resources and Services Administration: Migrant Health Program*. http://citeseerx.ist.psu.edu/viewdoc/download?doi=10.1.1.197.5482&rep=rep1&type=pdf.

Licona, Adela C., and Marta Maria Maldonado. 2014. "The Social Production of Latin@ Visibilities and Invisibilities: Geographies of Power in Small Town America." *Antipode* 46(2): 517–36.

Mahler, Sarah, and Patricia R. Pessar. 2001. "Gendered Geographies of Power: Analyzing Gender Across Transnational Spaces." *Identities* 7:441–59.

Menjívar, Cecilia. 2000. *Fragmented Ties: Salvadoran Immigrant Networks in America*. Oakland: University of California Press.

———. 2002. "The Ties That Heal: Guatemalan Immigrant Women's Networks and Medical Treatment." *International Migration Review* 36(2): 437–66.

Menjívar, Cecilia, and Daniel Kanstroom, eds. 2013. *Constructing Immigrant "Illegality": Critiques, Experiences, and Responses.* Cambridge, U.K.: Cambridge University Press.

Moraga, Cherrie. 1981. "Theory in the Flesh." In *This Bridge Called My Back: Writings by Radical Women of Color,* edited by Cherrie Moraga and Gloria Anzaldúa, 22–57. Watertown, NY: Persephone.

Nelson, Lise, and Nancy Hiemstra. 2008. "Latino Immigrants and the Renegotiation of Place and Belonging in Small Town America." *Social and Cultural Geography* 9(3): 319–42.

Park, Yoosun, Rupaleem Bhuyan, Catherine Richards, and Andrew Rundle. 2011. "U.S. Social Work Practitioners' Attitudes towards Immigrants and Immigration: Results from an Online Survey." *Journal of Immigrant and Refugee Studies* 9(4): 367–92.

Portes, Alejandro. 1998. "Social Capital: Its Origins and Applications in Modern Sociology." *Annual Review of Sociology* 24(1): 1–24.

Probyn, Elspeth. 1996. *Outside Belonging.* London: Routledge.

Radford, Jynnah. 2019. "Key Findings About U.S. Immigrants." Pew Hispanic Research Center. June 17. www.pewresearch.org/fact-tank/2019/06/17/key-findings-about-u-s-immigrants/.

Sandoval, Chela. 2000. *Methodology of the Oppressed.* Vol. 18. Minneapolis: University of Minnesota Press.

Schmalzbauer, Leah. 2014. *The Last Best Place?: Gender, Family, and Migration in the New West.* Stanford: Stanford University Press.

Seccombe, Karen T. 2011. *"So You Think I Drive a Cadillac?" Welfare Recipients Perspectives on the System and its Reform.* 3rd ed. Boston: Allyn and Bacon.

Sepúlveda, Enrique III. 2011. "Toward a Pedagogy of *Acompañamiento*: Mexican Migrant Youth Writing from the Underside of Modernity." *Harvard Educational Review* 81(3): 550–73.

Shutika, Debra Lattanzi. 2011. *Beyond the Borderlands: Migration and Belonging in the United States and Mexico.* Oakland: University of California Press.

Smith, Barbara Ellen, and Jamie Winders. 2007. "'We're Here to Stay': Economic Restructuring, Latino Migration and Place-Making in the U.S. South." *Transactions of the Institute of British Geographers* 33(1): 60–72.

Trudeau, Daniel. 2006. "Politics of Belonging in the Construction of Landscapes: Place-Making, Boundary-Drawing and Exclusion." *Cultural Geographies* 13:421–43.

U.S. Census Bureau. 2010. "Profile of General Population and Housing Characteristics: 2010." Accessed July 20, 2018. https://factfinder.census.gov/faces/tableservices/jsf/pages/productview.xhtml?src=CF.

———. 2013. "Summary File. American Community Survey." Accessed March 1, 2014. http://ftp2.census.gov/.

———. 2015. "Summary File: American Community Survey, 5 Year Estimates, 2011–2015." Accessed June 14, 2018. www.census.gov/programs-surveys/acs/technical-documentation/table-and-geography-changes/2015/5-year.html.

Valencia, Ramón R., and Daniel Solórzano. 1997. "Contemporary Deficit Thinking." In *The Evolution of Deficit Thinking: Educational Thought and Practice*, edited by Ramón R. Valencia, 160–210. London: Falmer Press.

Vega, Sujey. 2015. *Latino Heartland: Of Borders and Belonging in the Midwest*. New York: New York University Press.

Weigt, Jill. 2018. "Carework Strategies and Everyday Resistance Among Mothers Who Have Timed-Out of Welfare." In *Marginalized Mothers, Mothering from the Margins*, edited by Tiffany Taylor and Katrina Bloch, 195–212. Bingley, U.K.: Emerald Publishing.

Williamsburg-James City County School Division Administrative Staff. 2019. "FY 2020 Budget Discussion." Presentation at Budget Work Session, Williamsburg-James City County School Division. January 22. Williamsburg, Virginia.

Yoshikawa, Hirokazu. 2011. *Immigrants Raising Citizens: Undocumented Parents and Their Children*. New York: Russell Sage.

Yuval-Davis, Nira. 2006. "Belonging and the Politics of Belonging." *Patterns of Prejudice* 40(3): 197–214.

———. 2011. *The Politics of Belonging: Intersectional Contestations*. Thousand Oaks, Calif.: Sage.

CHAPTER 6

Finding Home / *Haciendo Familia*

Testimonios *of Mexican Male Farmworkers in Central California*

YVETTE G. FLORES

> We all tell stories about our lives, both to ourselves and to others; and it is through
> such stories that we make sense of ourselves, of the world, and of our relationships
> to others.
>
> —Steph Lawler, "Narrative in Social Research," 2002

Introduction

Although transnational male migration from Mexico to California has occurred steadily since the Mexican Revolution (Gonzales 1995) and has ebbed and flowed depending on the United States' need for agricultural labor and Mexico's political and social realities (Consejo Nacional de Población 2015), there is limited information on these men's mental health or the ways in which they negotiate changes in their family relations, cope with loneliness and isolation, and form social networks of support in their new context.

Through a mixed-methods study, my collaborators and I investigated experiences of migration, mental health, and family relations among eighty migrant and return-migrant men from Mexico (see Flores et al. 2019).[1] This chapter offers findings derived from in-depth, semi-structured interviews with ten men who participated in the California cohort of this larger study. These *testimonios* reveal that the men who had no spouses or children in the United States built social support networks to assuage the losses related to migration, to address their longing for their homeland, and through solidarity, reduce their sadness. The men created *familia* out of their shared experiences of uprootedness. All the men had migrated initially to help out their parents financially and saw the hardships they experienced as a worthwhile sacrifice.

I argue that these *testimonios* provide a deeper understanding of the men's experiences of migration, family life, and mental health than what can be gleaned from quantitative measures. These narratives challenge limited and racialized notions of the "machista" Mexican, working-class males or dangerous, "illegal," "bad *hombres*," propagated in public discourse, and reveal how these men obtained resources to sustain themselves and their families, enacting traditional gender scripts that they had learned from an early age. Finally, the narratives offered by these men shed light on how masculine understandings of self-sacrifice for the sake of one's family gave rise to a form of resilience and inner strength that allowed them to cope with and persevere under extreme conditions of exclusion and economic exploitation.

Gender, Masculinity, Migration, and Belonging

Elsewhere, my collaborators and I have addressed the complexity and heterogeneous nature of transnational migration processes and the role of gender and masculinity in the experiences of immigrants (Flores et al. 2019). In our larger study, we found that Mexican agricultural workers made sense of their migration experience in terms of their masculine gender role. They saw migration as a way to fulfill hegemonic rules of masculinity to be the economic providers for their families. Therefore, I conducted in-depth interviews with ten men to explore this finding further and to identify how the men coped with the challenges created by their migration and difficult work conditions.

The findings of the larger study echo those of Mexican scholars who investigated gender and migration in Mexico beginning in the decades of the 1980s and 1990s (see Vega 2009; Rosas 2008). Studies grounded in theories of masculinity conclude that work, sending remittances, and the authority and control that men exercise over their families even from another country, as well as the courage to brave a dangerous journey to the United States, reflect culturally constructed values of Mexican masculinity and male identity (Flores and Valdez-Curiel 2009; Vega 2009; Rosas 2008). However, most of these studies neglect the psychological impact of migration on men and relied on samples largely composed of adults, even though many males migrate as adolescents (Vega 2009).

For example, Hernández's (2012) study of Mexican boys and youth detained at the border concludes that adolescent male migration reflects internalized values regarding masculinity, which are inculcated in boys since infancy. These boys are taught that they are responsible for their families regardless of the cost or personal sacrifice, and that it is their duty to support their parents. Therefore, they migrate to fulfill that obligation as well as to work to generate the capital necessary to marry and form their own families. Hernandez's findings challenge the notion that cultural and social constructions of masculinity and their attendant role expectations are relevant solely for adults, since it is evident that for rural Mexican men such expectations form during childhood and prevail throughout their life.

Psychologists have argued that a gender perspective provides a more nuanced understanding of the meaning and purpose of migration in the lives of men and women (Flores et al. 2019; Espin 2015; Falicov 1998). The social construction of masculinity and femininity creates differences in individuals' quality of life and experiences. It is important to note, however, that internalized notions of masculinity are neither rigid nor immutable; instead, masculinity is constructed daily and modified historically in response to societal changes and men's perception of themselves and in relation to others (Flores et al. 2019; Ramirez 2011; Vega 2009; Rosa 2008). Thus men learn, adjust, and practice their gender role assignments according to what others expect of them, and according to what they consider to be characteristics of an ideal man (Flores 2013; Connell 2003). While dominant social constructions of hegemonic masculinity constitute men as individuals with power and privilege, such constructs render invisible immigrant men, men of color, and others who belong to marginalized groups on the basis of social class or sexuality (Ramirez 2011; Connell and Mitterschimidt 2005; Connell 1997).

Some scholars exploring the relationship between masculinity, stress, identity, and overall mental health among Latino men in the United States call for a more nuanced analysis of hegemonic masculinity (Lu and Wong 2014). Utilizing the Minority Masculinity Stress Theory, Lu and Wong (2014) find that the (largely educated) Latino men in their sample contested the stereotypical depictions of machismo that abound in U.S. social science. Most of the men continued to value achievement, which they defined in terms of providing for their loved ones. Their stress resulted largely from the social and cultural devaluation that minimized or denied their contributions and limited their ability to succeed.

Ramirez's (2011) exploration of masculinity among Mexican immigrant *jardineros* (gardeners) underscores the importance of contextualizing men's enactment of masculinity in terms of their social class, social position, and the racialized nativism and citizen hierarchy they have to negotiate in their daily work. In their study of Latino immigrant men in the U.K., which did not include Mexican men, McIlwaine (2010) argues for an intersectional analysis of men, masculinity, and their negotiation of gender roles.

Therefore, I consider it critical to examine immigrant men's relationship to work in terms of their intersectional identities (Hurtado and Sinha 2018) and their social and geographical location. Specifically, I wanted to examine how masculinity is enacted among immigrant men from rural communities who are currently residing in rural destinations in Central California, where the men live in relative isolation from European Americans, interacting mostly with other immigrant men in their communities.

In most Mexican rural families, men have been assigned the role of provider charged with meeting their family's economic needs. When the social and economic realities of their communities impede men's fulfillment of their expected role, they must evaluate their options in order to enact it (Flores and Cervantes Pacheco 2016). In this context, transnational migration appears as an attractive option, especially in the case of communities with long histories of transnational migration, where "*irse al norte*" (going North) has become an adolescent rite of passage (Rivera-Heredia, Obregón, and Cervantes 2009).

Migration and Mental Health

Psychological studies of transnational migration consider it a stressful life event that impacts all who participate in it, including the migrant and those left behind (Falicov 2015; Ayón, Marsiglia, and Bermudez-Parsai 2010; Rivera-Heredia, Obregón, and Cervantes 2009; Salgado 2007; Achotegui 2002). Most binational studies of Mexican migration have focused on the physical health of migrants and the health disparities they face once in the United States (Consejo Nacional de Población 2015), without consideration of the role of gender in immigrant health or psychological adjustment. Various studies indicate that, especially for those who are unauthorized, the migration process may create adverse consequences for migrants' mental health, given the challenges they face prior to and during migration and settlement in a new social context (Consejo Nacional de Población 2015; Falicov 2015; Kirkmayer et al. 2010). Torres and Wallace (2013) among others note that the stress of departure, anticipation of leaving loved ones behind, as well as the push factors to the migration, including social and political violence in Mexico, can cause additional stress. Moreover, concerns about detection and detention during the journey, the potential encounter with violence while en route, and possible deportation exacerbate migrants' apprehension. Furthermore, worries regarding whether or not they may find employment once settled into their new location, and the degree of social support they may find, all pose significant risks to the mental health of migrants (Flores et al. 2019; Flores 2015).

Once settled in the United States, Mexican immigrants also face multiple challenges, including changed systems of meaning and diverse ways in which the culture of origin, social supports, and even physical geography nuance the daily life of individuals and promote or discourage a sense of belonging (Falicov 2014, 1989). These changes can contribute to psychological distress. For example, immigrants from rural areas may find it easier to adapt to a rural community than to a large urban center. Not only may migrants find the kinds of available jobs to be familiar, but they may also be accustomed to the geographical terrain and climate of these areas and find social spaces easier to navigate, allowing them to recreate support networks prevalent in their communities of origin (Espin 2015). In addition, communication problems and difficulties in cultural adaptation due to language and value differences, including ideas about masculinity and gender role performance, pose significant threats to their emotional well-being. Augmenting these are the experiences of racism, classism, and discrimination from the majority population, which may reduce employment options and demonize their masculinity, ancestry, and thus their sense of self (Consejo Nacional de Población 2015; Wong and Lu 2014; Ramirez 2011; Ayón, Marsiglia and Bermudez Parsai, 2010). Therefore, it is essential to assess how men cope with these challenges and what psychological and cultural resources they utilize to mitigate their distress. Likewise, it is important to determine to what extent, if at all, the men develop belonging in their new context.

The process of migration requires a renegotiation of relationships across borders, within the new social context, as well as "a reconstruction of social networks" and the cultural and socioeconomic systems of migrants (Bhugra 2003; Rogler 1994). The transitions and adaptations required of immigrants may increase their stress and lead to mental health problems over time (Consejo Nacional de Población 2015; Jablensky et al. 1981). A report from the *Consejo Nacional de Población* (2015) notes that 8 percent of newly arrived Mexican immigrants described experiencing sadness, longing, and symptoms of mood and anxiety disorders, whereas 15.5 percent of Mexican immigrants who have lived more than ten years in the United States reported symptoms of anxiety, depression, hopelessness, or despair. Likewise, on average 14 percent of immigrants from Latin America who have lived more than ten years in the United States experience some feelings of hopelessness or anxiety compared to European Americans (11.6 percent; Consejo Nacional de Población 2015).

Psychologist Oliva Espin (2015) highlights the importance of memory, and what she terms "the geography of memory," in the construction of a sense of self among immigrants. Espin notes that many immigrants remain suspended in between countries and "geographies" and must find ways to cope with their uprooting. For men, a focus on work and their gender role of provider may assuage the longing and desire for the homeland and family left behind. Their role as provider may create continuity in terms of who they were and currently are—those in charge (*los encargados*) of their parents, spouses, and/or children's economic well-being. And while masculinity studies point to the detrimental aspects of hegemonic masculinity which are rooted in the subjugation of women, this research highlights dimensions of masculinity embodied by rural-origin immigrant Mexican men that produce healing and solidarity. Revealed here are ways in which the masculine role of economic provider produces resilience and endurance among agricultural farmworkers that enable them to persevere in the face of exclusion, "unbelonging," and economic exploitation. Despite the physical borders and economic necessities that prevented these men from returning to Mexico, their role as self-sacrificing breadwinners enabled them to maintain social connections with their families and attachments to their homeland, challenging their marginalization in the United States and producing meanings that fostered positive identities and solidarity.

Study and Methods

The data for this analysis is drawn from a larger study, which took place between 2012 and 2015 and employed mixed methods and a community-based participatory approach to investigate how Mexican immigrant men in the Central Valley of California and their compatriots in Michoacán, Mexico, perceived their migration's effect on their family relations as well as how they experienced emotional distress (Flores et al. 2019). We conducted interviews and focus groups with forty agricultural workers in Central California. From this sample, ten men were invited to participate in in-depth interviews held every six months for three years. Participants were selected based on their depression scores (mild to moderate)[2] and their willingness to remain in the study for the three-year period. The longitudinal perspective garnered from our contact with these men over three years' time permitted us to examine the impact of seasonal work, food insecurity, and the drought on their emotional well-being.

Based on existing literature and the themes that emerged in the focus groups, I developed an interview guide, which I used to facilitate a discussion of the men's initial reason for migration, how they addressed their health concerns, and the impact of their migration on their well-being. The interview guide was then reviewed with local *promotoras* (community health workers) who collaborated with the author in other research projects (see de la Torre et al. 2013). The interview questions were also vetted by local informants who gave input on language use, given the literacy level of the participants.

All interviews were audiotaped, transcribed, and analyzed by the principal investigator utilizing the ATLAS.ti program (version 6) for data reduction (Taylor and Bogdan 1987). The interviews were conducted in Spanish, either in person or by telephone depending on the men's availability due to the seasonal nature of their jobs. Those conducted in person were held at the local Senior Citizen Center. Each participant was presented with a twenty-five-dollar gift card at the conclusion of the interviews. Snacks and refreshments were always available.

The men in the selected sample had lived in the United States for at least ten years and lived alone, with other men, or with their families. While all of the men had mild to moderate symptoms of depression, none of them expressed having any anxiety. All of them described making use of psychological resources, primarily religious coping and *auto-control* (self-control) to face whatever vicissitudes of life they encountered. Although they all reported having strong networks of social support, most of the men described difficulties utilizing the social supports available to them.

FIGURE 8.1 Research participants, August 2018. Photo by Dr. Hector Rivera Lopez.

Interviewees ranged from thirty-five to seventy-two years of age. Five of the men had migrated to the United States between the ages of sixteen and twenty, two had migrated between the ages of twenty-one and twenty-five, and three had migrated after age twenty-five. Five of them had traveled back and forth to Mexico during the 1990s, but once border crossing became more difficult, they had stopped going to visit their families. The older men had adult children whom they had not seen for years. Eight of the ten men had only completed elementary school; one had finished high school and one had a college degree from Mexico. All the men worked in the fields. Two drove tractors or other farm equipment, the rest planted and harvested crops. One of the men lived with his wife and daughter, who had recently arrived in the United States; the rest lived in rented rooms or in shared apartments with other men.

For immigrants, mental health implies the ability to negotiate a new social context that likely will create challenges, pose risks, and produce potential threats to their emotional and physical health. The *testimonios* of these immigrant men offer a window into their agency and cultural wealth, as they describe in their own words the impact of migration on their physical and emotional well-being, the loss of connection created by family separation, the psychological resources they utilize to negotiate challenges, and how they create *familia* and belonging in an often-hostile context. *Testimonios* are a means for those on the margins to assert themselves as political and social subjects by narrating and giving voice to their experiences. By presenting their *testimonios*, the men in this study had an opportunity to visualize their lives and stories (Latina Feminist Group 2001). The men's *testimonios* offered narratives of longing and uprootedness, their sacrifice for the well-being of others, and the re-making of family ties.

Research Site

The study took place in a rural, agricultural community in Central California where the majority of the 7,200 residents are either Mexican or of Mexican origin. The town is twenty-two miles off the main highway and is accessible via country roads from nearby communities. The primary source of employment is agriculture. The community has one health center and one recreation center, a small grocery store and two gas stations; one service station includes a small convenience store. There are no pharmacies, department stores, or movie theaters in the town. There are two Mexican restaurants located in the center of town. The local health center has no Spanish-speaking staff. The residents live in single-family homes, migrant housing, or apartment buildings. As the U.S. principal investigator,[3] I had spent six years doing fieldwork in this community prior to conducting this study; thus I was well known by the men, as well as to the *promotoras* and community leaders who vetted and approved the study.

FIGURE 8.2 Research participants pictured with author. December 2017. Photo by Dr. Hector Rivera Lopez.

FIGURE 8.3 Participant and Dr. Hector Rivera-Lopez. Photo by Dr. Yvette Flores.

Results

The first question I posed in the interview asked why they had migrated to California and what they were expecting to find in the United States that Mexico was not providing. Most of the men responded that their first motivation to migrate to California was to improve the quality of life of their families in Mexico. They described their role as the "*encargados de sus familias*" (those in charge of responding to their family's economic needs). Juan, aged thirty-five, who had worked in California since age nineteen, stated his goals as follows: "*Darle una vida mejor a mi hijo* [give my son a better life]" and "*y ayudar a mis padres* [help my parents out]." Juan had planned to come to California for only a short time; however, when he learned that his girlfriend was pregnant, he decided to stay longer in order to provide for her and his child, and to continue to help out his parents. He did not meet his son until the boy was three and had seen him only a few times since then, as returning to Mexico became more arduous and unsafe. He sent remittances to his parents, partner, and son every month. He along with three other men shared a house on the edge of town.

The consensus among the ten men was that Mexico did not provide them with the educational and employment opportunities to offer their families a dignified standard of living, much less help them actualize their dreams and expectations. Some of the older men interviewed had migrated with prior agreements (*cartas*) that were sanctioned by the U.S. government as part of the Bracero program.[4] These workers were brought to the United States to work in the fields, and once the farming season ended, they could return to their country of origin. Many of these men never intended to stay in the United States indefinitely. They came motivated to provide their families with financial support to improve their living conditions in Mexico. However, they could not get ahead financially and had remained in California.

Some of the men realized when they returned to Mexico that they "had changed" and no longer felt they belonged in their communities of origin (*yo ya no me sentía a gusto allá*).

Nine of the men originated from *ranchos*, rural communities in Michoacán, Mexico, that provided limited work opportunities; many of their parents subsisted on the crops they planted and traded for other goods. All of them grew up in poverty, without running water or electricity. One of the men I call Benito was over sixty years old and had been living in the United States for more than thirty years. He had decided to migrate to California in search of the "Dream of the North" ("*El Sueño del Norte*") or "an opportunity to make it possible for his family to have access to an improved way of life." He had worked for over thirty years and had nothing to show for it. But, he quickly added, his parents had lived well with his assistance, and he had educated all five of his children, who were now professionals. When asked if he planned to return to Mexico, Benito hesitated before answering that he would, when he got older and could no longer work.

Migration and Well Being

When asked about the impact of the migration on their health, many of the men spoke of loneliness (*soledad*) and that "money was not everything" ("*El dinero no lo es todo*"). Javier, age forty-two, reflected on what most of the men spoke about, the ever-present desire to return home: "*Me dan ganas de regresar pero pienso en mi hijo* [I have the desire to return, but then I think of my son]." Javier remained in the United States because he wanted to educate his children. His youngest son was starting *preparatoria*, high school, and he wanted to see him graduate. He planned to return to Michoacán to see his son graduate and remain there, hoping that with his savings, he could start a business.

The men who lacked authorized immigration status could not return home for visits, even to say good-bye or bury a deceased parent. José stated: "*Mi mamá se murió. Yo no pude ir a su entierro* [My mother died and I could not go to her funeral]." When asked how he coped with the loss, he stated that he used self-control to manage his loneliness and isolation; "*hay que aguantarse* [one has to hold on]," he said.

Although the men were not asked about their immigration status, they all disclosed whether they "had papers" or not. Only two of the men had legal residency. One had obtained it during the amnesty program and the other was sponsored by his employer. The men who were unauthorized migrants lived with some fear of detection and deportation. The older men recounted that in their early years in the United States employers exploited them more and often called immigration officials prior to paying them. If they were detained or deported, the farm owner would not pay them for the work they had done. Benito noted that times were better now; although massive deportations were occurring throughout the United States, they were not as afraid, as long as they did not leave the community or get into legal problems. However, many of the men reported wage theft; that is, employers who refused to pay them for overtime work or for activities that were not specific to their job, such as laying down irrigation pipe, even though this was essential for the cultivation of crops.

Many of the men had suffered physical injuries on the job. Their unauthorized status largely precluded seeking health care when injured or ill. Most of the growers did not provide health insurance, and the local health center did not have Spanish-speaking staff. Benito stated that he had seen a male doctor for a while, paying him out of pocket. However, the doctor had retired and a young female physician had replaced him. Benito stated: *"¡Yo no puedo ir a ver a una señorita para que me revise mis partes privadas, no! Me quedo sin ir al doctor.* [I can't go see a young woman and have her examine my private parts. No, I just will not go see the doctor.]"

The ten men described the worst type of injury as the kind that affected their spirit, resulting in hopelessness, sadness, longing for family, and feelings of impotence when, despite their efforts, they could not get ahead financially. The men worked in difficult conditions and in extreme weather. The men stated that the cold and the heat were just reminders that their families depended on them to survive. For example, Sergio stated that whenever he felt overwhelmed by the heat, he thought of his mother who needed medicine for diabetes. He had to push through and keep working. (*"Pos, cuando siento que me vence el calor, pienso en mi viejita que necesita medicina para su diabetes, y me aguanto. Tengo que echarle ganas."*) The men described working despite feeling ill or being in pain because their family needed them. Most of the men worked more than fourteen hours, six or seven days a week. Many of them were not aware of or did not acknowledge the health implications and the impact that working in the fields imposed on their bodies and spirit. Most of the time they relied on traditional healing practices to attend to their physical ailments.

In the psychology of these men, complaining about physical pain is a sign of weakness and lack of *"fuerza de voluntad"* (will power). The idea of not having the strength to face adversity is a source of shame that needs to be avoided at all costs. This belief is embedded in the core value of respect (Ramirez 2011). A man who respects himself never quits. Even if that means that his health will be compromised. The saying *"estamos aquí prestados* [we are here on loan]," which several of the men expressed helped them to "keep going" and not quit, even when physically ill. This attitude, often described in the literature as fatalism or stoicism, instead reflected the men's commitment to the economic betterment of their families despite the physical toll (Drew and Shoenberg 2011).

Narratives of Longing and Uprootedness: Longing for the Homeland

Most of the men described life as a sacrifice and discussed how *"El sueño americano"* that brought them to the United States no longer exists. They longed to return home but remained in the United States because their families in Mexico still needed their financial support. For the older men, the death of their parents left them no reason to return. While they struggled financially in the United States, most concurred that life in Mexico would be more difficult, especially lacking the resources to go back and establish a business or have their own home.

Despite their longing for an eventual return "home," the men expressed profound gratitude to the United States. Julián, a fifty-four-year-old man, stated, *"este país me ha ayudado con trabajo para ayudar a mi familia* [this country has helped me have work to help out my family]." Few of the men considered how their absence affected those left behind, as they focused primarily on the economic benefits of their absence. A few of the men did state that children also needed the presence of a father, but they had to sacrifice that connection for the economic survival of their family.

The ten men offered narratives of a "dual existence." Their hearts and spirits were connected to Mexico but their bodies resided in the agricultural fields where they worked. All the men had migrated initially as young adults or late adolescents to support their parents. While those who were unauthorized had been able to travel home to Mexico during their first few years in the United States, as the passage North became more expensive and dangerous, they could no longer afford to do so. Thus they relied on memories of home, occasional letters, and phone calls to maintain contact with their loved ones. They felt that they belonged "*ni aquí ni allá* [neither here nor there]" (Espin 2015).

José, who grew up in Mexico City, had been employed as a computer analyst, but lost his job during the 1980s Mexican economic crisis. Without prospects for employment, he decided "to try his luck" in the United States. He knew some men from his community who had migrated to the rich agricultural valley of California. He arrived with limited knowledge of English; thus he could only find work in the fields. He never married and worked to support his aging parents and to save for his eventual return to Mexico.

An articulate man, over the course of his interviews José shared his sadness and his sense of uprootedness. Yet he remained in California because his mother had a heart condition and required surgery. His siblings did not want her to have the surgery for fear that she would die. His mother phoned him and asked for his opinion. As the eldest, his mother confided and trusted him more. He supported his mother's decision to have the surgery. Although he had wanted to go see her before the procedure, his mother pleaded with him to remain in California, as the border crossing had become increasingly dangerous, and José complied. When Jose's mother died during surgery, his siblings became furious with him and blamed him for her death. As all the siblings were married with children of their own, José felt obligated to assume financial responsibility for her surgery and subsequent burial. He sold a small house he had purchased in Mexico and used his life savings to cover the expenses. He described the sadness, devastation, and regret he felt at not seeing her before she passed. He coped with the loss by attending AA meetings, even though he did not drink. During a subsequent interview, José spoke about the stigma Mexican men hold against using mental health services. He added that they needed that support, as men alone in a foreign country, but did not seek services due to male pride. "*Tenemos que cambiar nuestras ideas; si necesitamos ayuda, debemos de buscarla. No hay que tener tanto orgullo.*" "We need to change our ideas," he stated. "If we need help, we should seek it. We don't need to be so proud."

Sacrifice for Others

Most of the men shared similar stories of longing and loss. The notion of sacrifice for the family was central to their masculinity. Visualizing the happiness of their families is the reward for the suffering and deprivation experienced. The compensation was seeing their children attain an education, their parents improve their living conditions via remittances, and seeing (or hearing about) their family's happiness and to celebrate from afar the accomplishments that were made possible because of their efforts. All the men noted that their loneliness and difficult living situations were worth the sacrifice.

The men who had married and formed families of their own often felt guilt that they could not provide for their parents as much. Thus they sacrificed by working longer hours, following the crops as needed to be able to sustain themselves, their spouses, and children, and continue to support their parents. Many of the men coped with stoicism and self-control; they swallowed their emotions and pretended not to feel. They did not complain about living with other men in shared rooms, or as boarders in other people's houses. They lived frugally and saw the sacrifice as worthwhile because their families in Mexico lived relatively well. Sergio stated, "*hay que sacrificarse por la familia, para eso vinimos a este pais, para que ellos estuvieran mejor. No tiene caso estar aquí gozando si ellos están sufriendo.* [We have to sacrifice for our families (in Mexico), that is why we came to this country so they could have a better life. There's no point being here having a good time if they are suffering.]." These men, as those in Ramirez's (2011) sample, viewed their masculinity as intimately connected to their work; they came to the United States to work, not to be "*guevones*" (slang for lazy).

Some of the men admitted to using alcohol to cope and oftentimes overspending on alcohol such that they could not send as much money to their families. They felt tremendous guilt. Benicio, age seventy-two, recounted how he came to the United States as a bracero; thus, initially he had "papers" and could travel safely between Michoacán and California. But when his contract ended, and he did not return to Mexico, he became undocumented. The woman he had married in Mexico and whom he visited annually joined him in the United States when he could no longer return for visits. They had two children in Mexico who eventually joined him in the United States; but once their children grew and left the rural community, his wife left him and returned to Mexico. He had been alone since. He admitted that his drinking might have been a contributing factor to the end of his marriage, but denied that it was the principal reason she left him. "*Sí, pues, mi vieja me dejó porque no le gustaba aquí. Ella prefería estar con su mamá. Pues, sí, a ella no le gustaba que yo tomara, pero esa no fue la razón principal por la que se fue.*" He believed she simply did not like the United States and preferred to be with her mother in rural Michoacán. Despite his advancing years, he continued to work in the fields. Having no family to support, he appeared content with earning enough money to live. He had no plans to return to Mexico. Admittedly his life in the United States had been difficult, but worth the sacrifice. "Why would I complain? [*Para que me voy a quejar?*]," he asked. "*Sí, ha sido duro vivir aquí, lejos de la tierra de uno, pero valió la pena el sacrificio. Mis padres vivieron mejor porque yo estaba acá.* [Yes, life here has been hard, far from one's homeland, but it was worth the sacrifice. My parents lived better because I was here.]"

Migration, Family Disruption, and Reunification

While all the men conceded that their migration disrupted family life, only one of the men addressed the impact of separation on their wife and child. Higinio had migrated as a young man to help support his parents; on a return visit to his hometown, he met a woman with whom he fell in love. They exchanged letters for two years, and on another visit, they married. Higinio had been able to obtain legal residence as a result of the amnesty program of 1986. He visited annually, as he could travel freely between the two countries; when they had a daughter, he felt even more compelled to continue working in California to support them.

As his daughter grew, she began to complain about his absences. She cried every time he left Mexico. He felt suspended between countries and felt tremendous guilt about putting her and his wife through such sorrow. Thus he petitioned for them to migrate legally. However, his daughter had a difficult time adjusting to the United States at age eleven. She did not speak English, and the school she attended offered minimal academic support. Higinio poignantly spoke about his distress and feelings of impotence that he could not provide better for his family. While his wife and daughter were living in Mexico, he lived with other men and spent little money on housing. However, upon their arrival, he had to rent a house. His expenses grew and his wife had to seek work. "*Estoy contento que mi señora y mi hija están conmigo, pero ahora tengo más presión económica. Mi señora tiene que trabajar porque no nos alcanza con mi salario. Me da vergüenza que no la puedo mantener y que ella tiene que trabajar, pero al menos estamos juntos por ahora.* [I am happy that my wife and daughter are with me, but now I have more financial pressure. My wife has to work because my income is not enough. I am ashamed that I can't support her and she has to work, but at least we are together now.]"

Since his wife had to work, it meant that Higinio's daughter enjoyed less of her presence and support. Thus he dedicated all his free time to his daughter. They often took long walks together and often were seen at the Friday *tiangis* (flea market) in the summers. Higinio worried about his daughter's future in the United States. He knew the community where they lived offered limited educational opportunities after high school; for their daughter to study, she would need to leave the community. He dreaded the potential family separation. However, he continued to believe that whatever sacrifices needed to be made would be worthwhile as long as they benefited his daughter's future.

Most of the men who had been (or were) separated from their families did not see their presence in Mexico as necessary to their families' well-being. Higinio, on the other hand, saw the impact of his absence on his daughter as well as the challenges posed by reunification.

Haciendo Familia

The psychology of the men was centered mainly on the welfare of their families. In their minds, family always came first. Thoughts about their family and what their labor could provide for them appeared to provide them with a "super energy" to help them face any obstacles that might interfere with their provider role. Several of the men stated, "*mi familia me da la energía para seguir adelante.*" This attitude could be described as the intergenerational legacy of the archetype of the "Warrior," a posture in life that nothing except death will stop them from achieving their goal. The energy of the "Warrior" is a value that is shared by all the men interviewed. They look after each other and provide support among themselves when a "Warrior" is wounded.

The men relied primarily on each other for social support. As Ramirez (2011) also found in his study of "*jardinero* masculinity," the men supported each other through actions, not with words. The men in our study did not sit around together and discuss their needs. They observed each other and provided assistance when they saw the need, without being asked. A few attended Alcoholic Anonymous (AA) meetings, even if they did not have a substance abuse disorder, as they found social support there and learned strategies to cope with their loneliness. Joaquin, one of the men interviewed, had migrated at age sixteen; he had no family and had lost his legs due to untreated diabetes. At age forty-seven, he was ill and had no health or disability insurance or a way to make a living. The other men took care of him; they found an old wheelchair and fixed it for him so he could get around. Although homeless, the other men made sure he had a place to sleep at night and shared their earnings with him so he could buy food. Joaquin was stoic. He had stopped communicating with his family in Mexico when he could no longer send remittances. He did not want them to know of his situation.

The men had built community and found support in their shared loneliness (*soledad compartida*). Many said: "*Aquí a todos nos falta la familia pero nos apoyamos . . . nos convertimos en familia. Aquí nos hacemos familia.* [Here we are all without our families, but we support each other. We become family.]" This solidarity was made possible by the fact that they worked together, they originated from the same ranchos in Michoacán, and often lived together or near each other.

These men built family with each other to assuage their loneliness and create belonging. They did not feel they belonged to the United States or to Mexico; they belonged to the fields and to the community in which they lived. Benito stated: "*Ya no somos de México y nunca fuimos de acá. México está en el corazón y en los recuerdos. Aquí nosotros somos la única familia que tenemos.* [We no longer belong to Mexico and we never belonged here. Mexico is in our hearts and memories. Here, we are the only family we have.]" For the men interviewed, their belonging was created by bonds of solidarity with each other. It was not so much *pertenencia* (belonging) to a place but their shared struggle. Their *familia* in the community allowed them to face multiple injustices, inclement weather, loneliness, and isolation.

Conclusions

The men who participated in this study offered narratives of resilience and shed light on the ways in which masculinity shapes their migration experiences and their adaptation to a new cultural context. Their stories point to the nobility and sacrifice of men who migrate to support their families. Work in the agricultural fields of California offers low pay ($10 per hour, which was the minimum wage in California at the time of the study). Some of the farmers offer low-cost housing; other men rent rooms from families or live in apartments shared by several men. While a few succumb to addiction to manage the stress, loneliness, and culture shock, most continue to send remittances to their families and see their loneliness and isolation as a worthwhile sacrifice as long as their families are doing well. Many of these men find community among each other and created *familia.* I interviewed a father-son dyad who had been away from the rest of the family for two decades. As the father aged, his son joined him in the fields to help him work.

Few of the men had access to health-care services; none had access to mental health support. Their lack of English fluency, limited financial resources, and barriers to services threatened their health. They coped with resignation, their religious faith, and the firm belief that although the "American dream" was dead, they needed to prevail so that their children could have a better future.

The men interviewed held onto traditional views of masculinity and family; they saw their primary role as providers for their families. Their identity was rooted in the hegemonic masculinity prevalent in rural Mexican communities; they viewed their personal sacrifice as essential for the well-being of their loved ones. Drawing on their cultural values, the men forged kinship ties with each other. They relied on their social networks, constructed as family, to endure the loneliness and isolation caused by their migration, living in an isolated rural community, and the nature of their work in the fields.

They held onto values of solidarity and *compañerismo*; they helped each other in times of illness, scarcity of jobs, and when they experienced losses. Some held on to the dream of returning to Mexico someday. Others felt they belonged neither here nor there, so remained in the local community *por ahora* [for now]. The men's *testimonios* shed light on how the men cope— through social networks, their faith, and through adherence to the fulfillment of their masculine gender role. They rely on the psychological resource of *auto control*, of *aguantar* or endurance, in order to fulfill their cultural mandate because they see it as central to being a good man, spouse, son, or father. By enacting their gender role, they sacrifice for others; by relying on their value of family, they create a support system that sustains them.

Their "geography of memory" helped them maintain continuity with their life in Mexico while residing in California (Espin 2015). Their focus on sacrifice for others allowed them to face the stressors created by the last presidential election in the United States. During the 2016 elections, Mexican men were demonized and cast as rapists and murderers. The men took the discourse in stride. "*Pura política* [just politics]," they would say. They worried more about possible raids if Trump were elected. After the elections, the men vowed to withstand the possible increase in racism and hate crimes. They sought support from each other to take care of their belongings, "just in case they got deported." They continued to live their life. As of this writing, four years after the conclusion of the project, nine of the men remain in the community. José returned to Mexico City and is now working with a group of deported men who run a t-shirt shop and welcome deported compatriots in order to help them adjust.

While these narratives may be somewhat unique to immigrant Mexican men in a rural, U.S. context, I believe that the men reflect universal themes rooted in patriarchal notions of masculinity. The men's histories reflect universal themes of resilience, resistance, and commitment to thrive despite structural racism and the longing for the homeland and loved ones left behind. Despite their geographical and at times social isolation, these men formed community with each other, supported each other during difficult times, and forged belonging. They formed kinship ties to help assuage the sadness of family separation. Utilizing cultural values of interdependence, honor, respect, and sacrifice for others, the solidarity of these men contested prevailing narratives of Mexican men's dysfunction. Their testimonies shed light on how Mexican immigrant men can create *familia* with each other and construct networks of support to nurture their resilience, and to promote belonging, if not to the country in which they live, to the shared reality of being Mexican male agricultural workers.

These men created community as they engaged in the gendered activities associated with providing for their families. Through network-building and enacting social roles of economic providers, these farmworker men forged meaningful attachments with each other and their families which gave them the strength to endure in the contemporary context of increasingly restrictive policies that limit access to dignified work, health care, and social services.[5]

Notes

1. The author acknowledges the contribution of the research team, in particular Ericka Cervantes-Pacheco PhD and Hector Rivera-Lopez PhD, the *promotoras*, and especially the men who shared their lives and *testimonios*.
2. None of the men met the criteria for major depressive disorder or any other psychiatric disorder based on the standardized instruments. However, the ten participants had symptoms of depression that ranged from mild to moderate.

Of the sample of forty men, only one had severe depression and was not interviewed but was offered therapy instead.

3. The author was known to the men due to her long-term involvement in the community. They had engaged with her previously in focus groups co-facilitated by a male psychologist. Individual interviews to elicit the men's *testimonios* began once the men had developed trust, *confianza*, in her. As Ramirez (2011) notes, researchers must be mindful of the class (and gender) differences and the distance these can create in our investigations.

4. The Bracero Program was a series of laws and binational agreements beginning in 1942, which provided Mexican laborers with special permits to work in the United States, primarily in agriculture (Bracero History Archive 2021).

5. I continued to visit the community and offer workshops to the men after the conclusion of the study. The COVID-19 pandemic interrupted these visits. Follow-up contact by phone was conducted to offer support and inquire about their health and concerns. As essential workers, the men continued to work in the fields, often without proper protective equipment. None of the men became ill; however, several lost relatives in Michoacán who succumbed to the virus.

References

Achótegui, Joseba. 2002. *La depresión en los inmigrantes. Una perspectiva transcultural*. Barcelona, Spain: Mayo.

Ayón, Cecilia, Flavio F. Marsiglia, and Monica Bermudez-Parsai. 2010. "Latino Family Mental Health: Exploring the Role of Discrimination and Familismo." *Journal of Community Psychology* 38(6): 742–56.

Bhugra, Dinesh. 2003. "Migration and Depression." *Acta Psychiatrica Scandinavica* 108(Suppl. 418): 67–72.

Bracero History Archive. 2021. "Bracero History Archive." Roy Rosenzweig Center for History and New Media, George Mason University, the Smithsonian National Museum of American History, Brown University, and the Institute of Oral History, University of Texas, El Paso. Accessed September 7, 2021. http://braceroarchive.org/.

Consejo Nacional de Población. 2015. *Migration and Health: Mexican Immigrants in the United States*. Mexico City, Mexico. Consejo Nacional de Población.

Connell, Raewyn. 2003. *Masculinidades*. Mexico City: Universidad Autónoma de México, Programa Universitario de Estudios de Género.

Connell, Robert W. 1997. "La organización social de masculinidad." In *Masculinidades: Poder y Crisis*, edited by Teresa Valdés and José Olavarría, 31–48. Chile: FLACSO.

Connell, Robert W., and James W. Messerschmidt. 2005. "Hegemonic Masculinity: Rethinking the Concept." *Gender and Society* 19(6): 829–59.

de la Torre, Adela, Banafsheh Sadeghi, Richard D. Green, Lucia L. Kaiser, Yvette G. Flores, Carlos F. Jackson, Ulfat Shaikh, Linda Whent, and Sara E. Schaefer. 2013. "Niños Sanos, Familia Sana: Mexican Immigrant Study Protocol for a Multifaceted CBPR Intervention to Combat Childhood Obesity in Two Rural California Towns." *BMC Public Health* 13(1): 1–12.

Drew, Elaine M., and Nancy E. Schoenber. 2011. "Deconstructing Fatalism: Ethnographic Perspectives on Women's Decision Making About Cancer Prevention and Treatment." *Medical Anthropology Quarterly* 25(2):164–82.

Espín, Olivia M. 2015. "A Geography of Memory; a Psychology of Place." In *Gendered Journeys: Women, Migration and Feminist Psychology*, edited by Olivia M. Espín and Andrea L. Dottolo, 29–53. New York: Palgrave Macmillan.

Falicov, Celia Jaes. 1989. *Latino Families in Therapy: A Guide to Multicultural Practice*. New York: Guilford Press.

———. 2014. *Latino Families in Therapy: A Guide to Multicultural Practice*. 2nd ed. New York: Guilford Press.

Flores, Yvette G. 2013. *Chicana and Chicano Mental Health: Alma, Mente y Corazon*. Tucson: University of Arizona Press.

———. 2015. *Psychological Perspectives for Chicano and Latino Children and Adolescents*. Austin: Sentia Publishers.

Flores, Yvette G., and Enriqueta Valdez Curiel. 2009. "Conflict Resolution and Intimate Partner Violence Among Mexicans on Both Sides of the Border." In *Mexicans in California: Transformations and Challenges*, edited by Ramón A. Gutiérrez, Patricia Zavella, Denise Segura, Dolores Trevizo, and Juan Vicente Palerm, 183–215. Champaign: University of Illinois Press.

Flores, Yvette G., Lisceth Brazil-Cruz, Hector Rivera-Lopez, Rosa D. Manzo, Monica Siañez, and Ericka Ivonne Cervantes Pacheco. 2019. "Aquí en Confianza (Here in Confidence): Narratives of Migration, Mental Health and Family Reunification of Mexican Immigrant Men in the California Central Valley." In *Community-Based Participatory Research: Testimonios from Chicana/o Studies*, edited by Natalia Deeb-Sossa, 153–78. Tucson: University of Arizona Press.

Gonzáles, Butrón, and Maria Arcelia. 1995. "Las mujeres en Michoacán." In *Estudios de género en Michoacán. Lo femenino y lo Masculino en perspectiva*, edited by Miriam Aidé Núñez Vera, María Arcelia Gonzáles Butrón, and Cecilia Fernández Zayas, 157–79. Morelia, Michoacán, Universidad Autónoma de Chapingo, Universidad Michoacana de San Nicolás de Hidalgo, Centro de Investigaciones y Desarrollo en el Estado de Michoacán.

Hernández, Oscar Misael. 2012. "Migración, masculinidad y menores repatriados en la frontera Matamoros-Brownsville." *Trayectorias* 14(33–34): 76–94.

Hurtado, Aida, and Mrinal Sinha. 2018. *Beyond Machismo: Latino Intersectional Masculinities*. Austin: University of Texas Press.

Jablensky, Assen, Norman Sartorius, Walter Gulbinat, and G. Ernberg. 1981. "Characteristics of Depressive Patients Contacting Psychiatric Services in Four Cultures." *Acta Psychiatrica Scandinavica* 63: 367–83.

Kirkmayer, Laurence J., Megha Sedhev, Rob Whitley, Stéphane F. Dandeneau, and Colette Issac. 2009. "Community Resilience: Models, Metaphors and Measures." *Journal of Aboriginal Health* 5(1): 62–117.

Latina Feminist Group. 2001. *Telling to Live: Latina Feminist Testimonios.* Durham, N.C.: Duke University Press.

Lu, Alexander, and Y. Joel Wong. 2014. "Stressful Experiences of Masculinity Among Young U.S.-Born and Immigrant Latino American Men." *Culture, Society & Masculinities* 6(2): 111–28.

McIlwaine, Cathy. 2010. "Migrant Machismos: Exploring Gender Ideologies and Practices Among Latin American Migrants in London From a Multi-Scalar Perspective." *Gender, Place and Culture* 17(3): 281–300.

Ramirez, Hernan. 2011. "Masculinity in the Workplace: The Case of Mexican Immigrant Gardeners." *Men and Masculinities* 14(1): 97–116.

Rivera, Heredia, Maria Elena, Nydia Obregón Velasco, and Ericka Ivonne Cervantes Pacheco. 2009. "Promoción de la salud. Consideraciones para la intervención con los migrantes y sus familias." In *Aportaciones a la Psicología de la salud,* edited by Jennifer Lira, 225–54. México: UMSNH.

Rogler, Lloyd H. 1994. "International Migrations: A Framework for Directing Research." *American Psychologist* 49(8): 701–8.

Salgado, Nelly. 2007. "Migración México-Estados Unidos: Retos y oportunidades en salud." *Salud Pública en México,* 49, edición especial, XII Congreso de Investigación en Salud Pública. México: Instituto Nacional de Salud Pública.

Taylor, Steve J., and Robert Bogdan. 1987. *Introducción a los métodos cualitativos de investigación.* Barcelona: Paidós.

Torres, Jacqueline M., and Steven P. Wallace. 2013. "Migration Circumstances, Psychological Distress, and Self-Rated Physical Health for Latino Immigrants in the United States." *American Journal of Public Health* 103(9): 1619–27.

Vega Briones, Germán. 2009. "Masculinidad y migración internacional: Una perspectiva de género." *Aldea Mundo* 14(28): 53–64.

PART III

Resistance Through Claims-Making and Cultural Expression

CHAPTER 7

Belonging and Vulnerability in San Francisco

Undocumented Latinx Parents and Local Claims-Making

MELANIE JONES GAST, DINA G. OKAMOTO,
AND JACK "TREY" ALLEN

In U.S. public and policy arenas, Latinx populations are often viewed as "illegal," "criminal," and "unassimilable foreigners," even when they have citizenship or legal status and protections under the law (Flores and Schacter 2018; Brown 2013; Chavez 2013). Furthermore, undocumented and temporary-status Latinxs face both social and legal exclusion, along with the constant threat of deportation by the state (Menjívar and Abrego 2012). Due to federal immigration policy, undocumented Latinxs feel and anticipate "legal violence"—"the normalized but cumulatively injurious effects of the law" (Menjívar and Abrego 2012, 1380). Even Latinx young adults who have spent all or most of their lives in the U.S. experience attacks against their membership and fears of problems with authorities within a hostile national climate (Flores-González 2017; Gonzales 2016). Such messages signal the precarious state of belonging and membership of Latinxs in U.S. society and its institutions (Flores-González 2017).

While restrictive policies and hostile rhetoric toward Latinx populations have ramped up at the national level, some cities and communities have attempted to counter the federal climate with inclusionary efforts and policies (García 2019; de Graauw 2016; Marrow 2012). In this study, we focus on the city of San Francisco, California, where immigrants, regardless of legal status, have opportunities to engage in local decision-making and access rights, protections, and resources. Recognized as a "welcoming" local government (Welcoming America 2018), San Francisco has adopted policies and practices aimed at making public programs accessible to immigrant and underserved populations. Some of these local policies include bilingual education in public schools, city-funded health care and housing, and other public programs such as municipal identification cards for all residents to access local services (de Graauw 2016). As a self-designated "sanctuary" city, San Francisco restricts front-line workers and the police from aiding Immigration and Customs Enforcement (ICE) with investigations or arrests unless required for criminal violations (Ridgley 2008). San Francisco also has an established network of community-based organizations (CBOs) and activists working for immigrant and underserved populations, making it an ideal place to study undocumented Latinx immigrant agency and belonging, or the state of being recognized as a community member with rights and freedoms afforded to other community members (Glenn 2011).

As nonprofit organizations, CBOs provide support catered to the unique needs and backgrounds of local immigrant populations (Gast and Okamoto 2016; Cordero-Guzmán 2005). Through sustained advocacy work and close interactions, CBOs work with community members to build their capacities, act on concerns, and engage in "claims-making" or making demands and requests of authorities and polities in local arenas (Gast, Okamoto, and Nguyen 2021; Coll 2004). While others have identified barriers to immigrant claims-making in employment, health care, and politics, we focus on how undocumented CBO participants, mainly mothers, begin to "make their rights real" by claiming entitlement to services and support afforded to other community members in local programs and institutions (Bloemraad 2018; Gleeson 2016). Through local claims-making acts, we argue that undocumented CBO participants are expanding the boundaries of belonging and community membership beyond legally defined citizenship (see also Mendez and Deeb-Sossa 2020; Coll 2004). We also highlight the limits of local claims-making for belonging in U.S. institutions, as undocumented Latinx immigrants anticipate legal and institutional exclusion in the national climate, making belonging constantly precarious and negotiated (Menjívar and Abrego 2012). Our study has further implications given the uncertain economic, health, and housing climates low-income immigrants face during and after the COVID-19 pandemic.

We examine the following research questions: How do CBOs shape the claims-making and belonging of undocumented Latinx parents, mainly mothers, in local San Francisco programs and institutions? How do parents negotiate claims-making experiences and processes of belonging in the city? While past research demonstrates the strategies and practices CBOs use to empower and serve immigrants, we know less about how immigrant CBO participants come to understand claims-making and make their own requests and voice concerns in programs and institutions. As an example, in her work on low-income Mexican and Central American women, Coll (2004) found that participating in a CBO helped these women to cultivate feelings of community membership and collectively articulate new ideas about belonging and entitlement. While CBOs can help immigrants feel connected and share collective concerns, few studies examine how CBOs inform immigrants' actual claims-making attempts in local programs and institutions.

We conducted multistage in-depth interviews and fieldwork at *Adelante Familias* (AF), a CBO in San Francisco serving low-income immigrant families, to examine how undocumented Latinx parents from Mexico, Central America, and Peru develop and negotiate claims-making in local programs and institutions through their CBO involvement. Although a majority are mothers from Mexico, we use the gender-neutral "Latinx" term to encompass the one father and other Latin American parents. We interviewed parents early on in their contact with AF and then again one to two years later to understand how their perceptions and experiences evolved. At the time of initial interviews, these parents averaged eleven years in the United States but still described feelings of exclusion in city programs and institutions. Over time, through their involvement in the CBO, they gained tools to access and make claims in local programs and institutions as city residents. Yet these parents negotiated conflicting messages regarding their *local* inclusion and claims-making and their and their family's exclusion, disempowerment, and precariousness in a hostile *national* climate.

Immigrant Advocacy and Community Organizations

Advocacy and social-movement organizations have played key roles in contesting anti-immigrant policies and encouraging immigrants to express their collective voices. Studies have examined immigrant organizing within labor unions (Gleeson 2013), the undocumented student movement (Nicholls 2013), and the 2006 uprising against legislation criminalizing undocumented immigrants (Pallares and Flores-González 2010). Advocacy organizations work to portray immigrants as credible, nonthreatening, and deserving of legal citizenship, as well as other rights and benefits. Social-movement organizations deploy positive narratives about DREAMers and provide them with a source of empowerment and agency (Terriquez 2015; Unzueta Carrasco and Seif 2014). In doing so, these organizations contest how the state defines "deserving" citizens and help immigrants to assert their voices, affect policy-making, and understand their ability to create change (Patler 2018).

Unlike social-movement organizations, CBOs often encompass both advocacy and direct-service goals by providing a space for immigrants to develop networks, mobilize and assert their voices around shared issues, and gain access to public programs and services. Through referrals and public-service contracts, CBOs directly link immigrants and their children to public agencies (Gast and Okamoto 2016; Cordero-Guzmán 2005). Importantly, these local organizations hire staff with community ties, enabling CBOs to address issues specific to the neighborhood or community needs.

We contribute to literature on advocacy and community-based organizations, which heavily centers on the role that leaders, activists, and organizations play in shaping immigrant rights and empowerment (de Graauw 2016; Ramakrishnan and Bloemraad 2008). While local organizations can powerfully define and defend immigrants' social legitimacy, immigrants themselves also play key roles when they make individual demands and participate in local programs and institutions. In particular, when immigrants access and make requests in public assistance, healthcare, schools, and other programs, they are claiming entitlement to services and support afforded to other community members, changing the boundaries of who "belongs" and can claim rights and demands.

We unpack the process of claims-making in the local setting of San Francisco, and discuss implications for belonging and membership in the United States. When individual immigrants make claims of local public programs and institutions, they are not only accessing benefits and rights afforded to other community members, but also facilitating and realizing their inclusion and membership in San Francisco. Yet, as Bloemraad (2018) notes, claims-making involves a "relational process of recognition" where institutional actors and community members must recognize the claimant *and* claim—for example, a claim to benefits or resources—as legitimate (14). Through local claims-making acts, undocumented parents in San Francisco assert their city membership, while still negotiating their belonging and recognition in U.S. society and institutions. As others have noted, "belonging is not a 'reified fixity,' but an ongoing, dynamic process that involves everyday practices" and relationships fostering a sense of community and attachment (Mendez and Deeb-Sossa 2020, 177). Thus, through claims-making acts in local programs and institutions, undocumented parents facilitate their belonging, but simultaneously experience institutional relationships where they and their children lack power and legitimacy. We examine this process of making claims while negotiating belonging in the U.S. among undocumented Latinx parents in San Francisco with formal access and rights.

Immigrant Claims-Making in Public Programs and Institutions

As a self-declared "sanctuary" city with a history of immigration alongside inclusive policies providing immigrant access and protections, San Francisco's welcoming context should enable immigrant participation in local programs; yet research suggests that the process is not necessarily smooth (de Graauw 2016; Gast and Okamoto 2016; Marrow 2012). U.S. immigration and border-control policies have reinforced anti-immigrant rhetoric about "alien invaders" and the "flooding" of immigrants from across the Mexican border (Chavez 2013). In 1996 and into the 2000s, federal welfare and immigration reforms restricted immigrants' access to public benefits and services, and strengthened deportation efforts (Golash-Boza 2012). Past research links anti-immigrant rhetoric and policies to significant increases in fears associated with the use of public programs by noncitizen and legal immigrants (Fix, Capps, and Kaushal 2009). Even if eligible for state-funded or local programs, undocumented immigrants face anxieties related to receiving public assistance and medical services (Van Natta et al. 2019; Berk and Schur 2001). Immigrant parents are especially concerned that using public services will put them at risk of losing future benefits or will jeopardize the ability of themselves or family members to gain future permanent residency status (Park 2011).

Undocumented Latinxs face other barriers to making requests in public programs and institutions even when they have formal access through local policies or healthcare reforms. Public discourse about Latinx immigrants' "undeservingness" portrays them as morally corrupt and draining on (white) Americans (Brown 2013, Chavez 2013). Such racialized, broad-based language, along with a hostile federal enforcement system, permeates institutional interactions, conveying messages of marginalization and a lack of belonging, even for Latinxs with citizenship status (Flores-González 2017; García 2017; Menjívar and Abrego 2012). Gender also intersects in that low-income, Latina mothers are often deemed undeserving of public assistance with "out-of-control" fertility based on stereotypes about Latina hypersexuality (Chavez 2013). Intersectional stigmas and discrimination affect Latinas' perceptions of public programs and health care (García 2017; Gast and Okamoto 2016).

It is important to consider undocumented Latinxs' vulnerability and precariousness (both perceived and real) when analyzing their local claims-making. The anticipation of federal exclusion and negative treatment could affect how undocumented Latinx immigrant mothers manage claims-making opportunities and rights recognition even in generally inclusive settings like San Francisco. When making claims of authority figures and workers in local institutions, immigrants must interact in close contact and provide personal information, which could increase fears and anxieties. Such fears and anxieties are constantly negotiated, even when claims-making has been successfully met or recognized.

Data and Methods
Adelante Familias

We use in-depth interviews and fieldwork observations over four years in a nonprofit CBO to understand the perceptions and experiences of Latinx immigrant participants over time. *Adelante Familias* (AF) is a program housed within a CBO formed by activists and community leaders in the 2000s to address gentrification and affordable housing for the low-income community in surrounding neighborhoods. AF's mission is to inform, engage, and empower low-income immigrant families through advocacy campaigns, leadership programs, language classes, and bilingual monthly informational meetings. AF additionally serves low-income families by providing direct services, including food bags, bus passes, backpacks, and clothing for low-income children, as well as housing, legal, and employment assistance through contracts with local agencies.

AF is in a neighborhood near San Francisco's financial district, where low-wage employment opportunities in hotels, restaurants, and offices encouraged recent influxes of immigrants. A majority of the participants initially came to AF for the direct services, especially the children's material aid, and they later learned about the advocacy campaigns and leadership programs. Given gendered expectations about childrearing, most AF participants are mothers. In Spanish and other languages, AF staff engage participants by discussing housing, education, political, and outreach campaigns prior to providing direct aid and assistance in the monthly meetings (see Gast and Okamoto 2016).

Multistage Interviews and Fieldwork

Over the course of six months during 2009–2011, the first two authors and research assistants volunteered and attended monthly, sometimes weekly, meetings and workshops at AF. The first two authors also interviewed staff and program directors and distributed interview sign-up sheets in Spanish, English, and Tagalog to recruit CBO participants. Between 2011 and 2014, a team of bilingual-research assistants conducted initial and follow-up interviews with twelve Filipinx and twenty-nine Latinx parents who participated in AF; we focus on the Latinx parents in this chapter.[1] Prior to initial interviews, almost all respondents had not engaged in advocacy or political organizations. The follow-up interviews allowed us to understand the temporal ordering of organizational involvement and perceptions of claims-making and belonging.

Our respondents reflect AF's client population. All but one father were mothers in their thirties or older, with an average of eleven years of U.S. residency. Seventy percent came from Mexico and 90 percent were undocumented (the rest had temporary visas or unknown documentation). A majority had less than a high-school diploma and a monthly income under $2,000, indicating their poverty status.[2] About half had used public assistance or health care at one point, and several had previously been homeless. About one-third were taking care of children on their own. Just over 70 percent had U.S.-born children; over half had mixed-status or undocumented children.[3] All were eligible for local health care as San Francisco residents. The parents of U.S.-born children were eligible for state and city programs such as CalWORKS or CalFresh food stamps.

Each interview lasted a half hour to three hours and was conducted in private rooms at the AF community space. We use pseudonyms to protect the anonymity of the staff, parents, and organization. Questions focused on participants' migration and adaptation experiences in the United States; school, CBO, and public program involvement; employment, income, and expenses; reasons for participating in CBOs and public programs; and perceptions of treatment in CBOs, programs, and institutions such as public schools, health care settings and hospitals, and work in San Francisco. A majority had attended AF for only a few months or less at the time of initial interviews. Almost all of those interviewed during follow-up interviews were still participating in AF (one to two years after initial interviews).

Data Analysis

We used the program Dedoose to broadly code interview transcripts and fieldnotes for topics related to confidence, information, skills, and assistance gained, involvement in the CBO and other public programs, and perceptions of local immigrant treatment. Next, the first author engaged in more focused, inductive analysis and developed thematic memos about the relationship between CBO involvement over time and the parents' participation in public institutions and programs. The first two authors reviewed and discussed the thematic memos, refining our emerging themes. The authors wrote subsequent thematic memos while triangulating between the fieldnote and interview data with parents and organizational staff and developing themes that reflected and expanded upon existing literature. Notes logged throughout our discussions served as the basis for documenting analytic directions and informing the writing and analysis.

Undocumented Latinx Parents' Sense of Exclusion Prior to Adelante Familias

During initial interviews, we asked parents about their perceptions of access to public programs, education, and other support systems for their families. While some parents or their children participated in bilingual-education and community programs, most parents lacked knowledge of the many rights, protections, and services afforded to immigrant families in San Francisco. These parents also conveyed a sense of exclusion and powerlessness when considering city public programs and institutions. The Latinx parents were fearful of any institutional interactions that could lead to disclosing personal or family members' information and, in their minds, possible problems with ICE.

Monica arrived in San Francisco in 2003 from Mexico through Arizona. She now lives with two undocumented children who are enrolled in local colleges and a U.S.-born daughter in middle school. During the first interview, Monica explained how she lived in constant anxiety for several years ("I didn't trust anyone") and has only recently become involved in AF and other programs. Still, she conveyed a sense of exclusion: "For us Latinos, it is more difficult than for others. In health care, for example, in food stamps, and in many things. No, you cannot ask for help . . . because you do not qualify . . . [or] you regret having gone." Like Monica, other mothers mentioned receiving (often inaccurate) information from family members or coworkers about their exclusion from public programs and lack of protections. Some mentioned initial fears of participating in AF and other CBOs, even though these organizations did not ask for documentation status or work with ICE. As those responsible for childrearing, such presumed exclusion prevented these mothers from crucial economic and healthcare resources for their children. Contrary to the sentiments conveyed by Monica and others, undocumented immigrants with U.S.-born children are eligible for CalFresh food stamps, public health care, and housing assistance. Local programs are not allowed to share information with immigration authorities.

Prior to attending AF, parents said they were wary of asking questions and making requests of institutional professionals and workers. Martha, a Mexican mother also with mixed-status children, described her many fears prior to coming to AF, including fears of speaking to AF and public-program staff: "I thought that a person didn't have a right to anything here. It's not my country. . . . I didn't know where to go to complain, because, how should I say, people are afraid. Afraid that, it's better to say nothing because I don't want anything to happen to me. You think that you don't have rights here." Although most parents had lived in San Francisco for more than six years at the time of initial interviews, they were unaware of the city's inclusive policies and protections for undocumented immigrants, and anticipated exclusion. Thus, despite residing in a sanctuary city, these undocumented parents did not feel protected and able to access services, rights, and resources like other city residents. These reports are particularly troubling given their poverty status and, for many, single-parent status.

"Losing the Fear": Gaining Rights and Support Through Adelante Familias

During follow-up interviews one to two years later, AF participants transformed fears attached to their undocumented status and redefined their relationship with local programs and institutions. Through AF, immigrant parents learned about their (and their children's) rights and protections in public assistance, schools, health care, and housing, and gained confidence in approaching city programs and institutions. Furthermore, parents gained strength and empowerment from their support by AF and the local community, which was particularly beneficial for mothers who previously felt that they and their family lacked access and support.

After participating in AF, parents highlighted how AF and other community and public programs "do not ask for papers." They also spoke of feeling welcomed and included in AF meetings and campaigns. For instance, Inés, a Mexican mother with mixed-status children, believed that AF elevated the status of undocumented immigrants by teaching about their rights: "They [at AF] give you information about your rights or that you are . . . an immigrant but you are like the ones who live here. The fact that you don't have papers doesn't make you feel less." During each monthly meeting, AF staff spoke in Spanish and asked parents to share their concerns and problems with housing, employment, school, and health-care systems. Sharing and listening to others helped them grow confidence and assert their voices, translating their individual problems into collective ones. As one parent described, AF is "a space for people to listen to us." Consuelo, a Mexican mother with undocumented-teenager children, underscored how AF staff created a "safe space" for parents: "[AF staff] say: 'Today is confidential. You can stay here. You can talk openly and say what you feel.'" To Consuelo, these conversations helped her to leave each meeting "with a relieved soul."

AF helped parents see the collective nature of their problems and understand that they were supported through local services and protections based on their city residency; access and claims-making in local institutions did not need to be defined by citizenship status. For instance, Pertrona, a Mexican mother of three U.S.-born children, described how community organizations helped her to apply for food stamps for her children. Prior to participating in AF and other community organizations, Petrona thought that she and her family would "get into problems and maybe even [with] immigration [ICE]" if she applied for food stamps. Through community legal advisors, she learned that public workers could not ask about documentation status "because people here who don't have documents and are illegal still have rights. And [their] kids have rights." Likewise, Ilana, a Mexican mother of three mixed-status children, said she learned that "San Francisco has a lot of help for all of us," referring to the fact that undocumented immigrants can access city public services and assistance.

Ten years prior to the initial interview, Mercedes, a thirty-six-year-old mother from Mexico, came by herself to join her husband in San Francisco. Four years later, her son was born in the U.S., and they paid for her daughter to be brought from Mexico. Mercedes learned English and, through parents of her children's friends, heard about AF. Prior to coming to AF, Mercedes was extremely anxious around public workers, especially since her husband had been deported a few years ago. Undocumented women like Mercedes must, often alone, manage fears and anxieties for their entire family when their partners experience deportation. More than 90 percent of U.S. deportees are men, even though about half of all undocumented persons are women (Golash-Boza 2016). In the follow-up interview, Mercedes described how AF transformed not only her individual fears, but also how she viewed undocumented-immigrant rights as a whole. Through AF and its contacts, she gained assistance from an immigration lawyer to create a "pending case [with] immigration" for naturalization and learned about rights for her family, such as city-health insurance: "We are learning that we have rights. . . . If we needed help with immigration lawyers, they can help us. They [also] advised me about the rights we have as employees because the laws are changing constantly. They also told us . . . we have rights to, how do you say it? [Health] Insurance . . . things like that. This information helps you because . . . when you realize it, you can do something."

By using the term "we," Mercedes emphasized the collective "rights" afforded to undocumented immigrants, including her family, in the city. She also understood that local agencies, activists, and policies were working to support and protect undocumented immigrants, which helped diminish her anxieties. AF helped translate San Francisco's inclusive policies, programs, and organizations for mothers like Mercedes, and encouraged newfound feelings of agency.

Parents like Mercedes began to make requests in legal aid, educational, health care, housing, library, and after-school programs, and extended their voices outside of AF. Marcela, a Mexican mother of three U.S.-born young children, explained her transformation through AF and how she had gained the confidence to make requests of public workers: "At first, you are fearful. . . . You don't have a lot of confidence. But now, it's like you feel more confident, you know where, you know how to ask, of the [AF] workshops that you've taken. . . . They give you that strength and that courage that, that you need to know that you can . . . lose the fear. Now, I do feel with the capacity of going and asking . . . what I want, and this and that."

Likewise, Selena, a Mexican mother of three mixed-status children, summed up the powerful role of AF for undocumented families: "We receive the information and we know that no, you do not have to have fear of the things. And well I tell you that you get more comfortable and you know that you count on organizations to support yourself. . . . So, I would say that . . . [in] a phrase, 'Information is power.'" AF helped the Latinx parents transform their knowledge, confidence, and skills to make requests and claims for city services and programs. This was particularly powerful for mothers who recognized their access to public programs for their families.

Although almost all parents in our study had resided in San Francisco for several years, it was not until they participated in AF that they felt more confident and understood their access and rights in the city. Through AF and its referrals to other agencies, these parents transformed their initial sense of exclusion and learned how to claim entitlement and support in San Francisco. As others have argued, local organizations and inclusive interactions mitigate the effects of nation-state citizenship boundaries and restrictive policies (García 2019; Marrow 2012; Coll 2004). Next, we discuss the negotiated aspects of claims-making as parents still anticipated exclusion and, at times, lack of belonging even with their improved local access and tools for claims-making.

Negotiating Belonging and Vulnerability Along with Claims-Making

AF did more than teach parents about their access to public programs; AF also taught parents to assert their individual and collective voices in the city. AF staff regularly encouraged and helped parent participants write letters to landlords, city supervisors, and other authority figures and show up at community forums and rallies at City Hall. During one AF meeting, José, a staff member, urged parents in Spanish to attend a City Hall rally: "Please, go. It's important for us as a community, that they know that we also have problems." José explained that the wealthy and powerful should not be the only ones to make demands and shape city decisions. By directly asking parents about their needs and concerns, and encouraging their engagement, requests, and voices in city campaigns, issues, and institutions, AF staff taught parents the importance of local claims.

One specific AF campaign involved fighting budget cuts to bilingual education in public schools with other organizations and activists. AF worked to educate parents about the campaign and encouraged their participation in city-budget meetings. AF staff asked parents what bilingual education meant to their families and what programs they would like to see. One AF staff member explained: "We involve the families to do campaigns and stuff like that so they can take the lead. We show them what to do, not to be scared or anything." Selena, a Mexican mother noted previously, shared what she had learned through campaigns: "AF can help us to fight, to have a voice more to say, 'Okay, we do not agree [with the budget cuts], but we also count as people, we are members of this community, so, no, we do not think it is fair.'" Thus AF helped the parents engage with institutional decision-making, elevate their voices, and connect with community networks working on behalf of immigrants so that their claims-making would be recognized.

In other campaigns, including on housing and educational policies or the U.S. Census, AF staff taught parents how to assert their voices in U.S. society and political structures. Mothers began to see that, as undocumented immigrants, they could make changes to better the lives of low-income immigrants and their families. For instance, Verónica, a Honduran mother with two undocumented children, learned that "union is strength" in the city and that they could collectively fight landlords "vacating [evicting] unjustly." Mercedes, whose husband has been deported, ascertained that undocumented immigrants need not be restricted by "illegality" and could influence decision-makers and authority figures: "It is not only that we are illegal. We have rights. . . . You learn and can influence people to do something in order to change things." Mercedes learned not only how to voice concerns and access support as a single mother, but also how to create change as a resident and community member. These women articulated a new relationship with the city, one that was not defined by their undocumented motherhood.

Others spoke of gaining confidence and learning how to approach landlords and employers to address individual concerns. AF's workshops addressed an array of San Francisco's policies and programs, including tenant-rights policies and affordable-housing programs. AF provided blueprints for collective claims-making and for making individual requests of authority figures as parents, employees, and tenants. In one workshop, AF staff outlined tenant rights in San Francisco while catering the discussion to low-income immigrants who often experience problems with landlords. AF staff taught parents to approach landlords by first writing letters and documenting the days and times of conversations and details of the issue or concern. AF also encouraged parents to bring any concerns and documents, including tenant consent forms, to AF for help with translation or legal action.

For mothers, reframing their city-institutional relationships helped them associate empowerment with their maternal role in their children's schooling. For instance, Ilana, a Mexican mother described previously, indicated that she felt responsible for her son's education, but had anxieties involved with school interactions prior to attending AF. Through AF, she learned that she could speak to school officials without disclosing documentation status ("You can express yourself without fear"). She went on: "We have that right to say what is good for my son, what changes we would like [to teachers]." Other mothers spoke of losing "fears of speaking" and gaining confidence through knowing how to ask questions and address school problems.

However, opportunities and tools for claims-making, even in a sanctuary city like San Francisco, do not negate the legal exclusion, vulnerability, and stigmas experienced or perceived by these parents. In fact, while parents learned strategies for asserting voices and making demands, some believed that these actions put them at greater risk or did not change the likelihood of exclusion and problems. Despite repeated assurances from AF staff about safety from immigration authorities during city events and rallies, some parents attended AF meetings but avoided campaign activities, as they feared "television cameras" that could record their presence or other risky interactions. As one parent noted, "Maybe if I have my papers I would be more comfortable participating. . . . I don't want to be arrested by the police." Other parents, in follow-up interviews, mentioned remaining fears after learning about undocumented parent access to city programs. Martha, the Mexican mother who transformed her fears after initially feeling that undocumented immigrants lacked rights, remained cautious about political organizing and accepting food stamps because she did not want to do anything "wrong" in the eyes of the government. Even while AF helped parents to feel more confident and assert their voices as undocumented immigrants, these parents were still on guard, especially in contexts where contact with the police or government authorities remained uncertain.

The constant presence of legal violence in the federal climate meant that parents still anticipated exclusion and federal enforcement even while they realized and worked to facilitate their own local inclusion. When we asked, in follow-up interviews, about undocumented experiences in public assistance, housing, health care, and police enforcement in San Francisco, parents conveyed conflicting messages about their city access and protections and the broader exclusionary climate heard in the media or through family and friends. Petrona, described previously as obtaining food stamps assistance through local CBOs, still felt that her undocumented status represented a lack of entitlement in public programs afforded to citizen residents: "Once you have documents you have a greater ease to do certain things. They will help you more, not because you don't deserve it or they don't want to help, but . . . the rules that exist. . . . For example, with the work permit, they require it anywhere . . . and your social security number. And that is where they discover everything." To Petrona, even city public workers who "want to help" are required to question documentation status, opening the door for "discovery" at the federal level.

In a hostile federal climate, mothers highlighted worries about their undocumented children's futures. As one distraught mother described, her efforts to help her daughter in education were meaningless given the contexts of legal exclusion and limited opportunities for the undocumented: "[My daughter] wanted . . . to study nursing, and her counselor told her . . . not a good idea. Because when she begins her internship, she will have to show social security. She does not have it. Everything she had studied would be ruined." Mothers of undocumented and mixed-status children negotiated both their own and their children's vulnerability and marginalization in the United States, even while working toward their inclusion in city programs and institutions. The many anxieties related to their children's futures greatly affected how they understood belonging and recognition in the United States, since they carried the weight of interacting with institutional representatives on behalf of the family.

Mothers balanced their newfound claims-making tools with the reality that institutional contact made their entire family vulnerable. A few mentioned that, while they had rights in San Francisco, they still did not have driver's licenses and could experience problems when traveling outside of San Francisco. Marcela, noted previously as feeling confident through AF to approach teachers and public authorities, also stated that she remained "in the shadows" and lacked legitimacy in U.S. institutions: "One feels that sometimes you are in the shadows. And they [people with papers] can go more freely, they can have better jobs. They have a better life. . . . And those of us that do not have papers, well, no. . . . You do not have as much rights, you cannot demand." Marcela indicated that her developing claims-making abilities in the city did not translate to a sense of belonging where she could fully access community rights and make demands for her family.

Racism as a broad-scale exclusionary force also signaled to the Latinx parents that they would be continually homogenized and marginalized as a group (see also Gast, Okamoto, and Nguyen 2021; García 2017). Victoria, a Salvadoran mother of mixed-status children, felt more confident about health care and public programs through AF, but was still wary of interacting with authority figures because of experiences with racism: "There is much racism . . . just because one has the physical features of a Latino." She had also heard from family members about discrimination towards the undocumented by the police and public program workers in San Francisco: "Although you can apply for low-income apartments, for food stamps, to Medi-Cal, to whatever type of service, the social worker will prioritize those with papers." Likewise, Jacinta, a Peruvian mother of three undocumented children, had been involved in AF campaigns and other advocacy organizations and used public programs for years. Despite her claims-making efforts, she understood that authority figures used markers of race and legal status to categorize those "looking Latino" as inferior and illegitimate, shaping her continued anxieties toward program workers: "We Latinos are afraid of presenting ourselves." Diego, a Honduran father, highlighted stereotypes against "Hispanics" affecting his institutional interactions, echoing the mothers' sentiments. These parents understood the value of localized claims-making and how to assert their voices in schools, public programs, and city institutions, but still felt, in specific cases, powerless and marginalized.

Discussion and Conclusion

Our research on low-income undocumented Latinx parents, mainly mothers, in the "sanctuary city" of San Francisco contributes to an understanding of how immigrant CBO participants engage with claims-making and nego-tiate belonging or the state of membership and rights recognition afforded to other community members (Glenn 2011). Using in-depth interviews and fieldwork in a local CBO, we examine how these parents realize and ad-vocate for their inclusion, rights, and membership—part of the process of belonging—while still negotiating feelings of exclusion in public programs and institutions. We argue that conflicting messages, regarding their and their family's *local* support, as well as exclusion and disempowerment in a hostile *national* climate, limit how local claims-making translates into feel-ings of belonging. Our multiyear study highlights how undocumented Lat-inxs' negotiations and processes of belonging in San Francisco are dynamic and unresolved, involving making demands to shape their own inclusion, as well as disillusionment despite city-wide formal rights and protections.

Local CBOs enhance and support immigrant claims-making acts; thus they are part of the process of immigrant belonging and rights recognition. Although the parents in our study had resided in San Francisco for several years, it was not until they participated in AF's meetings that they gained confidence and assertiveness in local programs and institutions. As AF par-ticipants, these parents learned to disassociate the fears and anxieties tied to undocumented status, facilitating newfound requests for resources and sup-port from institutional workers and programs. Through AF, undocumented Latinx parents were able to transform initial feelings of exclusion and engage with local claims-making. The CBO, local programs, and the inclusive city policies provided the possibilities for undocumented parents to access and realize much-needed support within the city—important for the mothers responsible for childrearing. In other words, the context of San Francisco's nonprofit organizational infrastructure, community activism, and local in-clusive policies, as well as these parents' voices and agency, facilitated their claims-making with employers, landlords, teachers, and workers in public assistance or health-care facilities. While past work has focused on the fears, anxieties, and stigmas faced by undocumented immigrants, as well as how advocacy organizations and policies shape the contexts immigrants navigate, our study details how undocumented immigrants themselves learn to make claims through a CBO while also responding to U.S. institutional realities and the federal climate.

Yet increased claims-making does not automatically produce belonging or the state of being recognized, heard, and treated with legitimacy, for example, in public programs and institutions (Bloemraad 2018; Glenn 2011). Constant surveillance, exclusion, and discrimination toward undocumented Latinxs as part of the broad-scale anti-immigrant climate subjugates them to everyday "legal violence" and racial oppression across different institutions (Menjívar and Abrego 2012). While undocumented Latinxs in our study began to shift boundaries of belonging through claims-making acts and asserting their voices, they still felt and anticipated future problems for themselves and family members, especially in interactions with public assistance and the police and in travel outside San Francisco. Furthermore, perceptions of and experiences with racism across different institutions conveyed messages of marginalization and powerlessness regardless of actual rights, national origin, length of residency, and local support (see also García 2017).

It is possible that more extensive time at AF could change the parents' anticipation of future exclusion and marginalization. However, even the parents who had participated for a few years in AF's campaigns still mentioned anticipating discrimination or immigration problems. During follow-up interviews, mothers noted family members' vulnerabilities and the need to protect and manage their undocumented or mixed-status children's precariousness in U.S. institutions. Furthermore, while we cannot directly link perceptions to public program use, we found that, at the time of follow-up interviews, some mothers still limited their use of public assistance (like food stamps) because of fears or anxieties. The efforts of local organizations and policies to facilitate immigrant access and empowerment remain incomplete as undocumented Latinxs, especially mothers, face legal and social exclusion toward themselves and their children in U.S. society and institutions. CBOs and local activists must not only improve access and protections but also empower immigrant mothers in navigating widespread racism, anti-immigrant sentiments, and intersectional stigmas affecting themselves and their children (Gast and Okamoto 2016). Such work is crucial as low-income immigrants face compounding constraints and uncertainties amplified by the COVID-19 pandemic.

Despite living in a sanctuary city with immigrant-friendly policies and participating in an advocacy organization, low-income, undocumented parents manage federal vulnerability and exclusion with each new claims-making opportunity as city residents. Although these Latinx parents did not encounter a level of hostility found in more restrictive cities, they still underscored a "hyperawareness" of legal violence and exclusion found in the

United States (García 2019; Menjívar and Abrego 2012). For these parents, vulnerability and precariousness are intensified, at times, as they engage in claims-making and assert their voices with authority figures in San Francisco. Moreover, mothers of undocumented children constantly negotiate the effects of the federal climate for their children, even while they facilitate claims-making and institutional support for their children. The larger implications of our study point to the importance of understanding how undocumented parents simultaneously negotiate belonging, vulnerability, and exclusion across intersecting community, institutional, and policy contexts in the United States.

Notes

1. We interviewed a total of twenty-one Latinx participants in the second wave. Female Spanish-speaking research assistants conducted interviews on their own or accompanied the first author as a translator.
2. In 2013, the federal poverty level for a family of four was $1,962 per month.
3. We did not directly ask about documentation status for respondents or family members. We did ask about migration experiences and where children were born. Respondents often shared migration details, including crossing the border without documentation.

References

Berk, Marc L., and Claudia L. Schur. 2001. "The Effect of Fear on Access to Care among Undocumented Latino Immigrants." *Journal of Immigrant Health* 3(3): 151–56.

Bloemraad, Irene. 2018. "Theorising the Power of Citizenship as Claims-Making." *Journal of Ethnic and Migration Studies* 44(1): 4–26.

Brown, Hana. 2013. "Race, Legality, and the Social Policy Consequences of Anti-Immigration Mobilization." *American Sociological Review* 78(2): 290–314.

Chavez, Leo R. 2013. *The Latino Threat: Constructing Immigrants, Citizens, and the Nation.* 2nd ed. Stanford: Stanford University Press.

Coll, Kathleen. 2004. "Necesidades y Problemas: Immigrant Latina Vernaculars of Belonging, Coalition, & Citizenship in San Francisco, California." *Latino Studies* 2(2): 186–209.

Cordero-Guzmán, Hector R. 2005. "Community-Based Organisations and Migration in New York City." *Journal of Ethnic and Migration Studies* 31(5): 889–909.

de Graauw, Els. 2016. *Making Immigrant Rights Real: Nonprofits and the Politics of Integration in San Francisco.* Ithaca, NY: Cornell University Press.

Fix, Michael E., Randy Capps, and Neeraj Kaushal. 2009. "Immigrants and Welfare: Overview." In *Immigrants and Welfare: The Impact of Welfare Reform on America's Newcomers,* edited by Michael E. Fix, 123–52. New York: Russell Sage Foundation.

Flores-González, Nilda. 2017. *Citizens but Not Americans: Race and Belonging among Latino Millennials*. New York: New York University Press.

Flores, René D., and Ariela Schachter. 2018. "Who are the 'Illegals'? The Social Construction of Illegality in the United States." *American Sociological Review* 83(5): 839–68.

García, Angela S. 2019. *Legal Passing: Navigating Undocumented Life and Local Immigration Law*. Oakland: University of California Press.

García, San Juanita. 2017. "Racializing 'Illegality': An Intersectional Approach to Understanding How Mexican-Origin Women Navigate an Anti-Immigrant Climate." *Sociology of Race and Ethnicity* 3(4): 474–90.

Gast, Melanie Jones, and Dina G. Okamoto. 2016. "Moral or Civic Ties? Deservingness and Engagement Among Undocumented Latinas in Non-Profit Organisations." *Journal of Ethnic and Migration Studies* 42(12): 2013–30.

Gast, Melanie Jones, Dina G. Okamoto, and Emerald T. Nguyen. 2021. "Making Requests: Filipina/o and Latina/o Immigrant Claims-Making and Racialization." *Ethnic and Racial Studies*. 44(7): 1211–30.

Gleeson, Shannon. 2013. "Shifting Agendas, Evolving Coalitions: Advocating for Immigrant Worker Rights in Houston." *WorkingUSA* 16(2): 207–26.

———. 2016. *Precarious Claims: The Promise and Failure of Workplace Protections in the United States*. Oakland: University of California Press.

Glenn, Evelyn Nakano. 2011. "Constructing Citizenship: Exclusion, Subordination, and Resistance." *American Sociological Review* 76(1): 1–24.

Golash-Boza, Tanya. 2016. "The Parallels Between Mass Incarceration and Mass Deportation: An Intersectional Analysis of State Repression." *Journal of World-Systems Research* 22(2): 484–509.

Golash-Boza, Tanya Maria. 2012. *Immigration Nation: Raids, Detentions, and Deportations in Post-9/11 America*. Boulder, Colo.: Paradigm Publishers.

Gonzales, Roberto G. 2016. *Lives in Limbo: Undocumented and Coming of Age in America*. Oakland: University of California Press.

Marrow, Helen B. 2012. "Deserving to a Point: Unauthorized Immigrants in San Francisco's Universal Access Healthcare Model." *Social Science & Medicine* 74: 846–54.

Mendez, Jennifer Bickham, and Natalia Deeb-Sossa. 2020. "Creating Home, Claiming Place: Latina Immigrant Mothers and the Production of Belonging." *Latino Studies* 18(2): 174–94.

Menjívar, Cecilia, and Leisy J. Abrego. 2012. "Legal Violence: Immigration Law and the Lives of Central American Immigrants." *American Journal of Sociology* 117(5): 1380–421.

Nicholls, Walter. 2013. *The DREAMers: How the Undocumented Youth Movement Transformed the Immigrant Rights Debate*. Stanford, Calif.: Stanford University Press.

Pallares, Amalia, and Nilda Flores-González, eds. 2010. *¡Marcha!: Latino Chicago and the Immigrant Rights Movement, Latinos in Chicago and the Midwest*. Urbana: University of Illinois Press.

Park, Lisa Sun-Hee. 2011. "Criminalizing Immigrant Mothers: Public Charge, Health Care, and Welfare Reform." *International Journal of Sociology of the Family* 37(1): 27–47.

Patler, Caitlin. 2018. "'Citizens but for Papers:' Undocumented Youth Organizations, Anti-Deportation Campaigns, and the Reframing of Citizenship." *Social Problems* 65: 96–115.

Ramakrishnan, S. Karthick, and Irene Bloemraad. 2008. *Civic Hopes and Political Realities: Immigrants, Community Organizations, and Political Engagement.* New York: Russell Sage Foundation.

Ridgley, Jennifer. 2008. "Cities of Refuge: Immigration Enforcement, Police, and the Insurgent Genealogies of Citizenship in U.S. Sanctuary Cities." *Urban Geography* 29(1): 53–77.

Terriquez, Veronica. 2015. "Intersectional Mobilization, Social Movement Spillover, and Queer Youth Leadership in the Immigrant Rights Movement." *Social Problems* 62(3): 343–62.

Unzueta Carrasco, Tania A., and Hinda Seif. 2014. "Disrupting the Dream: Undocumented Youth Reframe Citizenship and Deportability Through Anti-Deportation Activism." *Latino Studies* 12(2): 279–99.

Van Natta, Meredith, Nancy J. Burke, Irene H. Yen, Mark D. Fleming, Christoph L. Hanssmann, Maryani Palupy Rasidjan, and Janet K. Shim. 2019. "Stratified Citizenship, Stratified Health: Examining Latinx Legal Status in the U.S. Healthcare Safety Net." *Social Science & Medicine* 220: 49–55.

Welcoming America. 2018. "Our Network." Accessed January 9. www.welcoming america.org/programs/our-network.

CHAPTER 8

Strategic (Il)legibility

The Marginalization and Resistance of Latina Community-Engaged Artists in Chicago

MICHAEL DE ANDA MUÑIZ

Women and people of color in the arts often confront the devaluation of their work as well as blocked access to resources, networks, and institutions necessary for their artistic and financial success (Miller 2016; Tator et al. 1998). Globally, the median valuation for women-made art is about 27 percent lower than that of men (Brown 2019). Of the artists featured in eighteen major U.S. art museums' collections, 12.6 percent are women, 15 percent are people of color, and 2.8 percent are Latina/x/o (Topaz et al. 2019).[1] Indeed, the arts are structured by gender and race hierarchies that position white men as the archetypical artists. And because of this, Latinas experience challenges to their legitimacy as artists.[2] In this chapter, I ask: How and why are Latina community artists marginalized within the arts? How is their inclusion in the arts challenged, and how do they resist such marginalization?

Drawing on two years of ethnographic research in Chicago, I argue that devaluation, contested access, stereotyping/pigeonholing, and illegibility limit Latina community-engaged artists' belonging in the arts, and these artists strategically maintain belonging through the simultaneous use of illegibility and legibility. Their artistic labor is valued less financially, and their community-engaged artwork garners far less artistic value or prestige. They struggle to gain and maintain access to arts spaces. Dominant stereotypes frame what others expect of Latina artists and limit the support and opportunities they receive. When their work is not recognizable or knowable according to dominant values and ideologies, they are denied resources and pushed out of the arts. Each of these experiences is impacted by discourses

about gender and race that structure the arts and produce narrow understandings of Latinas and Latina art.[3] However, Latina community-engaged
artists also strategically claim space in the arts.

These artists claim belonging in the arts by using a source of their
marginalization—legibility and illegibility. The ways in which they make
themselves and their work legible at times and illegible at others allow them
to create space for themselves and other marginalized groups in the arts.
Therefore, what I call, "strategic (il)legibility" is a form of disidentification
(Muñoz 1999)—a simultaneous engagement with, while working against,
dominant artistic institutions and values. It is informed by a strategic and
fluid mode of resistance, "differential consciousness," that resists binary categories (Sandoval 2009).

I define a "community-engaged artist" as an artist who regularly produces
artwork, such as murals, sculpture, photography, performance, and music,
for *and* with community members. This does not include artists who merely
exhibit their individual artwork in community spaces. Rather, to be engaged,
one must collaborate with community members throughout the creative
process. As Victoria Martinez, a thirty-one-year-old Mexican American
community-engaged artist, explains: "There are some artists that I question. . . . In general, their idea of community art is getting pictures in front
of a mural with kids and you're in the middle. Like that's wrong. Because it
takes a lot of relational ideas and memories and footwork to produce a well
created community-based project. . . . It is important to work with people
and to survey them as much as you can to integrate what their desires are,
what their thoughts are."

Community-engaged artists organize art programming that is accessible,
relevant, and impactful for Latina/x/o communities. They curate experiences
that strengthen community ties and tap into creativity that many community
members did not recognize that they possessed.

I focus on Latina community-engaged artists because these artists have
received scant attention in both the scholarship on Latina/x/o art and that
pertaining to gender and race in the arts. Examining experiences of "illegibility" among Latina artists highlights the specific obstacles and forms of marginalization that contribute to the lack of Latina representation in the arts.
I contend that these experiences do not lead Latina community-engaged
artists to fully assimilate to dominant artistic values, nor does it prompt them
to completely leave the arts. Instead, they develop strategies to simultane-

ously engage with and work against dominant artistic values and institutions. "Strategic (il)legibility" captures complex forms of artistic resistance that transcend the assimilation/rejection dichotomy. These theoretical interventions may also apply to Latina/x/o social and political struggles for inclusion in other cultural realms.

Gender and Race Marginalization in the Arts

Research finds that both sexism and racism structure the arts and that devaluation, contested access, and stereotypes push nonmale and nonwhite artists into the margins. Historically, women have been underrepresented in the arts and excluded from male-dominant professional networks (Wreyford 2015). Women struggle to promote themselves (Scharff 2015; Banks and Milestone 2011) and obtain paid work as artists (Bielby and Bielby 1996). They are confined to less-valued positions and genres (Alacovska 2015) and face exclusion from museum and gallery exhibitions (Saltz 2006). Overall, less societal value is placed on women's artistic production, as evidenced by the association of men with fine art and women with crafts (Collins 1979). Ideologies about the archetypical artist, collective judgments about aesthetic value, and the structure of artistic careers are gendered to favor male artists and creative workers (Miller 2016).[4]

The arts are also structured to center and benefit white people. Tator et al. (1998) argue that the marginalization of artists of color is reinforced by a larger social system of racism in which nonwhite groups are denied access to institutions, resources, and expression. Elite art institutions are "white sanctuaries" that maintain white supremacy and normativity, reassuring white people of their dominant position in society (Embrick, Weffer, and Domínguez 2019). When artists of color do gain access to arts institutions, they are frequently "ghettoized" through race-specific exhibitions that position artists of color as outside the mainstream art world, not meeting dominant artistic standards, and inherently different and inferior (Blackwood and Purcell 2014; Hall 1997). Structural racial inequities are directly related to the fact that the administrators of museum and arts foundations are overwhelmingly white, arts in communities of color are underfunded, and museums and galleries have historically locked out artists of color (Helicon Collaborative 2017; McCambridge 2017; Pindell 1987). Due to political and economic shifts, such as privatization and public divestment from the arts, art institutions are more dependent on private funding and attendance, and even those museums created by and for communities of color have had to appeal to elitist and Eurocentric artistic systems of valuation (Dávila 2012; Noriega 1999).

Research on the marginalization of women and people of color in the arts suggests that artists who are women of color, and Latinas more specifically, must contend with multiple systems of oppression within the arts world. Gender and race fundamentally impact the value that artworks and artistic labor are given; what opportunities, spaces, and networks are accessible; and what assumptions are made about artists. This chapter does not make generalizable claims about the condition of Latina or women of color artists. Rather, I examine Latina community-engaged artists' experiences to reveal the ways that dominant gender and race discourses manifest and impact their lives. The historical exclusion of Latinas/xs/os from the arts has resulted in the development of Latina/x/o community arts. Latina/x/o artists have found that it is in their own communities that they have the space and support that mainstream arts institutions have denied them. Furthermore, Latina/x/o community art practices have also generated critiques of and alternatives to mainstream artistic conventions.

Latina/x/o Community Arts

In Latina/x/o communities, artwork raises consciousness, beautifies low-income neighborhoods, provides youth with extracurricular activities, and heightens Latinas/xs/os' sense of belonging and community pride (Wherry 2011; Selbach 2004; Holscher 1976). Latina/x/o community artists have long been central to the processes of "placemaking/placekeeping" in which Latinas/xs/os claim belonging in their communities, engage in local political issues, and resist their communities' cultural erasure and displacement (Lin 2019; Bedoya 2014; Wherry 2011; Dávila 2004). They use various mediums, such as mural, music, mosaics, sculpture, and landscaping, in order to demonstrate that their communities have the power to shape the physical spaces in which they live (Viesca 2004; Gude and Huebner 2000). Latina/x/o community-based art practices have also historically countered the exclusionary, mainstream culture of institutional art (Grams 2010).

Latina/x/o-centered museums and galleries around the United States were born from community-based movements that created alternative spaces for Latina/x/o artists who were denied access to mainstream arts institutions (National Museum of Mexican Art 2019; Cordova 2017; Dávila 2004; Moreno 2004). These spaces redefined how Latina/x/o art was valued and made art more accessible and politically relevant to working-class Latina/x/o communities (Cordova 2017). However, like the communities themselves, these movements and spaces are not monolithic.

Latina/x/o community art movements employ different strategies to support Latina/x/o cultural production and representations. Some create formal institutions, such as museums, galleries, and nonprofit organizations (Grams 2010, 53–59). In order to acquire large national grants, increase attendance and patronage, and gain prestige, they often must bureaucratize, or adopt hierarchical administrative structures, provide measurable evidence of their success, and emphasize voices and support from outside of their communities (Moreno 2004; Halley and Valdez 2000). As a result, they can stray from their original missions by compromising the values of their communities and abandoning a commitment to innovative, avant-garde artistic expression (Halley and Valdez 2000).

Other movements increase community input and participation in public arts, such as murals and installations (Grams 2010, 53–59). They reject bureaucratization and the funding opportunities that come along with it in order to maintain grassroots, collectivist approaches to community art (Halley, Valdez, and Nava 2001). For example, they will not apply to grants that come with "strings attached" or stipulations that dictate how the organization must run and what kind of projects they must produce. Yet, Latina/x/o community artists' strategies do not always abide by neat dichotomies of bureaucratization/collectivism and assimilation/rejection. Scholarship by Latina/x/o feminist and Queer scholars reveals artistic strategies that allow for alternative modes of dealing with dominant discourses and institutions.

Latina/x/o Feminist and Queer Resistance Strategies

Latina/x/o feminist and Queer scholars illustrate the various ways that Latinas and Queer Latinas/xs/os experience and resist the intersection of racism, sexism, and heterosexism in dominant white society and Latina/x/o communities (Anzaldúa 2012; Hames-Garcia and Martínez 2011). Latina/x/o artists have been central to the development of alternative resistance strategies (Hurtado 2000; Muñoz 1999). Feminist and Queer Latina/x/o activists and artists engage in alternative strategies of resistance that move "within and between multiple sites of struggle" and challenge "conventional notions of oppositional subjectivity" (Cotera, Blackwell, and Espinoza 2018, 1).

Two theories of Latina/x/o resistance are particularly relevant for this chapter: Chela Sandoval's (2009) differential consciousness and José Esteban Muñoz's (1999) disidentifications. Chela Sandoval (2009) theorizes that feminists of color have a "differential mode of oppositional consciousness." This consciousness is the "refusal of U.S. third world feminism to buckle under, to submit to sublimation or assimilation within hegemonic feminist praxis" (Sandoval 2009, 340). While hegemonic (white) feminist praxis uses single-issue, single-approach politics, a differential consciousness allows women of color who are feminists to "read the current situation of power and to self-consciously choose and adopt the ideological form best suited to push against its configurations" (Sandoval 2009, 348). As a result, feminists of color engage in fluid and coalitionary political activism.

Muñoz (1999) highlights a strategic form of resistance that operates on its own terms, outside the framework of hegemonic discourses. Focusing on the work of Queer artists of color, he defines disidentification as a "survival strategy that works within and outside the dominant public sphere simultaneously" (Muñoz 1999, 5). It is "the third mode of dealing with dominant ideology, one that neither opts to assimilate within such a structure nor strictly opposes it; rather, disidentification is a strategy that works on and against dominant ideology" (Muñoz 1999, 11). Disidentification serves as an option for those excluded from both hegemonic identities and counter-identities.

Sandoval's (2009) and Muñoz's (1999) conceptualization of resistance strategies as fluid and contextual are useful for my explanation of how Latina community-engaged artists resist marginalization and push-out in the arts. These artists reject the established options of either assimilating to or leaving the arts. Depending on the context and their goals, they strategically choose how to work with and against dominant discourses. I find that it is through the strategic use of legibility and illegibility that Latina community-engaged artists are able to make a space for themselves in the arts.

Legibility

Legibility "refers to the ability to be recognized as legitimate and worthy of resources within institutions" (Sweet 2019, 412). To be knowable and recognizable is an essential component of social domination. Said (1978) and Bhabha (1994) each discuss the ways that the dominated are made knowable. For example, the West justifies its political and economic domination by making the non-West legible as irrational, childlike, and different (Said 1978). And mimicry, when colonial subjects take on the beliefs and practices of their colonizers, represents "[the dominant group's] desire for a reformed, *recognizable* Other" (Bhabha 1994, 122; emphasis added).

Additionally, Sweet (2019) finds that low-income women of color who are victims of domestic violence and rape can only access state resources, such as immigration visas or child custody, by being legible as victims of their own individual "depression, low self-esteem, and psychological failure" (415). Framing their victimization in ways that do not affirm racialized, gendered, and classed stereotypes about low-income women as irrational and irresponsible renders them illegible as credible victims and denies them resources. In this manner, an individual is primarily legible when they conform to hegemonic discourses that maintain and justify unequal social relations.

Politicians, corporate actors, and writers have attempted to counter Latinas'/xs'/os' legibility as threats to U.S. culture, economy, and safety by asserting Latina/x/o social, political, and economic inclusion (Dávila 2008). These "Latino spin" narratives make Latinas/xs/os legible as "just 'another ethnic group' that is equally well-equipped to display . . . 'Anglo protestant values' . . . and their belonging as undoubtedly American" (Dávila 2008, 3). Latino spin reproduces the strategy of mimicry (Bhabha 1994, 122) in which Latinas/xs/os are made legible as reformed, recognizable Others that are almost the same, but not quite middle-class, white US citizens. In this way, Latina/x/o belonging is conditional and reinforces existing social hierarchies.

As analytical concepts, legibility and illegibility are fruitful for this study. They help explain artists' experiences of not having their work understood by others and how artists strategically maintain belonging in the arts while also working against hegemonic institutions and values. Latina community-engaged artists claim belonging by strategically making themselves and their work legible as legitimate and deserving of space and resources according to hegemonic frameworks. At the same time, they maintain the illegibility of their devalued practices, such as political artwork, and counterhegemonic politics and goals, such as making the arts more accessible to working-class communities of color, illegible, so as to avoid the institutional denial of spaces and resources. These practices hold the potential to transform Latina/x/o communities' access to and engagement with the arts. This simultaneous use of legibility and illegibility facilitates artists' access to spaces and resources that they then share with marginalized communities. In other words, they seek individual belonging in order to actively work against structural exclusions.

Research Methods

This chapter is informed by more than two years of ethnographic research with seventeen Latina community-engaged artists in Chicago.[5] My introduction to and relationships with these artists began in 2013 when I met an artist from Little Village, a predominantly-Latina/x/o working-class neighborhood in Chicago. We shared political, artistic, and community values and interests, and she invited me to participate in an art project. Through this project, I learned that other Latina artists were regularly organizing and leading art projects and events with and for community members, such as free community workshops, youth art programs, and art shows. However, I noticed that Latino street artists and Latina/x/o artists who solely produced work for traditional art institutions were receiving the most media attention and institutional recognition.

I built relationships with many artists and began participating in art projects before conceptualizing this study. Many of my interviews and conversations were those between friends, community members, or comrades, rather than researcher and participant. Furthermore, artists noted that, as a Chicano community member who is committed to decolonial, Queer, and feminist politics, they trusted me with personal information.[6]

From May 2016 to September 2018, I attended art exhibitions and events, parties, informal gatherings, artist meetings, collective meetings, community marches and actions, and community workshops and panels, among other events in which Latina community-engaged artists participated. I conducted in-depth formal interviews with ten artists, held informal conversations with an additional seven artists, and collaborated with eight artists on art projects and community workshops. I used two phases of coding to analyze transcribed interviews and field notes. The first phase involved open coding in which I identified concepts, themes, and examples. The second phase involved directed coding based on the most prevalent concepts and themes in my data and past research.

Reflective of Chicago's Latina/x/o population, twelve artists in my research are Mexican/Mexican American/Chicana, three are Puerto Rican, and two are a mix of other Central and South American nationalities. Their ages range from their mid-twenties to sixties. Most were raised in the city of Chicago. Some migrated to Chicago from other parts of the United States and Latin America as adults. Thirteen artists are formally trained artists, and eleven are full-time professional artists, such as performers, photographers, painters, and sculptors, and/or art educators and teaching artists. The rest are not formally trained, nor full-time professional artists, but still regularly produce artwork.

Marginalization: Devaluation, Contested Access, and "Stereotyping/Pigeonholing"

Devaluation

Due to gender and racial inequities within the arts, the artists in this study have frequently experienced the devaluation of their artwork by other artists, institutional gatekeepers, and Latina/x/o community members (Miller 2016; Tator, Henry, and Mattis 1998). Nearly all have a story about organizations asking them to produce artwork or perform artistic labor for free. They have been told "You will get great exposure," "I thought you made art because you love it, not to make money," or even "Don't you care about your community?" But as Elvia Rodriguez Ochoa, a forty-nine-year-old Mexicana, aptly put it, "People die of exposure. . . . Yes, I love this. But the gas company doesn't accept love as a form of payment."

Beyond economic value, Latina community-engaged artists and their work are devalued within the arts by being passed over for awards and recognitions or having their artwork disparaged as "crafts." But one of the most common experiences results from artists' devotion to teaching as central to their artistic practices. Silvia González, a thirty-one-year-old Chicana, shared her frustration in this regard: "I had always felt like art educators were never valued or even seen as the same as a painter or the same as a photographer. So, in some ways I felt more validated as a photographer than as an art educator even though I was doing all of it. And it still happens where if I tell people I'm a photographer, 'Oh what kind of photography?!' If I tell people I'm an art teacher, it's like 'Ohhhh . . . how's that?'"

The devaluation of teaching is ironic given that most artists develop their craft under the guidance of art educators. Nevertheless, many of the artists have felt the pressure to separate their teaching from their independent practice and put more energy towards independent artistic production. The devaluation of their work leads to the artists' contested access to mainstream and community arts spaces.

Contested Access

The artists in this study have varying access to arts institutions. Some are consistently denied access and others are securely within institutions. Amara Betty Martín, a thirty-six-year-old Afro-Boricua artist, is often denied opportunities by arts institutions, such as curation, teaching, and exhibition opportunities, simply based on her lack of institutional credentials. She says, "I feel really pressured to get a degree. But it's not something I *want* to do. It's something I feel like I'll do because I'm pressured by economic reasons. Because I could have all these things on my resumé, but I don't have a degree. And [arts institutions] are kind of like 'Mmmm, I don't know.'" However, even with traditional arts training and credentials, Latina community-engaged artists' access to mainstream arts institutions is contested.

Maria Gaspar, a forty-year-old Chicana, shows her work in museums around the United States and has earned prestigious awards and fellowships, such as the *Chicago Tribune*'s 2014 Chicagoan of the Year in Visual Arts. After earning her Master of Fine Arts (MFA) in 2009, she pieced together temporary, part-time jobs at various arts institutions and organizations, such as a position as adjunct faculty at the School of the Art Institute of Chicago (SAIC). In 2015, she applied for a tenure-track position at SAIC and was excluded from the all-white group of finalists. Disappointed, she planned to leave SAIC until colleagues led by a tenured faculty member of color "made a fuss" and wrote a letter to the college dean. She was invited as a finalist, obtained the position, and is now tenured. Despite this, some colleagues and students at SAIC still frequently question her qualifications and the value and impact of her community work.

Latina artists' access to community arts spaces is also contested. Sexism among Latino community artists has long prevented and limited Latina artists' access to Latina/x/o community art spaces. For example, Elvia was part of two community art collectives and one community arts organization. She was the president of one collective, and the men in that collective voted her out of her position. She says, "[The men] didn't think I had the capacity to do all the projects that I was involved in. . . . That's the explanation they gave me." She believes that explanation on its own is sexist, because a group of men made a determination about her capacity as a woman. But she also believes that it was a cover for "deeper *machista* motives" because she says, "I was pretty much the only woman in the group for a long time. A lot of other women artists came and went but I was the one that tried to stick with it the longest." In addition to blocked access to community spaces, Latina artists experience stereotyping and pigeonholing, which also underestimate and devalue their capabilities.

Stereotyping/Pigeonholing

Latina community-engaged artists contend with preconceptions about who Latinas are and what kind of art they produce. Gendered, racialized, and classed stereotypes about working-class Latinas' otherness shaped critics' interpretations of their work. For example, Victoria Martinez attended a predominantly white art school in Minnesota and was regularly told that her work about her life, friends, and community was "very avant-garde" or "very outsider art." Stereotypes about Latina emotional excessiveness, such as being loud and angry, shape how the artists are viewed. When Silvia González sought out constructive feedback on her artwork, her professor asked, "Why do you always want to work from the place of anger? Why is all of your work so angry?" Experiences like these led many of the artists to feel extremely frustrated and isolated in art school.

Even within Latina/x/o communities, the artists from this study contended with narrow understandings of what kind of work Latina artists should be producing. There is an expectation that their work use imagery that explicitly marks their gender and ethnicity, such as references to Frida Kahlo, *calaveras*, or Latin American Catholic and nationalist symbolism. If Latina community-engaged artists approach art outside of this repertoire, then they are either pressured to draw on prescribed imagery or must engage in additional labor to justify their approach. For example, thirty-four-year-old Paulina Camacho Valencia was asked to lead a painting event to fundraise for a Latina/x/o organization helping undocumented youth. The organization wanted her to teach the group how to paint a sugar skull in the likeness of Frida Kahlo. Paulina objected because she believed the event should value the process of building community among her group through individually unique paintings. But the organization was adamant about her using this imagery. Paulina stood her ground and was willing to abandon the event, but, with only days until the event, the organization acquiesced. As evidenced by this example, failing to conform to dominant discourses and their assumptions not only renders artists illegible and unrecognizable to mainstream white artists, critics, but even, at times, to Latina/x/o community audiences.

Marginalization Through Illegibility

Devaluation, contested access, and stereotyping or pigeonholing involve the imposition of assumptions, meanings, or value onto Latina artists and their work. However, I find that the artists from my research regularly experience a different form of marginalization when their work is unrecognizable according to hegemonic race, gender, and artistic frameworks. Their illegibility when they do not produce art using a single discipline, such as painting or photography, or do not produce art for the dominant white and/or male gaze, compel artists to go to lengths to defend their artistic choices and can even result in their being pushed out of the arts.

For example, while critiques that artists receive in art school are central to their growth and creative development, Silvia González's classmates and professors in art school consistently told her, "I don't understand how to talk about your work, so I'm not going to talk about it." She recalls that after one of her final critiques, "Some people didn't know [how to react]. It was dead silent when the performance was over." At a time when Silvia felt her artistic practice was advancing, she was met with silence from classmates and faculty who did not want to engage with her work because it was illegible to them. Silvia reflects on this as an example of "how white supremacy manifests in academic spaces. How sometimes it's just difficult to be a person of color in these institutions with these ideas that I'm struggling with and unpacking. And then there's no one there to build with. I was making work that was more personal to me, more self-oriented, and more self-guided. And I think that's where people are like, 'I don't know who you are or what you're doing.' This unwillingness to understand or because you don't know it, it must not be talked about."

FIGURE 8.1 Maria Gaspar, *Textile Collage*. 2016, Chicago, Illinois. Image courtesy of Maria Gaspar.

While their white classmates received support, the artists' illegibility led them to be ignored by critics, coerced into engaging artistic themes that make white artists and gatekeepers comfortable, and unmotivated to continue producing art. Many seriously considered leaving the arts or temporarily stopped producing art. Latina artists are able to resist such marginalization by developing strategies that work with and against dominant discourses and institutions. One of the more innovative strategies involves actively working with legibility and illegibility in order to make the arts more accessible for themselves and others.

Strategic (Il)legibility

Artists in this study strategically claim belonging using both legibility and illegibility, or (il)legibility. They make themselves and their work legible to gatekeepers in ways that facilitate their access to arts spaces and resources. At the same time, they protect their belonging by maintaining the illegibility of artmaking that is devalued or challenges the exclusionary boundaries of the arts. In this manner, they protect themselves from being viewed as undeserving of space and resources. These artists do not make themselves legible for individual power or prestige but to redistribute resources and create access for communities commonly excluded from arts institutions and resources.

In order for this strategy to be effective, artists must know the language, ideas, and frameworks that will be recognized and valued in particular institutional contexts and use this knowledge to make themselves and their work legible to gatekeepers. Several artists noted the need to use "artspeak," or jargon and buzzwords commonly used in artist statements and exhibition catalogs, in their grant and fellowship applications. For example, they use words like "social practice," "performative gestures," and "site intervention" to describe their community-engaged projects in ways that conform to existing artistic frameworks even though, in practice, they diverge from mainstream artistic conventions. This language not only frames their work in legible ways but also provides cover for aspects of their work that are not valued. As a result, they are able to secure funding for projects that normally would not have the support of those resources.

The artists in the study also understand that artists garner legitimacy through legibility when they produce one-off artwork using a single artform to be exhibited within private collections, museums, or galleries. For example, the most revered artists are experts in a single, prestigious mode of art-making (usually painting) and have their expensive artwork held in elite, private collections (usually fine art museums or wealthy art collectors). Latina community-engaged artists are able to make themselves legible according to these standards but also maintain the illegibility of their practices as a whole by bridging disciplines and producing art through multiple modalities.

For Nicole Marroquin, a forty-nine-year-old Chicana who teaches in an elite art school, her interdisciplinary art practice serves as a "survival mechanism." She says:

> The day I got here everyone was like, "You're not going to make it. Here's a list of people who didn't make it before you. They don't tenure Latinas." So, you know why I write and I do clay and I do new media and I do other stuff . . . everything is because I didn't think there was a place for me and I was going to have to keep moving or stay undercover. I just need to make it so it's impossible for them to tell me I'm not good enough. Which is why I'm throwing on the [pottery] wheel now [mass producing mugs]. I'm like what's the thing nobody would ever value at my school. I'm just going to do that a lot. It doesn't resemble something they like.

In order to earn tenure and secure her position in the arts, she had to produce art in ways that her institution recognized as legitimate. Nicole makes herself and her work legible by engaging with established artistic traditions and frameworks, exhibiting singular sculptural pieces in local and international art museums, and securing art fellowships and grants. At the same time, she must keep illegible the aspects of her practice that the broader art community would devalue or not see as authentic art. Legibility enables artists to individually claim space and resources in the mainstream art world, and they keep the ways in which they work against the art world and stay true to their community principles illegible. Their individual uses of (il)legibility serve their communities' interests.

Nicole regularly uses art forms that are not valued within mainstream arts institutions. For example, she conducts oral history and archival research on the history of student activism in Chicago. She has used this research to create posters and develop an educational smartphone application that uses art and augmented reality technologies. During her interview, she was producing feminist-themed drinking mugs to sell and give to friends. Through "moving," "staying undercover," using multiple disciplines and drawing their attention to her more legible artwork, Nicole keeps these aspects of her practice unrecognizable to those with institutional authority at her university. Her strategic (il)legibility also undermines the exclusionary structure of the arts. Much of her artwork is attainable by working-class Latina/x/o communities. Again, she is largely able to do this illegible work as a result of making herself legible according to hegemonic artistic values.

Maria Gaspar's work also highlights how Latina community-engaged artists use strategic (il)legibility to challenge exclusion in the arts. From September 2017 to April 2018, Maria held a series of art workshops with men and women incarcerated at Chicago's Cook County Jail, the largest single-site pre-detention facility in the United States. These workshops produced a public art project that featured critical depictions of the criminal legal system. She gained and maintained permission to release incarcerated people from their cellblocks and provide them with normally banned art materials, readings, and audio/visual equipment. The artwork was then projected onto the concrete wall that surrounds the jail.

Maria was able to achieve the goals of the project by strategically making herself and the project legible as legitimate and nonthreatening. For example,

FIGURE 8.2 Chalkboard from planning session of Latina community-engaged artists. Photo by author.

jail officials explicitly told Maria that she would not have permission to do the project if the artwork would be "bashing" Cook County Jail or the sheriff. Maria emphasized that she was an award-winning artist, community member, and art professor who wanted to hold art classes and let participants share stories so that the public could see the complexities of life at the jail.

Maria made the critical and abolitionist politics of the project illegible, because jail officials and guards randomly reviewed materials and were present during workshops. She brought artwork and readings that were not explicitly critical of the criminal justice systems but facilitated critiques of mass incarceration. Through creative exercises, she trained participants how to keep their critiques of the jail illegible to officials through metaphors and symbolism. She was successful in maintaining illegibility, because jail officials publicly shared that they saw the project as highlighting the jail's necessary, important, and innovative work. However, community members who attended the project shared how the artwork made them reconsider and question the role of the criminal legal system in their communities. The project also made the arts more accessible to incarcerated people who are largely excluded from the arts. The project distributed art foundation resources and opened up opportunities in the arts for many participants. Some have participated on panels or have exhibited their work in museums and galleries.

Strategic (il)legibility allows artists to find a third path between being "sell-outs" that fully assimilate and being "true community artists" that completely disengage from arts institutions. Latina community-engaged artists have varying abilities to use strategic (il)legibility because some do not have credentials or positions within arts institutions or do not have knowledge of artistic terminology and funding structures. However, even those who harbor major qualms about working within mainstream institutions still work with and respect those artists who do regularly engage these institutions using strategic (il)legibility. For example, Amara Betty Martín, a community artist who has had limited access to mainstream arts institutions, has supported and contributed to projects organized by Maria Gaspar, an artist who is regularly within mainstream arts institutions.

(Il)legibility, Belonging, and Artistic Resistance

Devaluation, contested access, and stereotyping/pigeonholing exclude Latina community-engaged artists from belonging in the arts, because they are understood by mainstream institutions as not doing valuable work, not meeting standards, and only representing their marginality. Their belonging is also challenged when their work is unknowable or unrecognizable to other artists and gatekeepers—when they are illegible. They resist exclusionary institutional structures by disidentifying and using a differential consciousness to engage strategic (il)legibility. This entails making themselves and their work legible in order to claim space in the arts while also being illegible and working against structural inequities in the arts. They do so by strategically engaging and disengaging with dominant discourses and institutions. Beyond my case, this chapter points to the broader relationship between legibility and Latina/x/o belonging in the United States and the possibilities that artistic resistance offers.

Throughout U.S. history, middle-class white men have served as the implicit reference by which legal and social belonging are determined (Glenn 2002). Latina community-engaged artists' strategic (il)legibility offers an alternative to "Latino spin" narratives that claim belonging by assimilating to white, middle-class, conservative norms and requires us to critically reassess belonging, legibility, and illegibility. Should Latinas/xs/os seek to belong to a society and institutions built on white supremacy, heteropatriarchy, and classism? Does legibility necessarily lead to full and equal inclusion for Latinas/xs/os? Does illegibility always have to be a mechanism of exclusion or can it serve as a source of Latina/x/o resistance? Are assimilation or opposition the only two options? Artistic resistance is key to collectively exploring these questions, because the creativity, fluidity, and collectivity central to artistic resistance allow Latinas/xs/os to question assumptions and formulate new, complex relationships with hegemonic discourses and institutions. These relationships can help Latinas/xs/os formulate sophisticated critiques of existing social structures and develop a praxis that imagines, rehearses, and practices freer, more just social relations that abolish existing racial, gender, and class hierarchies and nourish and value intracommunity complexities.

Conclusion

Strategic (il)legibility counters mainstream tactics that seek to facilitate permanent Latina/x/o inclusion and belonging in hegemonic institutions and discourses. For Latina community-engaged artists, belonging is intentionally partial, because belonging to institutions and spaces that are not built for

Latinas/xs/os is not liberating, healthy, or affirming. Instead, belonging is a strategic means to redistribute resources from mainstream institutions to marginalized communities and to challenge existing hegemonic structures. This liminal place can facilitate new, creative possibilities for Latinas/xs/os outside of already-existing institutions and discourses.

This research points to the need to transform the ideologies and practices of both mainstream and community arts spaces that provide more resources and support for Latina community-engaged artists. I also hope that by sharing the artists' strategies, other community-engaged artists (Latina or otherwise) understand that they do not have to choose between assimilation and opposition and are inspired to develop their own disidentifying artistic practices. At a time with growing social, environmental, political, and economic crises, artists are needed to pose difficult questions to the public—questions that are not being asked or are being silenced—so that we may collectively come to new solutions and new futures for our communities and societies. With community-engaged art, we can collectively develop new frameworks to understand our past, present, and future, and new forms of community to achieve a better world.

Notes

1. I use "Latina/x/o" to refer to a mixed-gender group instead of "Latino," "Latina/o," or "Latinx" to (1) respect the continued importance of the "a" and "o" in the gendered lives and politics of many Latinas/os, (2) not reproduce the gender binary with "a/o" or "@," and (3) not erase the specific history and gender politics of the "x" by using Latinx as a catch-all term. While awkward and possibly distracting, I see written language as malleable and an important and necessary site for disruption and experimentation.
2. I use "the arts" to reference the network of various institutions, ideologies, positions, practices, networks, and actors devoted to the production and exhibition of creative activity, such as painting, sculpture, performance, and writing.
3. I define *discourse* as a system of knowledge that structures social relations and power (Foucault 1972).
4. See Miller (2016) for a detailed analysis of women's marginalization in the arts.
5. This research has been approved by the University of Illinois at Chicago Institutional Review Board (Protocol #2016-0305).
6. I understand social relations to be structured by the intersection of settler colonialism, white supremacy, and heteropatriarchy. I found myself politically having more in common with Latinas than with Latinos largely due to patriarchal views and practices still prevalent among Latinos.

References

Alacovska, Ana. 2015. "Genre Anxiety: Women Travel Writers' Experience of Work." *Sociological Review* 63(1): 128–43.

Anzaldúa, Gloria. 2012. *Borderlands/La Frontera: The New Mestiza*. San Francisco: Aunt Lute Books.

Banks, Mark, and Katie Milestone. 2011. "Individualization, Gender and Cultural Work." *Gender, Work and Organization* 18(1): 73–89.

Bedoya, Roberto. 2014. "Spatial Justice: Rasquachification, Race and the City." *Creative Time Reports*, September 15, 2014. http://creativetimereports.org/2014/09/15/spatial-justice-rasquachification-race-and-the-city/.

Bhabha, Homi. 1994. *The Location of Culture*. New York: Routledge.

Bielby, Denise. D., and William. T. Bielby. 1996. "Women and Men in Film: Gender Inequality Among Writers in a Culture Industry." *Gender & Society* 10(3): 248–70.

Blackwood, Andria, and David Purcell. 2014. "Curating Inequality: The Link Between Cultural Reproduction and Race in the Visual Arts." *Sociological Inquiry* 84(2): 238–63.

Brown, Taylor Whitten. 2019. "Why Is Work by Female Artists Still Valued Less than Work by Male Artists?" *Artsy*. March 8, 2019. www.artsy.net/article/artsy-editorial-work-female-artists-valued-work-male-artists.

Collins, Georgia C. 1979. "Women and Art: The Problem of Status." *Studies in Art Education* 21(1): 57–64.

Cordova, Cary. 2017. *The Heart of the Mission: Latino Art and Politics in San Francisco*. Philadelphia: University of Pennsylvania Press.

Cotera, María Eugenia, Maylei Blackwell, and Dionne Espinoza. 2018. "Introduction: Movements, Movimientos, and Movidas." In *Chicana Movidas: New Narratives of Activism and Feminism in the Movement Era*, edited by Dionne Espinoza, María E. Cotera, and Maylei Blackwell, 1–30. Austin: University of Texas Press.

Dávila, Arlene. 2004. *Barrio Dreams: Puerto Ricans, Latinos, and the Neoliberal City*. Oakland: University of California Press.

———. 2008. *Latino Spin: Public Image and the Whitewashing of Race*. New York: New York University Press.

———. 2012. *Culture Works: Space, Value, and Mobility Across the Neoliberal Americas*. New York: New York University Press.

Embrick, David G., Simón Weffer, and Silvia Dómínguez. 2019. "White Sanctuaries: Race and Place in Art Museums." *The International Journal of Sociology and Social Policy* 39(11/2): 995–1009.

Foucault, Michel. 1972. *The Archaeology of Knowledge and the Discourse of Language*. Translated by A. M. Sheridan Smith. New York: Pantheon Books.

Glenn, Evelyn Nakano. 2002. *Unequal Freedom: How Race and Gender Shaped American Citizenship and Labor*. Cambridge: Harvard University Press.

Grams, Diane. 2010. *Producing Local Color: Art Networks in Ethnic Chicago*. Chicago: University of Chicago Press.

Gude, Olivia, and Jeff Huebner. 2010. *Urban Art Chicago: A Guide to Community Murals, Mosaics, and Sculptures.* Chicago: Ivan R. Dee.

Hall, Stuart. 1997. "The Spectacle of the Other." In *Representation: Cultural Representation and Signifying Practices,* edited by Stuart Hall, 225–90. London: Sage.

Halley, Jeffrey A., and Avelardo Valdez. 2000. "Culture and Rationalization: The Impact of a National Foundation Initiative on a Community-Based Cultural Arts Center." *The International Journal of Cultural Policy* 7(1): 151–70.

Halley, Jeffrey A., Avelardo Valdez, and Steve Nava. 2001. "Resistance to Bureaucratization of Culture: Lessons from the Chicano Arts Scene." *Journal of Arts Management, Law, and Society* 31(3): 198–211.

Hames-Garcia, Michael, and Ernesto Javier Martínez. 2011. *Gay Latino Studies: A Critical Reader.* Durham, N.C.: Duke University Press.

Helicon Collaborative. 2017. "Not Just Money: Equity Issues in Cultural Philanthropy." *Heliconcollab.* July 1. https://heliconcollab.net/wp-content/uploads/2017/08/Not JustMoney_Full_Report_July2017.pdf.

Holscher, Louis M. 1976. "Artists & Murals in East Los Angeles and Boyle Heights: A Sociological Observation." *Humboldt Journal of Social Relations* 3(2): 25–29.

Hurtado, Aída. 2000. "Sitios y Lenguas: Chicanas Theorize Feminisms." In *Decentering the Center: Philosophy for a Multicultural, Postcolonial, and Feminism World,* edited by Uma Narayan and Sandra Harding, 128–155. Bloomington: Indiana University Press.

Lin, Jan. 2019. *Taking Back the Boulevard: Art, Activism, and Gentrification in Los Angeles.* New York: New York University Press.

McCambridge, Ruth. 2017. "Museums So White: Survey Reveals Deep Lack of Diversity." *Nonprofit Quarterly.* May 9, 2017. https://nonprofitquarterly.org/2017/05 /09/museum-boards-directors-whitest-getting-whiter/.

Miller, Diana L. 2016. "Gender and the Artist Archetype: Understanding Gender Inequality in Artistic Careers." *Sociology Compass* 10(2): 119–31.

Moreno, María-José. 2004. "Art Museums and Socioeconomic Forces: The Case of a Community Museum." *Review of Radical Political Economics* 36(4): 506–27.

Muñoz, José Esteban. 1999. *Disidentifications: Queers of Color and the Performance of Politics.* Minneapolis: University of Minnesota Press.

National Museum of Mexican Art. 2021. "About Us." Accessed August 31, 2021. http://nationalmuseumofmexicanart.org/ content/about-us-0.

Noriega, Chon A. 1999. "On Museum Row: Aesthetics and the Politics of Exhibition." *Daedalus* 128(3): 57–81.

Pindell, Howardena. 1987. "Testimony." Agendas for Survival Conference. Hunter College, New York. Statistics, Testimony and Supporting Documentation. June 28, 1987. https://pindell.mcachicago.org/art-world-surveys/statistics-testimony-and -supporting-documentation/.

Said, Edward W. 1978. *Orientalism.* London: Routledge.

Sandoval, Chela. 2009. "U.S. Third World Feminism: The Theory and Method of Oppositional Consciousness in the Postmodern World." In *Geographic Thought:*

A Praxis Perspective, edited by George Henderson and Marvin Waterstone, 338–354. London: Routledge.

Saltz, Jerry. 2006. "Where the Girls Aren't." *Village Voice*. September 19, 2006. www.villagevoice.com/2006/09/19/where-the-girls-arent/.

Scharff, Christina. 2015. "Blowing Your Own Trumpet: Exploring the Gendered Dynamics of Self-Promotion in the Classical Music Profession." *The Sociological Review* 63(S1): 97–112.

Selbach, Gérard. 2004. "Interview with Jennie E. Rodriguez, Executive Director of the Mission Cultural Center for Latino Arts, San Francisco, CA, United States, August 15, 2001." *Revue LISA* 2(6): 95–100.

Sweet, Paige. 2019. "The Paradox of Legibility: Domestic Violence and Institutional Survivorhood." *Social Problems* 66(3): 411–27.

Tator, Carol, Frances Henry, and Winston Mattis. 1998. *Challenging Racism in the Arts: Case Studies of Controversy and Conflict*. Toronto: University of Toronto Press.

Topaz, Chad M., Bernhard Klingenberg, Daniel Turek, Brianna Heggeseth, Pamela E. Harris, Julie C. Blackwood, C. Ondine Chavoya, Steven Nelson, and Kevin M. Murphy. 2019. "Diversity of Artists in Major U.S. Museums." *PLoS ONE* 14(3): e0212852.

Viesca, Victor Hugo. 2004. "The Battle of Los Angeles: The Cultural Politics of Chicana/o Music in the Greater Eastside." *American Quarterly* 56(3): 719–39.

Wherry, Frederick F. 2011. *The Philadelphia Barrio: The Arts, Branding, and Neighborhood Transformation*. Chicago: University of Chicago Press.

Wreyford, Natalie. 2015. "Birds of a Feather: Informal Recruitment Practices and Gendered Outcomes for Screenwriting Work in the UK Film Industry." *Sociological Review* 63(S1): 84–96.

CHAPTER 9

Dance in the Desert

Latinx Bodies in Movement Beyond Borders

MICHELLE TÉLLEZ AND YVONNE MONTOYA

> No, you don't belong . . . you don't look like us, you aren't like us.
> —Lydia, dancer and dance scholar[1]

> The first memory of dance is dancing to Gloria Trevi at the age of three. I had really short hair, but I would be like "*me voy a poner el cabello suelto*" and I would always dance.
> —Esperanza, dancer, choreographer, educator

> For me dance has always been a way to express my agency, for me to feel comfortable in spaces.
> —Laura, dance administrator

In this chapter, we argue that Dance in the Desert (DITD)[2] is a project that helps us understand cultural expression and community formation for Latinx people in a state, and region, that has effectively targeted brown bodies— regardless of citizenship—for years (Gonzalez de Bustamante and Santa Ana 2012).[3] Latinxs are the largest ethnic group in California and New Mexico and the second largest ethnic minority group in Arizona and Nevada (Kaiser Family Foundation 2019). Given the shifting demographics and its proximity to the Mexico/U.S. border, Arizona has become a battleground for social justice and human rights. The incendiary rhetoric in popular media directly impacts the embodied experiences of vulnerable communities, especially Brown and Black (im)migrants (Téllez 2016). Over the course of the last fifteen years, the Arizona legislature has introduced numerous anti-immigrant bills, two of the most widely known are SB 1070 the "show me your papers bill," and HB 2281, "the ethnic studies bill." Moreover, federal policies like 287G have allowed local governments to collude with federal policies on immigration enforcement, workforce raids, police brutality, and mass detention and incarceration, which, in Maricopa County, became known as former sheriff Joe Arpaio's reign of terror (Téllez 2016). Despite the eventual overturning of most of the draconian measures of the bills (Depenbrock 2017; Duara 2016), the effects of these policies continue to be felt long after their introduction. Arizona has become known as one of the most politically fraught states in the nation.

The arts community has often been at the center of creative and incisive responses to such political conditions and their material consequences. Artists based in Arizona and in the broader southwest region are no different. In this chapter, we look to the framework of cultural citizenship (Flores and Benmayor 1997; Rosaldo 1994) to understand how Dance in the Desert (DITD)—a Southwest regional gathering of Latinx dance makers (dancers, choreographers, arts administrators)—is claiming social space, and the right of belonging, through dance expression.

DITD was born in 2017 as a response to the lack of space for Latinx dance artists to convene either in the Southwest region or nationally.[4] DITD founder Yvonne Montoya notes that there is no Latinx equivalent to the *International Association of Blacks in Dance*, which hosts an annual conference and advocates for Black Dance on the national level. Nor is there an equivalent to the *Indigenous Choreographers at Riverside*, an annual gathering that brings Indigenous dance artists, Indigenous studies scholars, and dance studies scholars to connect, discuss, and share work.

DITD provides opportunities for Latinx dancemakers to come together, incubate new works, and build relationships—in a region where there is little to no foundation or individual philanthropy support for dance in communities. The long-term goal is to create a platform to promote and support Latinx dancemakers while also increasing advocacy, funding, mentorship, opportunities, networking, and scholarship. Not only does DITD work to fill the void that currently exists in the field of dance; it creates an opportunity for community making and building. Though still a nascent project, we thought it important to document and offer an initial analysis of the potential impact of DITD in the state and region. In this chapter, we will introduce the literature on Latinx dance, analyze our interviews with participants of DITD (dancers and choreographers), and end by discussing the long-term possibilities inspired by DITD. We build on the scholarship of Latinx dance and performance (Salinas 2015; Garcia 2013; Rivera-Servera 2012; Rivera-

Servera and Young 2010; Suarez 2011; Romero et. al 2009) yet recognize that robust dance scholarship about or advocacy for the Latinx dance community at large does not exist. This project seeks to further close that gap.

Belonging and Insistence

In the context of the increasing militarization of the U.S.-Mexico border, including mounting deaths of migrant border crossers, violence, subjugation, and family separation—Latinx communities in the United States fight to claim social space and spaces of belonging. Border states are at the center of these struggles where the intersections of gender, race, colonization, and capitalism play out in myriad ways. The cultural implications for the Latinx community are widely felt across experience and place. While the arts, in general, are largely unfunded, they are radically so for Latinx arts organizations and artists themselves. In tracing the development and potential impact of DITD, we draw on the notion of cultural citizenship (Flores and Benmayor 1997; Rosaldo 1994) to understand how this project makes legible the issues that are inherent in Latinx communities for dance artists but who are typically unable to bring them to the public. In sum, we show that grassroots responses, like DITD, to these social conditions are ways of demonstrating belonging.

Cultural citizenship means having a place and a voice in the public, and it asserts that even in contexts of inequality, people "have a right to their distinctive heritage" (Rosaldo 2009). This point is further made in Cepeda's (2010) analysis of the single "*Nuestro Himno*," a Spanish-language paraphrasing of "The Star-Spangled Banner" performed by a cohort of U.S. Latina/o and Latin American recording artists. She argues, "Situated within the context of the ongoing legal, socioeconomic, and political struggles of recent Latino immigrants, both the recording and the demonstrations constituted important symbolic gestures toward the (re)claiming of U.S. public space and the contested meanings of nation and belonging" (28). In other words, cultural citizenship is distinct from legal citizenship because it underscores the practices that give citizenship meaning in everyday interactions and experiences.

In Rivera-Servera's (2012) cultural study of U.S. Latinx dance in theatrical, social, and political contexts, he called these everyday interactions *convivencia diaria*. He analyzes the "quotidian exchanges among Queer Latinas/os of diverse backgrounds in spaces of social and cultural performance" as "potentially transformative events that yield equally powerful notions of commu-

FIGURE 8.1   Dancers performing *Braceros* by Yvonne Montoya inspired by Montoya's father who worked as a Bracero (migrant farmworker) during his early teens picking watermelon and cantaloupe in Yuma, Arizona, in the late 1960s. Photo Courtesy of Yvonne Montoya and Dance in the Desert. Photo by Dominic Arizona Bonuccelli.

nity, resource sharing, and potentially collective political action" (39). Interestingly, one of Rivera-Servera's sites of analysis is in Phoenix, Arizona, at a time that was about a decade before DITD comes to be. While he analyzes public space and cultural exchange in Queer bars, his concept of *conviviencia diaria* can be applied to the intentional space created through Dance in the Desert. Cultural citizenship is built through the relationships created in DITD as the artists bring to vision their stories. Cultural citizenship gives us the language to understand how ethnic communities can assert cultural difference as they claim belonging in the United States. Along with belonging, we add the notion of insistence to underscore the continued urgency and salience of this work—and as a way to express the tremendous commitment Latinx dancemakers in the southwest have to staking public space through cultural expression.

We also use this framework of belonging in order to highlight how our documentation makes an intervention in the literature and field of dance theory, particularly in the archives of dance history where Latinx dance is essentially erased. The experience of Latinx dancemakers must also form part of these narratives. Salinas (2015) similarly noted this absence in his analysis of the 2005 Public Broadcasting Service (PBS) national broadcast of *Visiones: Latino Art and Culture*, where he points out that of the twenty segments that comprise *Visiones*, three episodes are dedicated to U.S. Latinx dance practices. Two of the episodes feature Latinx dancers performing within the Euro-Western informed concert dance traditions of classical ballet and American modern dance, and the third segment focuses on New York street-inspired hip-hop dance culture. As such, Salinas (2015) argues that "the elevation of mainstream institutional 'white' dance forms within the documentary's Latino 'brown' grassroots focus at once devalues and disciplines non-white dance and dancers to subordinate 'othered' or 'ethnic' status, while also dismissing our important creative contributions to the diversity of Latino/a and American expressive cultural heritage" (13). Throughout his dissertation, he shows how Latinx concert dance and the expressive brown body is marginalized and overlooked by mainstream concert dance.

Salinas (2015) further argues that Latinx choreographies construct complex counternarratives that enable community self-definition, empowerment, and the formation of identities through what he calls a borderlands, or *frontera*, worldview. Salinas (2015) shows that grassroots dancemakers and companies, with long service histories in Latinx barrios, or working-class neighborhoods, work from those contexts to create choreographies that center Latinx experience and aesthetic values as counterdiscourse to contemporary American theatrical concert dance, while opening up physical and conceptual spaces for the brown body in traditionally white domains of artistic practice. The concept of cultural citizenship further helps us understand that while citizenship is contested and incomplete, culture is constantly shifting and evolving (Rosaldo 1997).

Figueroa's (2018) analysis of the only Latinx-centered dance troupe in the United States—the Ballet Hispanico of New York City—highlights the "cultural and artistic labor of Latinx artists accessing modern, post-modern, and contemporary dance styles" (vii). She asks, "How does concert dance converse with and serve Latinx publics within the US?" and "How do Latinxs in the US make use of concert dance to construct, revise, and (re)imagine modes of Latinx identity?" Most importantly, she poses the question, "How does dance serve Latinx bodies given the sociopolitical location of Latinxs within the US?" (7). These questions are important as social membership and citizenship for Latinx people are a continued site of confrontation and conflict. U.S.-based Latinx dance-makers, like the U.S. Latinx population at large, "occupy the liminal spaces of culture, race and citizenship, and their experiences and labor are easily disregarded and undervalued" (8).

Figueroa (2018) asserts that Latinx dance artists are active contributors to the remembrance, formation, and re-formation of Latinx identity and cultural heritage. In her work, Figueroa (2018) bridges dance theory (methodologies and the study of the body) with Latinx Studies (a lens that discerns structures of power and marginalization) by highlighting how the "primacy of the body in dance, as opposed to other art forms, makes it an exceptionally intriguing vehicle for Latinx expression because the process of colonization so often consigns Latinxs to the body through a history of manual labor, skin politic, and for women, sexual and procreative fears/responsibilities" (13–14). One of the major issues Figueroa sees is the lack of access to arts training and education, which is compounded by a larger failure to support and sustain Latinx artists, especially in the realm of dance.

Other work on Latinx dance includes Garcia's (2013) analysis of the everyday practices of salsa dancing in the city of Los Angeles, where she describes how the diverse modes of salsa dancing reproduce notions of Latinidad.[5] Through ethnographic inquiry, Garcia analyzes the social hierarchies of salsa while highlighting how dance can create opportunities for bodies to exist when these are often marked as not belonging. The work of Yvonne Montoya (2019), the founder of DITD, similarly offers a critique on what kinds of bodies are seen as aesthetically fitting but through a focus on contemporary and concert dance. She argues that Xicana bodies are at best exoticized and at worst othered. In her own experience, she redefines her own commitment to a practice that embodies her lived reality and that is suited toward an audience that is reflected in the Xicana identity.[6] In other words, she uses Xicana bodies, stories, and experiences at the center of her contemporary dance practice and performance. Finally, Suarez (2011) helps us understand that Latinx dance-making centers "border consciousness," or an understanding of shared, institutionalized Othering. Suarez (2011) locates Latina/Chicana dance-making within the theories of Chicana writers Gloria Anzaldúa and Cherríe Moraga.

These studies offer a language for and insight into the practices and experiences of Latinx dancemakers in the United States. Our work on DITD builds on these projects as we use cultural citizenship to anchor how we study "the aspirations and perceptions of people who occupy subordinate social positions" in relation to dance and community making (Rosaldo 1997, 38).

Methodology

While DITD is intended as a long-term project, for this chapter we are focusing on the data gathered from its first event held in 2018 at Arizona State University (ASU) in Tempe, Arizona, where Yvonne Montoya was completing a fellowship at the Herberger Institute for Design and Arts.[7] During this first gathering, Montoya organized two focus groups to get a sense of the state of the field for Latinx dancemakers. Focus groups were conducted in both English and Spanish in order to meet the various linguistic needs of the DITD cohort. Two ninety-minute focus groups comprised of dancers and dance administrators participating in DITD were held the morning of the last day of the gathering. Focus Group One had six total participants, and Focus Group Two had seven total participants. Participants ranged in age from sixteen to forty-five years old and included various gender identities, sexual orientations, and immigration statuses. Education and experience levels ranged from high school to terminal graduate degrees and high school to executive-level administrators. There were eight participants from the Phoenix metro area, Tucson and Douglas/Agua Prieta, and five were from out of state. All but one resided in the southwest. Various subgroups of Latinxs were represented, including Mexican American, Mexican immigrant, DACAmented, Colombian American, Puerto Rican, Ecuadorian American, Chicanx, and Nuevomexicanx.

There were three general areas of questions that we used during the focus groups. The first had to do with the dancemakers' relationship to dance, including their journey in the field and its significance to them, but we also asked about the role of mentorship and role models. The second set of questions was about the dance community in which they currently participated and their performance practice, including how they saw their future as a dance artist in terms of long-term sustainability and support. The last set of questions pertained to their experiences of discrimination, race, and culture in the field. We transcribed and pulled the themes from these focus groups for our analysis.

Dance in the Desert

DITD is an initiative that addresses systemic deficits in dance in the southwest by providing a space for creative expression through dance that redresses geographic isolation and centers local expertise. By providing a space for network building between dancemakers, funders, and administrators in the world of dance performance, DITD builds meaningful relationships among Latinx dancemakers that expand their access to social capital (Yosso 2005). For example, Gina, a Douglas, Arizona–based choreographer and dance studio owner, was personally invited by Montoya to participate in Dance in the Desert. During DITD's closed-door *plática*/discussion between Latinx dancemakers and dance administrators, Gina met the Cultural Participation Manager at ASU's Gammage Performing Arts Center, who announced that an application for the Molly Blank Fund Teaching Artist Program, which trains teaching artists in the Kennedy Center arts integration method, was currently open. Given the limited professional development opportunities for dance teachers in Douglas, Gina was interested in the program. In the end, two dance teachers from Douglas applied—Gina and another teacher in her studio. Both were accepted and are now trained in the Kennedy Center arts integration method, taking the tools they learned back to their dance community in rural Cochise County. Networking can radically change how one gets access to programs and funding, and Gina's participation in the program is the direct result of the relationships built through DITD.

FIGURE 8.2   Dance in the Desert Founder Yvonne Montoya welcoming guests to the community share-out at Arizona State University's Grant Street Studios in April 2018. Photo Courtesy of Yvonne Montoya and Dance in the Desert. Photo by Dominic Arizona Bonuccelli.

DITD comes at a critical point as the Latinx dance community is experiencing a moment of aesthetic innovation. Participants—dancemakers (choreographers, dancers, arts administrators)—build cultural citizenship (Rosaldo 1994) through their artistic expression that is rooted in their community experience (similar to Salinas's [2015] concept of *frontera* worldview) and developed through their relationships (through *conviviencia diaria*) with one another (Rivera-Servera 2012). In addition to building upon the strengths and momentum of the Latinx dance community, bringing together Latinx dancemakers provides an opportunity to address systemic deficits that exist both in the field of dance and in academia that directly impact Latinx and dancemakers of color. These include geographic isolation, disenfranchisement, and a lack of tangible and intangible resources such as few mentors, a lack of inclusion in dance archives, a paucity of dance scholars writing about the work of Latinx dance makers, and minimal resources to support the work in the communities they serve.

The first *Dance in the Desert: A Gathering of Latinx Dancemakers* took place from April 26 to 28, 2018, on the ASU campus. The gathering brought together fourteen Latinx dancemakers and eight Latinx arts administrators, funders, and scholars. Events included dance workshops, choreography sharing and feedback sessions, closed-door dialogues and discussions between dancers and dance administrators, dance performances, focus groups, a community share-out, and a closing *pachanga* (party). In May 2019, the second Dance in the Desert took place in Tucson, Arizona, where Arizona-based Latinx choreographers and dancers were invited to a choreography retreat and professional development series with the intention of supporting the development of new work. The third gathering is planned for the border cities of Douglas/Agua Prieta in May 2022 (postponed from 2020 because of the global COVID-19 pandemic) and will focus on professional development for dancers and a binational exchange between U.S.-based Latinx artists and Mexican dance artists.

Dance in the Desert 2018 began on a hot Arizona afternoon when a group of six dance artists gathered in a small classroom at ASU for an opening circle. Over the course of three days, dancers and choreographers shared experiences, exchanged ideas, and took up institutional space—on a university campus, in well-lit, airy dance studios—places that have never centered Latinx dance artists. Montoya's piece entitled "Bracero" opens the final day—a solo performer moving through stylized gestures as the voice of a man remembering his youth picking watermelon in the fields in Yuma comes over the speakers. The voice ends and the sound of a mechanized melody is heard as a line of dancers enters the performance space, as there is no stage, one by one. The dancers perform a series of sharp and controlled mechanized movements, conjuring images of pistons and machines. There is power and strength in the dancer's bodies and they move in and out of the floor. The dance ends abruptly with the dancer running forward and jumping in front of the audience as if to say, "We are here, and we are strong."

Following the dance, the community share-out begins with DITD participants—including some of the dancers who just performed and members of the audience—engaging in an hour and a half dialogue. After the share-out, the crowd moved to the Phoenix Hostel and Cultural Center in downtown Phoenix for a closing *pachanga*. Situated outside in the hostel's beautiful garden area, the gathering began with food and music as DJ Musa, a Latina DJ, plays the DITD community's requested songs. Then unannounced, the music of *Tejana* sensation Selena's "*Si una vez*" begins to blare on the speakers as dancers in several corners of the space begin to perform a choreographed dance in the middle of the mingling guests. Dancers in various parts of the garden move their hips, perform multiple turns, and dance stylized cumbias with each other and with audience members before gathering together for a unison ending. When that dance, entitled "*Veinte*" by Montoya, ends, solo performer Maya takes the mic from the DJ and performs "*Cafe con leche*," dancing to a poem she wrote about her journey coming to love her brown skin. This moment captures the spirit of DITD, where the movement of bodies that are otherwise policed, encaged, separated, and excluded is centered and their ability to freely express themselves is realized.

Dancing with Family, Searching for Space

For some reason, I was never good enough.

—Julia, dancer and choreographer

For the majority of Latinx dancers, dance "training" began at home in the living room with family or, as Esperanza said, in the "*cocina* . . . connecting with my elders, my abuelas, my *tias*, my *tios*, understanding what it meant to be a male Latino." Birthday parties or other family events are where they often saw their parents dance, "you learn *cumbia*, you learn *salsa*, you learn *merengue* but you learn all these things from just watching, mirroring, and, of course, emulating those that are your elders." Often, they were first introduced to folkloric traditions such as *folklórico Mexicano*, *Danza Azteca*, and *Flamenco*. However, the family-centered cultural expression was not translatable to the white-dominated dance world where issues of class, race, and immigration status continue to exclude Latinx bodies. Lourdes's story is a clear example of the contradictions faced by Latinx dancers. She explains:

> So then I started going to community college where I trained really hard. I was taking one class at a time, one style at a time. I started ballet, jazz, modern. And so every semester there was a different class that I took because I couldn't afford to take all of them. So you know, the situation. . . . I was undocumented at the time and I don't know if my parents gave me any, much knowledge, about like what to do because we were all like figuring out our place here. So I was taking one class at a time, and I ended up getting a private scholarship. I don't even remember how. I think the dance director at this community college just kind of started offering me things. And I never revealed myself to her. I'm sure she found out somehow, somewhere, so she had me take some classes all day and night and I ended up getting into the dance program there. Then I met a lot of people and she had professional choreographers come in and set work on the students for the professional dance company. One time she was like "Hey, there is an arts school in California that's here and they're doing auditions, you should go to it." And I went. I was much older than all the young kids that were there, they were like high-school seniors and I was older. So I auditioned for the arts school in California, and I got a notice that "oh, you're accepted, you just need to fill out the application to get into the school." So then I applied for that program and got a letter of me being denied because I'm a liability, because I was undocumented, and at that time that door closed for me.

Lourdes was temporarily shielded from the reality of her status with her teacher and classes at her community college. However, that comfort immediately vanished when she tried to pursue her goals beyond this safe space. While Lourdes's immigration status derailed her plans for continued dance schooling, Lydia's story about her audition for a dance program at the University tells a similar experience of exclusion.

Faculty was like "I've never seen anything like . . . wow, you just went there."
But this other person, this other gatekeeper held so hard, was like "No, you
don't belong. . . . You don't look like us, you aren't like us." And it just . . .
and while it was happening, I didn't feel it was racial, I didn't feel it was cultural, which is the reason I bring up the story. When I felt it was afterwards
because the person who came to my defense, a woman of color Flamenco
instructor, I went to her afterwards, a day or two later and thanked her, and
while I was thanking her I like burst into tears and that's when I realized how
much the attack was actually . . . had everything to do about my shade, and,
you know, perhaps my age, and my *caradura* to be like . . . you know, no, I
also deserve and belong, this is a public institution and I deserve and belong
and I have the discipline to also have dance education, you know. Just an
education, not a starring role, right?

While we are not conflating immigration status with racism, we highlight
how Latinx bodies are always seen as not-belonging regardless of citizenship.
Dancemakers from all genres reported racism and experienced shaming of
their racialized bodies. It was concert and competition dancers, however,
who described the most racism directly related to the racialized Latinx body.
For example, Gina, the owner of a competition dance school from Douglas,
Arizona, recalled a competition experience in Phoenix where dancers did
not receive scores or recognition for participation at the awards ceremony
of a competition. She shares:

*Vinimos a una competencia que nunca habíamos venido de esta compañía
y eramos los únicos mexicanos . . . yo se que todas las críticas son diferentes,
y realmente no te dicen, "te estamos calificando por tu raza o por como te
ves," pero realmente lo hacen . . . al momento de recibir los mios (premios), se
acabaron . . . Pero como allá vivimos en una frontera, somos muchos mexicanos, no habíamos tenido una experiencia tan así hasta el momento en que
venimos aquí. . . . Que no te dicen realmente, "te estamos calificando por tu
raza," pero lo hacen . . . al momento vernos diferente, al momento de que no
te veas güerita, que tu color de tu piel sea otro.* [We came to a competition
that we had never participated in from a company and we were the only
Mexicans. . . . I know that all the criteria are different, and they don't really
tell you, "We're rating you by your race" or "by how you look" but they really
do . . . at the time of receiving mine (awards), they ended. . . . But since we live

on a border there, we are many Mexicans, we had not had such an experience until the moment we came here.... What they do not tell you, "We are really rating you by your race," but they do it ... at the moment we see ourselves differently, the moment you don't look *güerita*, your skin color is different.]

In this testimony, the studio owner draws a link between the different treatment of dancers directly to race/ethnicity and colorism. The use of the words and phrases "*güerita*"[8] and "*color de tu piel sea otro*" demonstrates that the studio owner is cognizant of the conscious and subconscious racial biases in concert and competition dance that upholds young, white, thin, long bodies as the aesthetic ideal.[9] Brown-skinned Latinx dancers were judged, or in this instance not judged, as unworthy because their bodies did not adhere to mainstream dance's white Western Euro-centric aesthetic ideals. This exclusionary behavior on behalf of dance's gatekeepers serves to push out Latinx dancers. The message to these young dancers and studio owner is quite clear: "You are the Other, and you do not belong here."

Skin color is not the only basis for discrimination that racialized Latinx dancemakers' experience in concert dance. Body shape and size, particularly a shorter height and/or curvy bodies, also mark Latinx bodies as racialized and can be lightening rods for discriminating treatment. Regarding experiences as a dance student in a community college, one dancer recalls:

Modern, contemporary dance is very white.... I was probably the only Latina dancer there.... Feeling a lot of pressure on like what my body looks like, and so I was working, taking dance classes, but then also like working out afterwards, or like eating ... having a terrible diet because I was trying to keep up with the perception of what was in that room ... like my body and my figure wasn't supported by the dance teachers there, or like the choreography that was being set.... And I remember getting back like super exhausted, walking home, and I remember feeling tears and crying and feeling like "Why is this so hard?" and it is ... now I can say that it's race and culture in the dance world, like I was trying to keep up with that expectation that is set.

This dancer's testimony describes the excessive exercise and disordered eating, which many concert dancers of various racial/ethnic backgrounds experience. However, the testimony also highlights dance teachers' unfamiliar-

FIGURE 9.3 Dancer Reyna Montoya performing in *Viente* by Yvonne Montoya at Phoenix Hostel and Cultural Center, April 2018. Photo Courtesy of Yvonne Montoya and Dance in the Desert. Photo by Dominic Arizona Bonuccelli.

ity with Latinx bodies. Bodies of different shapes and sizes move differently, and not all movement looks good on or translates to all bodies in the same way. The dancer's observation that their "body and figure" was not supported or valued not only in technique classes, but also in choreography is an experience reported by almost all Latinx concert dancers interviewed. Furthermore, dancers share that a lack of familiarity with shorter and/or curvy bodies extended beyond the dance classroom into professional dance company spaces:

> Being in the company was a blessing and a curse, cause I felt I had a very traumatizing experience there throughout that time, just like constantly being put in the back, not being cast, not given enough feedback, I would go and seek feedback and I would ask the artistic director, "What do I need to do? I want to improve, if I'm not ready, just tell me what I need to work on so I can be cast." But it was always very shallow.

This dancer highlights a lack of understanding about how to incorporate Latinx bodies on stage, and a refusal to showcase and center them in performance. Furthermore, not receiving constructive feedback to improve dance technique in order to become a stronger dancer and company member suggests that the choreographer was either hiding or not casting the dancer, not based on ability, but rather on aesthetics, thus reinforcing the idea that only certain bodies belong on stage. Choreographers' ignoring Latinx dancers in class and the marginalization and erasure of racialized Latinx bodies on stages serves to push them out. This push-out, as dancer Juan shares, is felt more deeply for undocumented dancers:

> I think I've seen a lot of artists that come through here without papers, without documentation and their work becomes erased or their cultural worth becomes devalued, and they become, I've seen quite a few times artists taken advantage of . . . 'cause I think there's this element of being documented and having your body existing in space versus being undocumented and your body doesn't carry any type of presence, so I think that becomes a really big issue. So you're erasing not just the color but you're erasing the full body, which becomes a really colonial issue when you think of this happened to us . . . what, 500 years ago but we didn't learn about this 500 years ago? . . . It's the same thing, it's just happening from a different legal perspective.

Juan is able to trace—and connect—contemporary experiences with a longer history of colonial mechanisms that uphold particular aesthetic standards and hierarchical practices of exclusion. While access to legal citizenship for some Latinx dancers remains unattainable, participating in DITD offers a space of potential and access via *conviviencia* enacted through cultural citizenship.

Dancing in Community: The Impact of Dancing in the Desert

DITD has created a space of possibility for participants and beyond. The DITD Arts administrator, Linda, underscores the importance of the creation of this space but also what it signifies for dancemakers to be able to fully assert their creativity through their own experiences, without extractive practices or exclusion:

> I'm a migrant, I moved to the United States when I was thirteen years old and I grew up seeing brown bodies sort of normalized as performers and

as dancers, and moving to the United States that kind of disappeared for me for a while . . . later I became acquainted with artists that couldn't—for status reasons—who could not perform and earn a living professionally as dancers but who had incredible artistry . . . as a funder and as an arts administrator it's become—recently through supporting a convening—that it became really clear to me that I was not interested in the institution owning the cultural labor that we're supporting. It's really important to me that the institution does not own the labor and the cultural production, the creation aspect, that the brown bodies are producing.

During the focus groups, two dance projects were brought up as examples of spaces that they hoped the field could move more in the directions toward. Lourdes mentioned the BlakTinx Dance Festival—a project that merges Latinx and Black dancers.[10] By applying for grants and working with the founder of the project, she was able to bring it to Phoenix in 2017. Alicia, dancer and former dance teacher in their mid-thirties who is Phoenix-based and mixed-race, discusses another project:

This past year I worked on a project that was actually a theatre show that was brought up from Tucson called *Mas* about the Mexican American Studies program down there, where I was working . . . and there was a moment where I was like "Oh my god, we're all brown," like I couldn't even. . . . I've never been in a process where everybody was Latinx, and it made me so emotional, so comfortable, and it felt so fucking good, and I couldn't believe that it had to take thirty-five years for that to happen to me. I live in the Southwest, I've always lived in the Southwest, like . . . what? So, yeah, it is just so special, and it doesn't happen very often.

By recognizing the value that comes from being in a project where Latinx bodies and experiences are highlighted and included, dancemakers make claims to belonging on their own terms. Here we start to understand the impact of DITD. During the community share-out, one performer said, "The biggest takeaway for me was that we all have stories to tell, are all in this together. We need our voices heard and it's so important to have the support of our community; I am grateful to be here with you all and I'm grateful to know that I'm not alone." Alicia also reflected, "The biggest takeaway for me, which might seem very simple, but I just want to name it because it doesn't

happen very often in dance spaces, but being in a room with all Latinx dancers gives us a safe space to talk about all of the things that have happened
to us throughout our careers." Julissa, an Ecuadorian immigrant in her early
forties, highlights that "Dance in the Desert means a bigger, broader picture
of more Latinx choreographers and dancers, this is the place where we are
gathering and finding how to break these barriers, how to open the doors,
and how to move that forward."

DITD gives Latinx dancers the opportunity to reflect on their identities
and aesthetics in dance. For example, a community member stated, "Our
people don't perform all the time in theaters because our families don't want
to come there, our people do not want to come there, and how do we make
sure that [dance] is accessible and that it is not really rooted in a very specific
Euro-centric way or that it is not rooted in a social-economic-specific way?"
In other words, DITD members begin to contemplate how dancers can challenge what is traditionally seen as "presentable" in a theater setting. How
can different music choices be included (i.e., *banda* or *rancheras* instead of
experimental or classical)? How can colors of costumes, lighting design, and
movements (the undulation of hips and pelvis of *cumbia* and *salsa* rather
than the held pelvis of ballet and contemporary) better reflect Latinx culture
and experience?

DITD provided the space for dancemakers to think more deeply about
what might resonate for Latinx audiences. For example, one audience member stated that they prefer to see "digestible pieces" stating that "sometimes
pieces are very complex and I am not from the arts community so it might
be a little bit confusing or overwhelming to see a piece that is very complex
and I don't have the background to appreciate it." These statements show that
both Latinx dance artists and Latinx audience members desire to create and
experience dance work within aesthetics that are not only legible and meaningful for Latinx communities, but that are staged in accessible locations.
Another dancer commented, "I think this element of aesthetics and how it
is placed in our bodies is interesting. I think it shows up a lot in conversations about how Latinx dancers are represented in multiple styles. . . . What
about dances that are not contemporary, ballet, or modern? The ones that
we learned in the *cocina*. How are those (dances) translated in performance
settings and cultural settings?"

Salinas' (2015) borderlands/*frontera* cultural analysis frames how this
cultural mixing/blending is part of Latinx cultural production which is fun-

damental to claiming space, claiming rights, and resources. There are clear artistic and cultural strategies being employed here, but there is also a play with contradictions and ambiguity that blur the lines between discipline (traditionally defined) and culture. DITD participants are claiming a space and inclusion in the world of dance in this way. In other words, we see claims to cultural citizenship through cultural expression. Moreover, DITD responds to anti-Latinx rhetoric and cultural exclusion by providing a place, space, and resources for Latinx dancer artists to band together and contest erasure and institutional exclusion in the field of dance. Regarding the gross underrepresentation of Latinx in dance, arts administrator Claudia added:

> And then also the very low-hanging fruit of representation. Many of us here have not had dance instructors, or teachers that look like us, that are Latinx, that understand our histories or understand our cultural understandings and placement within the world. Having representation at every level of dance creation whether it's dance instructors or dance critics that can write or speak about our work with proper context and language, researches, educators at the elementary school level and at the graduate and professional higher education level. Not seeing ourselves represented disproportionately at every single level of stakeholder that helps to build dance.

DITD becomes an opening for dancemakers to tell their stories, with their *frontera* worldview, through their art and reminds those across the field about the power they have to transform what and how stories are told through dance. Claudia continues:

> I didn't realize I had any power as an arts administrator before this past year . . . and I know so many Latinx arts administrators in New York City, in the Alvin Aileys, in the Martha Grahams, in the Dance Theatre of Harlems, in this huge institutions and we're not organized, because we're all just surviving. . . . None of us know how much power we have because we have internalized the racism, the narrative of survival for so long.

Holding space for Latinx dance artists to gather in Phoenix and Arizona in and of itself is, in many ways, a radical act and a first step toward eliminating Latinx erasure in dance. While claims to belonging and cultural citizenship do not "supplant or obviate the need for broader movements that can challenge class or hegemonic rule, the creation of social space and the claiming of rights can lead to powerful social movements. Latinos are creating social spaces (both physical and expressive) that knit together self-defined communities" (Flores and Benmayor, 1997, 277). Commenting on this erasure, participants in the first DITD cohort created a social media hashtag for the gathering that has been used in subsequent years by various members of the collective: #weexist. For us, this insistence—despite the erasure and exclusion—to exist, to express, and to belong marks DITD as a project that, through its insistence, will persist.

Conclusion

In this chapter, we have looked at how the anti-immigrant policies of the State of Arizona created an anti-Latinx climate that was felt across the Southwest. We argue that grassroots responses to these social conditions, like Dance in the Desert, are ways of pushing against this climate by creating a public presence that demonstrates belonging through cultural citizenship. Participants in DITD can assert cultural difference as they claim belonging and give citizenship meaning in their interactions. DITD creates opportunities in the *conviviencia diaria*—opportunities for relationships and opportunities for reimagining how dancemaking artists can bring to vision their stories as they fight for aesthetic equity in a field that all but ignores Latinx dancers. We know the experience we highlight in our work is not singular. Dance artist Alicia Mulliken (2020) reaffirms what we have learned from the narratives of DITD dancemakers when she writes, "As a first-generation Mexican American woman of color in the dance world, I have experienced microaggressions that have caused significant barriers to my progress as a dance artist and damaged my emotional health as a person of color—and yet, what I have endured is only a drop in the bucket." Our research supports Mulliken's experience of barriers and microaggressions; most dancers in DITD reported feelings of isolation, burnout, and even exclusion, with a handful of dancers reporting that they had left the field at various points in their careers. DITD is important for Latinx dancemakers because it creates a space to demonstrate cultural citizenship (a much-needed sense of belonging, a place for dancers to come together, have a voice and be heard, and build community) in the face of racism and exclusion in the world of dance and in U.S. society.

We also traced the limited literature on Latinx dancemaking to demonstrate DITD's potential and impact—essentially the archives of dance history erase the experiences of Latinx dancemakers. This work begins to address this vacuum, directly contributing to fields of dance and Latinx studies by centering Latinx dance makers and their voices. Dance in the Desert 2018 was a catalytic moment for Latinx dancemakers in Arizona and beyond because it offered a place and space for Latinx dancemakers to come together, conduct research, and build relationships. For many, Dance in the Desert marked the first time that Latinx dancemakers experienced a sense of understanding and belonging among a community of peers—providing a space for dancemakers to claim their own spaces for Latinx bodies, culture, and aesthetics in dance.

We conclude that in a region, and field, where Latinx peoples are often invisibilized or, worse yet, demonized, Dance in the Desert is offering a counter experience—one that centers their insistence and belonging to both. By creating a space that centers the movement of Latinx bodies when these bodies are so heavily restricted, DITD is building a movement that advocates for inclusion and visibility. In so doing, DITD invokes the human right to mobility and expression of cultural traditions and creative practice—one that invokes a shared experience that can best be understood as cultural

FIGURE 9.4   Dancers performing in *Viente* by Yvonne Montoya at Phoenix Hostel and Cultural Center, April 2018. Photo Courtesy of Yvonne Montoya & Dance in the Desert. Photo by Dominic Arizona Bonuccelli.

citizenship. Dancemakers who are culturally excluded are making claims to space and inclusion through cultural expression. They are carving out a new space for themselves in this world of dance, defying and remaking white aesthetics, and challenging the institutional and cultural exclusion of their racialized bodies. DITD contributes to the cultural fabric of the nation by sharing the experiences of Latinx communities; by enacting border stories, histories, and movements; and by centering aesthetics that remain largely unseen or grossly misunderstood by the mainstream United States.

Notes

1.   All names are pseudonyms to maintain anonymity.
2.   Dance in the Desert was founded by Yvonne Montoya. The 2018 project orga-
     nizers were Yvonne Montoya, Erin Donohue, and Gabriela Muñoz. Dance in
     the Desert 2018 was supported by *Safos* Dance Theatre, AZ Artworker, an ini-
     tiative of the Arizona Commission on the Arts, Liz Lerman LLC, ASU's Dean's
     Creativity Council, and Projecting All Voices, an initiative launched by ASU's
     Herberger Institute for Design and the Arts and supported by ASU Gammage.
     The research from this project was supported by WESTAF, the National En-
     dowment for the Arts.
3.   Latinx is a gender-neutral term that refers to the panethnic group referenc-
     ing the multiplicities of cultural, racial, and national identities of peoples from
     Latin American origins living in the United States. While we use this term in
     our chapter, if we are directly quoting from another author we follow their
     terminology which may vary between Latina/o or Latino.
4.   Several local arts organizations supported Yvonne Montoya's idea for bring-
     ing together Latinx dancemakers in Arizona. Through Montoya's fellowship at
     ASU, she was able to leverage the resources like meeting rooms, dance studios,
     access to gallery space, and additional funding for the project, which involved
     writing a handful of grants and project proposals and presenting the project to
     ASU's Herberger Institute for Design and the Arts Dean's Creativity Council, a
     shark-tank inspired event wherein ASU faculty propose projects to a group of
     local investors for funding.
5.   While we don't engage with Latinidad in this chapter conceptually, we un-
     derstand Latinidad as a way to refer to, as Rivera-Servera argues (2012), "the
     ethnic and panethnic imaginaries, identities, and affects that emerge from the
     increased intersection of multiple Latina/o communities" (22). Yet, as Aparacio
     (2017) has argued, "Latinidad has been highly contested and defined in various
     ways and also been claimed as a hemispheric framework for the study of the
     Americas, as well as critiqued and rejected as a label that homogenizes the rich
     heterogeneity of our communities and inadequately, if at all, recognizes the
     inclusion of Afro-Latinas/os and mixed-race Latinas/os" (113).

6. Montoya uses Ana Castillo's spelling of Xicana with a "X" instead of a "Ch." Castillo incorporates the use of the Nahuatl "X" in the spelling of Xicana to honor the indigenous roots of Chicana identities. Furthermore, the "X" challenges binaries and calls for solidarity while rejecting separatist nationalist ideologies. For more information, see Castillo (1994).
7. Mireya Guerra assisted with data collection and transcription of focus groups.
8. Light-skinned or blonde.
9. The color of your skin was different.
10. The BlakTinx Dance festival originates from Los Angeles, California, premiering for the first time in 2013 produced by choreographer, Licia Perea; and has been an annual production at the Bootleg Theatre for the past six years. In 2015, BlakTinx expanded to Tucson, Arizona, and later in 2017 to Phoenix, Arizona, with an annual show since then. The festival strives to diversify programming and audiences in the local dance scene and beyond. In 2019, the festival changed its name from BlakTina to BlakTinx, to be more inclusive and gender neutral. The festival focuses on contemporary dance but draws from many genres. Choreographers are encouraged to show work that is personal to them, and speaks about the Black and Latinx experience (BlakTinx n.d.).

References

Aparicio, Frances. 2017. "Latinidad/es," in *Keywords for Latina/o Studies*, edited by Deborah R. Vargas, Lawrence La Fountain-Stokes, and Nancy Raquel Mirabal, 113. New York: New York University Press.

Artifact Video Productions. 2018. "Dance in the Desert 2018 Community Share Out." Arrielle Pagac. Videographer. April 28, 2018.

BlakTinx. n.d. "BlakTinx: A Movement Festival of Cutting Edge Work, Celebrating Black and Latinx Choreographers." Accessed September 15, 2021. www.blaktina festival.com.

Castillo, Ana. 1994. *Massacre of the Dreamers: Essays on Xicanisma*. Albuquerque: University of New Mexico Press.

Cepeda, María Elena. 2010. "Singing the 'Star-Spanglish Banner' The Politics and Pathologizations of Bilinugalism in U.S. Popular Media," in *Beyond El Barrio: Everyday Life in Latina/o America*, edited by Gina M. Pérez, Frank A. Guridy, and Adrian Burgos, Jr., 27–43. New York: New York University Press.

Depenbrock, Julie. 2017. "Federal Judge Finds Racism Behind Arizona Law Banning Ethnic Studies." *All Things Considered*. National Public Radio, August 22, 2017. www.npr.org/sections/ed/2017/08/22/545402866/federal-judge-finds-racism -behind-arizona-law-banning-ethnic-studies.

Duara, Nigel. 2016. "Arizona's Once-Feared Immigration Law, SB 1070, Loses Most of its Power in Settlement." *Los Angeles Times*. September 15, 2016.

Figueroa, Brianna. 2018. *Ballet Hispánico: Constructing Latinx Identity Through Concert Dance*. PhD dissertation. Austin: University of Texas.

Flores, William V., and Rina Benmayor, eds., 1997. *Latino Cultural Citizenship: Claiming Identity, Space, and Rights*. Boston: Beacon Press.

Garcia, Cindy. 2013. *Salsa Crossings: Dancing Latinidad in Los Angeles*. Durham, N.C.: Duke University Press.

Gonzalez de Bustamante, Celeste, and Otto Santa Ana. 2012. *Arizona Firestorm: Global Immigration Realities, National Media, and Provincial Politics*. Lanham, Md.: Rowman Littlefield Publishers.

Kaiser Family Foundation. 2019. "Population Distribution by Race/Ethnicity." The Henry J. Kaiser Family Foundation. Accessed December 4, 2019. www.kff.org /other/state-indicator/distribution-by-raceethnicity/.

Montoya, Yvonne. 2019. "Who Takes Center Stage?: Xicana Epistemologies in Contemporary Dance," in *El Mundo Zurdo 7: Selected Works from the 2018 Meeting of the Society for the Study of Gloria Anzaldúa*, edited by Sara A. Ramírez, Larissa M. Mercado-López, and Sonia Saldívar-Hull, 95–108. San Francisco: Aunt Lute Books.

Mulliken, Alicia. 2020. "Recognizing Systemic Racism in Dance." *Seattle Dances*. June 19, 2020. http://seattledances.com/2020/06/recognizing-systemic-racism -in-dance/?fbclid=IwAR0B_KjnFPNUWaMWh_Hkffs-E4RjTY7EFkMC1AjFU9 LAqjHExlK4Rv34sTM.

Rivera-Servera, Ramon. 2012. *Performing Queer Latinidad: Dance, Sexuality, Politics*. Ann Arbor: University of Michigan Press.

Rivera-Servera, Ramon, and Harvey Yong. 2010. *Performance in the Borderlands*. London: Palgrave Macmillan.

Romero, Brenda M., Norma Elia Cantú, and Olga Najera-Ramirez. 2009. *Dancing Across Borders: Danzas y Bailes Mexicanos*. Champaign: University of Illinois Press.

Rosaldo, Renato. 1994. "Cultural Citizenship and Educational Democracy." *Cultural Anthropology* 9(3): 402–411.

———. 1997. "Cultural Citizenship, Inequality, and Multiculturalism," in *Latino Cultural Citizenship: Claiming Identity, Space, and Rights*, edited by William V. Flores, and Rina Benmayor, 27–38. Boston: Beacon Press.

———. 2009. "Cultural Citizenship." Academic texts. The Hemispheric Institute of Performance and Politics. Accessed August 31, 2021. https://hemisphericinstitute .org/en/enc09-academic-texts/item/681-cultural-citizenship.html.

Salinas Roén R. 2015. *Choreographing Borderlands: Chicanas/os, Dance, and the Performance of Identities*. PhD dissertation. Austin: University of Texas.

Suarez, Juanita. 2011. "Spectres in the Dark: The Dance-Making Manifesto of Latina/ Chicana Choreographies," in *Fields in Motion: Ethnography in the Worlds of Dance*, edited by Dena Davida, 403–26. Waterloo, Ontario: Wilfrid Laurier University Press.

Téllez, Michelle. 2015. "A Reflection on the Migrant Right's Movement." *Social Justice and Conflict. A Journal of Crime, Conflict and World Order* 42(3–4): 200–22.

Yosso, Tara J. 2005. "Whose Culture Has Capital? A Critical Race Theory Discussion of Community Cultural Wealth." *Race Ethnicity and Education* 8(1): 69–91.

CHAPTER 10

A City of *Puentes*

Latina/o Cross-Generational Memories and Organizing
in the 2016–17 Struggle for Sanctuary

GILDA L. OCHOA

Donald Trump's inflammatory language, exclusionary policy proposals, and unrepentant mocking of diverse groups of people permeated the 2016 presidential campaign. Such rhetoric unleashed a climate of hate that reverberated across the United States. In the first three days after the election, there were two hundred reported cases of hate crimes, harassment, and intimidation. For example, Latina/o[1] school children were told, "Go back where you come from," by classmates and even teachers. Others were threatened with deportation and harassed with chants of "Build that wall"—in reference to Trump's promise to construct a wall along the U.S.-Mexico border (Southern Poverty Law Center 2016). This vile climate incited both fear and activism—including in the predominately Latina/o, working-class city of La Puente, California—my own community where I have lived and conducted research for nearly thirty years.

Within days of the election, La Puente resident Manuel Maldonado invited three community members—including myself—to his home to strategize a local response to president-elect Trump's proposed actions. Observing activists in nearby cities, we were inspired to make La Puente a sanctuary city. As part of our organizing, long-time community members and younger college students coalesced as the Puente Coalition.

Following weeks of organizing, on January 10, 2017, the Puente Coalition lobbied the La Puente City Council to become a sanctuary city supporting immigrants, people of color, Muslims, LGBTQ people, and people with disabilities. Two weeks later, the Coalition called on the Hacienda-La Puente

Unified School District to also declare itself a sanctuary. By February 2017, the district became one of the 11 percent of California school districts to designate itself a safe haven (California Department of Education 2017).

Drawing on our established relationships and collective knowledge, we were able to move quickly because of decades of Latina/o and immigrant rights organizing and the coalition that was built between older residents and younger students. Over one hundred of us showed up to city council and school board meetings and presented our sanctuary resolutions. While organizing did not always proceed smoothly, and elected officials changed key components of our resolutions, we still rejoiced in our collective power in mobilizing, creating space for community voices, pushing elected officials, and being part of a larger sanctuary movement.

This chapter focuses on this 2016–17 cross-generational organizing effort. Informed by participant observations at city council and school board meetings, in-depth interviews, and my own involvement, it details the multiple ways the Puente Coalition (1) shared and drew upon generations of knowledge, including frameworks by feminists of color and undocumented youth activists, and (2) coalesced across generations to publicly assert a sense of belonging in city council and school board spaces. Undergirding this discussion is an analysis of how generational memories, inclusive and intersectional lenses, along with public assertions of belonging, were crucial aspects of this organizing. By centering the coalition's organizing approaches and frameworks, this chapter offers practical insights into the potential of cross-generational activism. It also enhances understanding of recent sanctuary struggles and the role of Latina/o communities in the struggle for belonging, especially in the context of the rise in blatant white supremacist, cis-heteropatriarchy discourses and actions.

Latina/o Generational Studies, Intersectionality, and Activism

To understand the processes influencing cross-generational organizing, I build on Flores-González's (2017) use of generations as an analytical lens and draw upon scholarship on intersectionality, immigrant youth activism, and cultural citizenship. Flores-González (2017) distinguishes four types of generational studies that can be applied to Latina/o identities and activist approaches (23–24). However, missing in Flores-González (2017) categorizations is a fifth generational approach that I develop in this chapter—one that considers both cross-generational relationships and the role of distinct generational memories in influencing organizing.

Analyzing the cross-generational mobilizations that occurred in La Puente reveals not only how context matters in terms of the socio-political periods influencing age-cohorts (Flores-González 2017), but, as social movement scholars illustrate, cross-generational relationships also influence activism: from adultism within organizations to providing youth with adult mentorship and support for youth-centered spaces (Cabaniss 2019; Ransby 2018; Gordon 2010). Likewise, I argue that *why* and *how* organizers participate and coalesce across different generations are informed by generational memories.

Focusing on individual life trajectories, the Latina Feminist Group's (2001) framework of "genealogies of empowerment" highlights how the memories of homelands, communities, families, and cultural traditions inform "individual paths" and "early lessons as blueprints" for life (21, 25). Similarly, Gonzales (2014) employs the concept "genealogies of struggle" to illustrate how generations of geographically-specific knowledge and organizing informed the 2006 immigrant rights marches in Greater Los Angeles (50). He details how the ideologies and organizational strategies of the 2006 Latina/o activists were rooted in at least one of three struggles: the 1960s and 1970s Chicano Movement, Central American Activists in the 1980s, and the 1990s California anti-immigrant Proposition 187 (50–55). Together, these "genealogies of empowerment" and "genealogies of struggle" frameworks historicize beliefs, actions, and movements. They also enhance awareness of how generations of Latina/o activists build on earlier struggles. By combining both the Latina Feminist Group's focus on individual life trajectories and Gonzales' emphasis on political contexts, I use the concept "Latina/o generational memories" to analyze organizing frameworks and approaches.

In La Puente, key to Latina/o generational memories is how community members used storytelling and personal narratives in both private and public spaces to make visible erased histories, draw connections between groups, inspire change, and reclaim stigmatized identities. In so doing, community members exerted what Flores and Benmayor (1997) term "cultural citizenship" by claiming space, along with rights to the city and schools (see Deeb-Sossa and Moreno 2015). However, the stories, frameworks, and displays of cultural citizenship differed across generations. Older Coalition members often rooted their organizing in the Chicano Movement and the United

Farm Workers, remembering legacies of racial segregation and race-based activism. In contrast, younger activists tended to draw on their experiences being Central American, DACA-mented, and/or Queer activists. They also relied on more recent work by feminists of color and undocumented youth activists to advocate for intersectional approaches that consider people's multiple identities and the interlocking factors shaping experiences.[2] Coined by Crenshaw (1989) to center the "multidimensionality of Black women's experience," an intersectional framework critiques a "single-axis lens" that considers race, class, *or* gender and advocates instead for an analysis that considers the simultaneity of intersecting systems such as patriarchy, heterosexism, and racism (139). Since this approach acknowledges both the salience of intersecting factors *and* people's multiple identities such that some can be both immigrant and Queer, it is also what Collins characterizes as a "both/and framework" (1990).

Scholarship on immigrant youth activism illustrates the growing use of intersectional both/and frameworks. As Seif (2014) recounts, in the early 2000s, the UndocuQueer youth movement raised public consciousness about the intersectional experiences of undocumented Queer immigrants. According to Terriquez's (2015) analysis of LGBTQ participation in the undocumented youth movement, there was a self-perpetuating process such that greater acknowledgment of people's multiple identities increased political participation among marginalized subgroups (358). For example, immigrant youth's use of "the coming-out strategy" associated with LGBTQ rights fostered greater LGBTQ inclusivity, and it increased "intersectional mobilization" and "intersectional consciousness" of marginalized subpopulations within marginalized communities (346).

Growing preferences for a both/and framework over an either/or approach also reflect criticism of some earlier activists who tried to push for immigration reform by adopting an assimilationist approach that presented select undocumented immigrants as models that fit within an "individualistic trope of the American Dream" (Seif 2014, 99). Such binary constructions of so-called "good" versus "bad" immigrants were a response to the framing employed by "the anti-migrant bloc" of conservative politicians, academics, and political pundits (Gonzales 2014, 6–8). Immigration reformers responded to the antimigrant bloc's hegemonic criminalization of migrants by championing particular immigrant stories and arguing that not all immigrants are "bad." This reactionary framing allowed conservatives to set the terms of the discussion. It perpetuates the criminalization of immigrants and fuels hierarchies by privileging some over others, and it removes the focus from the historical and structural factors shaping migration by blaming individuals for their assumed choice in migrating (Gonzales 2014).

Taken together, focusing scholarly attention on activists' distinct generational memories and varied frameworks assists in understanding ideologies, approaches, and possibilities for change. In the case of the Puente Coalition, cross-generational alliances deepened political consciousness and analytical frameworks. Furthermore, as Terriquez (2015) found in her research, more inclusive and intersectional frameworks by members of the Puente Coalition created public spaces of belonging for multiply marginalized Latinas/os to proclaim their intersecting identities. This claiming of multiple identities, along with rights to the city and schools, are powerful examples of "cultural citizenship" (Flores and Benmayor 1997). In La Puente, the exertion of cultural citizenship is enhanced because of its generational and intersectional approaches.

Research Background

The Puente Coalition consisted of a core group of about fifteen people. From November 2016 through May 2017, we met regularly—oftentimes twice a week—to strategize, draft resolutions, recruit community members, do press work, and lobby elected officials. We also spoke at biweekly city council and school board meetings.

All Coalition members are Latina/o—the majority are of Mexican descent. Almost all are immigrants or the children of immigrants, and several college students identified at DACA-mented, based on their status under the Deferred Action for Childhood Arrivals policy. Ranging in age from twenty to eighty years old, about half of the members were over the age of fifty. The other half were college students or recent college graduates in their twenties. All of the older participants were U.S. citizens.

Almost all were college-educated, and a few had graduate degrees. Most had long ties with the school district—many as high school graduates, some as parents with children in the district, and a few as district employees. Our deep connections to the district provided us with an awareness of various histories of inequalities as we experienced or observed them. These connections also enhanced our knowledge of local officials and policies, facilitating our organizing. While our educational backgrounds did not reflect the La Puente community, they added to the social capital and sense of entitlement enabling the Coalition to push for belonging in the city and schools.[3]

La Puente, California

Located in Los Angeles County, La Puente is a predominately working- and lower-middle-class Latina/o city with about forty thousand residents. Eighty-five percent of residents are Latina/o—the vast majority are Mexican and Mexican American. However, there is also a sizeable population of Central Americans who have lived in the city for decades—including my family who left Estelí, Nicaragua, in 1950 and eventually moved to La Puente. The remaining La Puente residents are Asian and Pacific Islander (12 percent), white (4 percent), and Black (1 percent). Overall, 40 percent of residents are immigrants, and 79 percent speak a language other than English at home (United States Census Bureau 2019). Sixty-five percent of adults have received a high school diploma or higher, and the median household income in 2019 dollars was $65,000. According to the U.S. Census (2019), 14 percent live below the poverty line. At the time of the struggle for sanctuary, four of the five city council members were Latina/o—the majority identifying as Mexican American and one as white.

Most La Puente residents live within the Hacienda-La Puente Unified School District (HLPUSD) boundary—one of the largest school districts in the Eastern San Gabriel Valley, with more than 18,000 students. Like the city, about 80 percent of students are Latina/o. Twenty percent are English language learners—primarily Spanish-speakers—and more than 70 percent are on free and reduced lunch (California Department of Education 2018).

From the time of its unification in the early 1970s, the wealthier, whiter, and now more Asian American community of Hacienda Heights has been unequally represented on the five-person school board. Only three people from La Puente have ever been elected to the board, and they have never served together. In 2017, one board member was from La Puente; all other members were from Hacienda Heights.[4] This lack of representation is reflected in inequities across the district such that La Puente schools have fewer academic programs, systems of support, and educational opportunities (Ochoa 2004).

Methodology and Positionality

As a La Puente resident, my work is informed by personal experiences, academic scholarship, and the qualitative research I have completed since the 1990s (see Ochoa 2004). This chapter is based primarily on participant observations from November 2016 through May 2017. During that period, I participated in Puente Coalition meetings held in members' homes, the community center, and the public library. I was also a frequent speaker during the public communication sections of the city council and school board meetings. Along with my notes, I analyzed recordings from city council sessions, newspaper articles, and the sanctuary resolutions and petitions. Beginning in April 2017, I also conducted thirty oral histories, ranging in length from 70 to 120 minutes, with community members involved with the struggle for sanctuary and elected officials.

While I did not set out to research this struggle, as the weeks passed, I conferred with members of the Coalition, and we agreed that writing about this organizing is part of the process of (re)membering and space-making that was so integral to the Latina/o cross-generational organizing among the Puente Coalition.[5]

Latina/o Cross-Generational Organizing for Sanctuary

I am a fourth year at UCLA and also a beneficiary of DACA . . . I stand before you and ask you to protect our brothers and sisters, be they undocumented, immigrants, women, Muslim citizens—all of those that stand in the president's ire and fascist agenda.

—College Student

Whether you are undocumented or you are LGBTQ, or Muslim, or anything that people want to try and talk about or put you down for, La Puente welcomes you. Hacienda-La Puente Unified School District welcomes you.

—HLPUSD teacher

As captured in these calls for sanctuary—the first to the city council by a student and the second to the school board by a teacher—the activism inspired by the Puente Coalition reflected (1) a cross-generational alliance of La Puente-area residents with distinct genealogies committed to justice; and (2) inclusive and intersectional frameworks that became the public narratives for change. It was inclusive because the sanctuary resolutions and individual demands named multiple groups who were explicitly impacted by the political climate. In some cases, it was also intersectional when at the urging of younger participants, community members adopted Crenshaw's (1989) conceptual lens and Collins's (1990) "both/and framework," advocating for an analysis that considers the salience of multiple intersecting identities and factors.

The differing generational memories within the coalition enabled the group to draw upon a legacy of resistance from local communities, feminist scholars of color, immigrant activists, and the histories more generally of Chicanas/os-Latinas/os. This reservoir of knowledge facilitated inclusive, intersectional, and historical frameworks. As such, it countered the exclusionary discourses at the federal level that pitted groups against each other.

Key to this cross-generational organizing was a reframing of dominant narratives and the exertion of concrete strategies to create public spaces of belonging for multiply marginalized community members. We did this through our resolutions, slogans, and symbols. The results were the passage of sanctuary and safe haven resolutions and powerful—yet momentary—assertions of belonging through space-making and identity claiming in city council and school board spaces.

Generational Memories

Undergirding the push for sanctuary was an understanding that this struggle was part of a history of injustice and resistance. This connection to the past emerged continuously at planning meetings and in public venues. Such remembering is a "radical act" of preventing erasure and "creating a sense of legacy" (Blackwell 2011, 11). For communities who are exiled and have experienced "dismemberment" because of war, displacement, and the denial of legal status, such "re/membering" can connect people to national communities, social history, and immigrant experiences (Coutin 2016, 3). It can also create space to reimagine a "more just future" (Coutin 2016, 7).

The sharing of these memories is rooted in a commitment to stop the reproduction of exclusion and prevent further injuries. However, this remembering reflects community members' varied generational memories. For Coalition members, these memories are shaped by factors such as the contexts under which we came of age and our own positionalities, including as US-born, citizen, resident, DACA-mented or undocumented. The remembering of these histories and the distinct ways community members entered the struggle for sanctuary punctuates the strengths of some of the Coalition's cross-generational organizing. However, as powerful as such remembering was, what became apparent during the oral histories is that precisely because of our distinct positionalities, not all of us were able to share our memories.[6] This was the case for those trying to forget stigmatized identities and the scars of war. The silences surrounding such histories and the ethnic and age demographics of the group inadvertently centered the histories of older Mexican American and Mexican immigrant organizers with citizenship privilege thereby resulting in more silence, even if unintentionally.

The testimonio by Manuel Maldonado, one of the longest-standing organizers in La Puente who was active in the Chicana/o Movement of the 1970s, illustrates in particular how older organizers rooted their activism in a legacy of racial/ethnic segregation: "The years that we have suffered, I remember when we came here to the United States in 1963. There were drinking fountains in parks that said 'Whites Only,' and there were fountains that were rusted and dirty that said 'Mexicans and Blacks.' I remember going to restaurants and reading the signs that would say 'Pets OK, but Mexicans and Blacks Not Allowed,' and things like that push me."

As a child, Manuel migrated from Mexico with his parents. He vividly recalls the hostile climate where signs publicly marked his exclusion. As a La Puente student, Manuel experienced such blatant marginalization by educators too: "I remember when I was in high school one of the coaches called us 'taco benders;' they would call us 'beaners.' That really frustrated me. Coming from a teacher, coming from an educated person, speaking to your students that way is not right."

When Manuel's children started school, he encountered more injustices as his activism increased: "At one of the meetings, board member Sandy Johnson called our children 'riffraff'—'All the riffraff from La Puente, how can we give them these classes,' you know trying to diminish and undermine our children. At another board meeting that a lot of our parents attended because we were asking to have more honors classes, she tried to say it in a soothing way or tried to compliment the parents who went with 'I really appreciate you leaving the soap operas behind to attend the board meetings.'"

As we gathered in homes and community spaces, older and more vocal organizers like Manuel often recalled this legacy of struggle. This included remembering decades of Spanish-language exclusion, underrepresentation on the school board, and fights for bilingual education. Such recollections rooted current struggles to a longer trajectory toward transformation. The sharing of these histories also disrupted the politics of division by connecting some of the struggles surrounding exclusion and belonging encountered by long-time residents because of race, class, and geography with more recent immigrants.

Coming of age in the 1990s and 2000s, younger community members also offered their own forms of remembering. For example, during her January 2017 public comments at the city council meeting where the community's sanctuary resolution was on the agenda, Rocío Mendoza linked the anti-immigrant climate of the 1990s epitomized in California's Proposition 187 with the current political climate: "[Before this meeting], I walked over to the library. It brought me back to when I was eleven years old and Prop 187 had been approved, and I remember the anti-immigrant sentiment. The fear that we had, and I remember how much that library felt like a sanctuary. Just thinking about those parallels . . . and now I think about what's happening with some of our family members feeling that fear, that anxiety and we are constantly feeling that."

In the 1990s, as California was in a severe economic recession, Mexican and Central American immigrants were scapegoated. Politicians and television commercials fueled xenophobic beliefs that undocumented immigrants were spreading diseases, draining social services, and stealing jobs. This hostile climate resulted in the passage of Proposition 187 in 1994, which tried to eliminate social services to undocumented immigrants. By remembering this climate, Rocío connects political and economic time periods, continual patterns of scapegoating, and feelings of fear and anxiety. By recalling too the haven the library provided her, she strategically offers a retelling of how La Puente was a sanctuary in the past, advocating that the city should be designated as such in the current period to ease contemporary fears.

For slightly younger community members who came of age in the 2010s— and were directly impacted by current immigration policies, memories of out-right exclusion were more recent. For instance, in an open petition for sanctuary to the school board, college student Lucia M. shared: "My family and I suffered first-hand the separation of our family which caused a huge financial, emotional, physical, and mental burden for not only myself but for my work, family, friends, and extended family. Although my situation has been resolved, the scars left behind will heal but can never be erased. With the passing of this request [sanctuary in our schools] I can find peace in knowing that others will not have to endure the pains that my family will live with forever."

Lucia's comments reveal how not all sanctuary supporters were equally impacted by the current political climate or were in similar positions to share publicly because of possible repercussions or even the hardship that remembering can bring.

For some, like Lucia, memories are "scars." They can be impossible or traumatic to recall. This was the case for Yael who during her oral history described having a "bad memory." As our conversation unfolded, she explained: "In high school, just thinking about my [immigration status] would make me have anxiety attacks. . . . My status caused me internalized shame that I feel like I held onto for such a long time. I was like, 'I'm not telling anyone.' It was just this really heavy secret I had carried with me for my entire life."

The stigma associated with being undocumented led Yael to hide her identity and lie about crucial aspects of her life until college, where she found a supportive community of other undocumented students. However, the years of keeping this "really heavy secret" have taken a toll on her memory, making it difficult to recall aspects of her past.

Such processes of remembering were key to organizing. Sharing these histories connected community members together and across time. Likewise, by recalling past experiences, as Lucia M. described, there was an attempt at preventing the reproduction of "financial, emotional, physical, and mental burden[s]." However, since not all were able to share their histories because of the trauma associated with them or other forms of erasure, the histories of older Mexican American and Mexican immigrant citizens were often centered during Puente Coalition's meetings because these were the ones typically shared. This may have inadvertently silenced participants with differing pasts, and it may reflect some of the age and immigration status hierarchies observed in other activist groups (Cabaniss 2019; see Gordon 2010). However, in both the construction of the resolutions and during public comments at city and school board meetings, youth drew more publicly from their lived realities, immigrant rights activism, and knowledge of feminists of color to push for inclusive and intersectional sanctuary resolutions. As illustrated in the next two sections, by doing so, they asserted multiple identities and helped to expand the spaces of belonging for the expression of other marginalized voices.

Inclusive and Intersectional Framing

Throughout our activism, we argued that the sanctuary resolutions had to be "inclusive" and could not perpetuate the politics of division invoked by the federal administration. Moving beyond just an inclusive framework, younger participants also drew upon women of color scholars and UndocuQueer youth activists to advocate for an intersectional both/and lens.

In constructing the sanctuary resolutions, the Coalition emphasized various community struggles. For the city's resolution, the Coalition borrowed language from the nearby predominately Latina/o working-class city of Pomona that passed a resolution using a similar approach: "Declaring the City of La Puente a sanctuary city that supports and denounces potential threats to our City of La Puente residents who are immigrants, people of color, Muslims, LGBTQ people and people with disabilities; and reaffirming the City's commitment to diversity and safeguarding the civil rights, safety and dignity of all our residents."

For the school district, we first created an online petition and then presented our proposed resolution.[7] The petition called for "declaring HLPUSD a sanctuary/safe zone district that would protect disabled, immigrant, LGBTQ, Muslim, and female students from the stated threats of the incoming presidential administration." Nearly 250 community members signed the petition urging the board to "make a strong statement to assuage the fears and uncertainty in our community" by:

1. Protecting the information of students and families from inquiries by ICE [Immigration and Customs Enforcement] or any government agency into the legal status or religious affiliations of students and their families;
2. Pledging not to cooperate with ICE in the detention of students and employees;
3. Protecting and supporting LGBTQ, women, and disabled students and staff and carrying out the laws that support them (including bathroom laws);
4. Developing trainings for parents and classified and certificated employees;
5. Developing and implementing an ethnic studies curriculum that addresses race, class, gender, and sexuality throughout the curriculum.

The Coalition's inclusive resolution proved confusing to some elected officials. After initially presenting our community resolution at a council meeting on December 20, 2016, a council member instead proposed making La Puente a Sanctuary City for Immigrants. That proposal was modeled after a 2015 resolution from a nearby working-class Latina/o city. However, Puente Coalition members believed that in the current political climate adopting a resolution for only immigrants would be exclusionary. So, we met with the council member to explain our position.

This discussion was pivotal in delineating who would be included in the resolution, and it enabled a crucial distinction between an inclusive framework—that lists all impacted groups—and one that is also intersectional. The youngest attendee at that meeting, María José, a college student, took the lead by advocating for an "intersectional lens"—one that acknowledges people's multiple identities and the interlocking factors shaping experiences. María José expanded on how some members of the community are not only undocumented but may also identify as LGBTQ.

This discussion moved the group's understanding away from just an inclusive resolution to one that captured the nuances of identities and acknowledged multiple structures impinging on people's lives. Through dialogue, the collective understanding became that if we only advocated for immigrants, we were forcing people to select one identity—giving primacy to immigrant status and anti-immigrant policies over other aspects of peoples' backgrounds and the significance of intersecting systems such as patriarchy, heterosexism, and racism.

In refining the sanctuary resolution, María José also urged the Coalition to avoid prevailing either/or binaries of "the good immigrant" versus "the bad immigrant" that have permeated popular discourse and some immigrant rights organizing (see Nicholls 2013). To avoid reinforcing anti-immigrant discourses, she proposed eliminating the following phrase from the initial community resolution: "Most residents in the City, including the vast majority of immigrants, are law-abiding citizens and are, when crimes occur, themselves the victims of crime." While all in attendance agreed that such framing pits groups against each other, it took María José's explanation to ensure its removal.

When the same city council member wondered if another council member might oppose including LGBTQ people in the resolution because he is Mormon, supporters of our resolution would not allow the use of religion to exclude. Community members quickly explained that not all religions or religious people oppose the rights of LGBTQ community members. As evidence, the oldest attendee, a member of the local Methodist Church, passed around a written statement of her church's support for LGBTQ community members. This discussion allowed for the disruption of divisive approaches to inclusion that marginalize LGBTQ community members and impede change. Such politics of division are also either/or single-axis in that they focus on either documentation status *or* sexualities, or they falsely assume that religious people cannot also support or be LGBTQ community members.

Part of shifting the prevailing narrative involved including DACA-mented school employees in the sanctuary resolution for the school district—not just students who have been spotlighted nationally as more worthy of support. An emphasis on supporting seemingly innocent youth over supposedly culpable adults stigmatizes and criminalizes older immigrants (Gonzales 2014). Disrupting this framework, the Coalition intentionally included this statement: "The District will continue to protect the data and identities of any student, family member, or *school employee* who may be adversely affected by any future policies or executive action resulting in the collection of any personally identifiable information to the fullest extent provided by law" (emphasis added).

When they voted for sanctuary, the city councilors and school board members removed such actionable items, along with staff trainings and the creation of task forces, from the sanctuary resolutions. Nevertheless, the Coalition's intersectional, both/and framing successfully built on a legacy of resistance and undermined majoritarian narratives embodied by both Trump's exclusionary paradigms and liberal discourses pitting groups against each other. As such, at the urging of a younger generation of activists, the Coalition's framing expanded the parameters of inclusion and belonging beyond immigration and narrow constructions of so-called good immigrants, and it created space for more intersectional approaches. Such opening up of space was especially transparent during the public meetings where community members exerted our collective strength and rights to the city, including through clear assertions of marginalized identities.

Cross-Generational Forms of Cultural Citizenship: Space-Making and Asserting Identities

With their formal, top-down, bureaucratic structures and exclusionary institutional practices, city halls and school board chambers are not welcoming places, especially for community members from marginalized groups. Attendees are expected to sit passively in rows and observe elected officials conduct business. The only official space for active community participation is during the public comment portion of meetings when, after submitting written requests during a designated time slot, individuals have two to three minutes each to address elected officials at podiums. While headsets are available for simultaneous translation at school board meetings, no interpretation services are provided at La Puente council meetings. Uniformed police officers are also visible at both locations. At the school district, the police officer often towers over community members speaking at the podium. Despite this rigid structure and chilly environment, Puente Coalition and other community members pushed back against expected modes of comportment and asserted our belonging. Here too, distinct generational approaches were apparent in these displays of cultural citizenship. Older organizers drew upon legacies from the Chicano Movement, the United Farm Workers, and Dr. Martin Luther King. Younger activists provided testimonials as they publicly proclaimed their identities.

At the city council and school board meetings, older Coalition members called for supporters to wear red to convey solidarity and the urgency of achieving sanctuary. Word spread through social media and phone calls,

FIGURE 10.1 Spanish-speaking mothers advocating for sanctuary in the Hacienda La Puente Unified School District as a police officer watches, January 26, 2017. Photo by author.

and hundreds of people filled the two chambers. The symbolic display of Latinas/os wearing red and occupying these spaces sent a clear message to elected officials about the community's ability to act swiftly and exert our collective power.

Drawing on his experiences and media connections, long-time activist Javier Rodriguez drafted and disseminated press releases about the Coalition's resolutions. As a result, an hour before the city council vote, the parking lot and city hall lobby were filled with Puente Coalition members spreading the group's messages to Spanish and English-speaking reporters. This strategically enabled the group to frame the narrative and reach a wider audience.

In writing the resolutions, lobbying officials, galvanizing the community and the media, and then filling the chambers, the Puente Coalition destabilized the typical atmosphere at meetings by flipping the expected roles of community members and elected officials. During these meetings, as the mayor and school board president tried to continue with business as usual, community members did not easily comply. After each person spoke in favor of sanctuary, there were shouts and applause. At key moments, Puente Coalition member Marta Sámano led the community in clapping and chanting of "Sí, se puede." The use of this classic chant begun by Dolores Huerta in 1972 with the United Farm Workers—an organization with which Marta spent her early years working—was a reminder of the legacy of Chicana/o struggle and cross-generational knowledge. Chanting and clapping united the group and remade the chambers into a rally where community members were no longer passive observers. When the city council and then the school board weeks later voted for sanctuary and safe haven respectively, most in attendance burst out in cheers. After the successful city council vote, Marta Sámano led a chant of "Sí, se pudo [Yes, we did]." The community joined in for several rounds, until the mayor called for decorum. Afterward and before the end of the meeting, community members rushed to the lobby where we celebrated with hugs and selfies. The Puente Coalition successfully claimed a political space and representational presence conveying our sense of belonging.

As part of reclaiming the city hall, coalition members defined how we wanted the city to be known. Both during the press conference and at the meeting, the rallying call became, "We are a city of puentes [bridges], not paredes [walls]." As Enrique Ochoa insisted during his public comments:

FIGURE 10.2 Community selfie after sanctuary resolution passes in La Puente, January 10, 2017. Photo by Alonzo Campos.

"That's why it's called La Puente!" This framing was in opposition to Trump's plan to expand a border wall. Yet, since it was also directed at the city council, we claimed the name and normalized the idea that at its core La Puente is a place of sanctuary.

Community members who signed the petition and spoke at packed meetings echoed the collectivist ethos of Puente Coalition's resolutions. Written and oral statements were instrumental in claiming space, making connections, and asserting a sense of belonging. They also reflect the use of personal narratives adopted by youth in the immigrant rights movement to convey points and come out of the shadows (see Zimmerman 2016, 1895). Such comments on the petition to the school board are illustrative:

> I have family and friends that are undocumented. I'm Queer and a person of color, all mentioned identities are among those that are at threat under the new presidential regime. As an alumnus and a member of those communities under threat, I'm signing as a responsibility to help protect those identities and others that are current and future students (Antonio R.).

> As a member of the LGBTQ community I had it easy. I was very well supported by my friends and family. Not everyone else has the same opportunity

to be themselves without hate. Also, as a proud Latina I refuse to let families be separated (Bianca M.).

As with these written declarations, during oral communications, speakers often began by proudly proclaiming their identities and connections to the city and school district. This included undocumented students, Queer alumni, and people with disabilities. María José's statement to the city was emblematic: "I identify as undocumented—a DACA-mented student since 2012. But, in the face of this election of Donald Trump, a lot of us are in fear that the privilege that we've been granted can be revoked."

During her oral history, María José reflected on how it felt to share her identity in this way: "That first event, the introduction of asking city council for sanctuary, I think that was one of the first times that I remember I talked about being undocumented very publicly in La Puente. I had done it I think in very different scenarios outside of La Puente. Yea, but never here. That was really complex, very complicated, and it gave me a lot of different feelings."

The push for sanctuary and María José's involvement created space for proclaiming her identity verbally through storytelling but also physically showing up to the city and school board chambers. As María José observed, by participating in this struggle she became aware of the previously undisclosed status of her friends' parents:

A lot of my peers that I went to school with, their parents were also undocumented, but it wasn't something that was public conversation. I remember seeing some of their parents at that [city council] meeting too, and I was like, "Oh! Now I know." A lot of my parents' church community members are also undocumented, and they were there that night too. So, it was really emotional because I wasn't only speaking for myself and also kind of telling my parents story, but also telling the stories of so many people who lived through the same realities that they don't always share that history because it's terrifying to share because if it lands in the wrong ears it can be dangerous potentially.

Reflecting Puente Coalition's both/and framework that aimed to avoid the pitting of groups against each other, another student declaring her DACA-mented status at the city council meeting disrupted the narrative that only youth who are labeled DREAMers are worthy of support:

Fortunately, I was able to apply for DACA, but our president-elect Trump has alluded that we are still undocumented. I'm afraid. And it's not just feeling sad for my parents; it's for my community, for all the community. So that's why I decided to mobilize and organize and represent my peers. And not that I believe we are DREAMers. They call us DREAMers, but our parents are the original dreamers. Nuestros padres son los originales. Nuestros padres tuvieron el sueño. They had the dream to come to this country to leave everything behind.[8]

While most of the speakers emphasized their support for immigrant, undocumented, and LGBTQ community members, several also advocated for people with disabilities. Brian was the first to address the city council on the evening of the vote. After invoking Dr. Martin Luther King's dream "that one day his children will grow up in a society where they will not be judged by the color of their skin but by the content of their character," Brian called for the support of all dreamers who for him include people without official papers in the U.S. and those with disabilities: "I commend the Council for leading the fight to ensure that people with developmental disabilities are represented. That people with autism like myself—who have autism and Asperger—that regardless of someone's disability that they have the correct and reasonable access to pursue their dreams in life."

In the city council and school board chambers where La Puente and Latina/o families have a history of feeling ignored and where public discussions of immigration, sexuality, and disabilities are rare, there was a feeling of vindication. As one after another community member advocated for the resolutions and against a hostile national climate where such groups were blatantly targeted, community members erupted in applause and chants of "*Sí, se puede.*"

Using the city council, school district, and online public spaces to claim identities that are under assault, undocumented and LGBTQ community members specifically insisted that such spaces embrace them and their demands. As such, they "push[ed] the boundaries of historically exclusionary public sphere[s]" (Zimmerman 2016, 1895). Their powerful claims to space and belonging reflect similar approaches utilized by immigrant youth in cities, schools, and media sites throughout the United States. As part of larger movements, undocumented youth have declared their immigration status as ways to "contest the power of the law, which sustains itself through the silencing of migrants who live in the shadow" (Zimmerman 2016, 1892). By publicly naming their immigration status, undocumented community members "testify to their own experiences" and "make claims to citizenship as rights-bearing subjects" (Zimmerman 2016, 1895). As Seif (2014) writes in her work with UndocuQueer youth, "When people 'come out,' they often reclaim the language of stigma and insult" (95). Terriquez (2015) demonstrates that when immigrant youth organizers use "the coming out strategy" associated with LGBTQ rights there are "boomerang effects" such that LGBTQ activists may feel more included and more willing to come out, also increasing their political involvement. The inclusively designed resolution and the sharing of testimonials may have opened-up spaces of belonging for multiple marginalized community members to offer their stories and push for change in these public venues, even though these narratives were less visible in the more private spaces of the Puente Coalition meetings.

Conclusion

In response to the political climate and inspired by organizers throughout California, Latinas/os in La Puente successfully drew on decades of organizing to coalesce as the Puente Coalition. We activated our relationships and experiences to quickly mobilize and pressure elected officials to pass sanctuary resolutions. Public attacks on multiple communities, along with our cross-generational knowledge of historical inequities, feminists of color theories, and undocumented struggles, informed our inclusive and oftentimes intersectional both/and public framework.

During a time of heightened fear and uncertainty, our mobilizing united and inspired community members. It connected us to larger struggles throughout the U.S. and historically. The victories were a testament to the power of cross-generational community organizing. We demanded that those in charge do the right thing and not be collaborators in carrying out hateful policies.

For a period, the Puente Coalition organizing fostered public space for communities often on the margins in the city and school district to publicly proclaim multiple identities and share experiences—enhancing understanding and expanding discourse. Cross-generational alliances and generational memories were instrumental in this process. Within Puente Coalition meetings, older more established U.S.-citizen Mexican Americans and Mexican immigrants framed much of the storytelling about the legacy of racial/ethnic exclusion. These generational memories helped historize aspects of the contemporary struggles, but they left out other voices and memories. This limited the verbal participation of younger members within the Coalition. However, younger and DACA-mented students were crucial in refining the La Puente sanctuary resolution to be more intersectional, and they publicly offered their testimonials about what the current political climate means. As such, they complicated understandings and opened up space for additional voices.

The activism even provided opportunities for elected officials and others to push for change, although in fewer ways than we desired (Ochoa 2021).[9] Nevertheless, community members remain undeterred. Just as elected officials noticed the quick organizing of the Puente Coalition, the resolutions are now a base for community members to continue struggling.

For academics and community activists, this example provides an important illustration of the power and possibilities of cross-generational Latina/o organizing and the roles of distinct memories, frameworks, and ways of expressing cultural citizenship—including from the symbols, chants, and stories shared. Ignoring these generational variations in scholarship and organizing perpetuates the very silences apparent in Puente Coalition meetings when particular memories and voices were centered. It also hides cross-generational strengths and how such organizing—especially when informed by inclusive and intersectional frameworks—can enhance political consciousness, increase participation of historically excluded groups, and facilitate institutional change.

Notes

1. Unless referring to a specific group, I use the term Latina/o throughout this chapter. I use Latina/o not to conflate the heterogeneous experiences of people included in this panethnic category but instead to be inclusive and to draw upon a term used often by La Puente community members. At the time of this writing, Latinx is increasingly common on college and university campuses. Latinx is important for disrupting gender binaries, but at the time of this organizing it was not used by the community members who are the focus of this chapter.
2. This reflects patterns by other youth activists such as Black Lives Matter (see Ransby 2018).
3. Thanks to Paula Ayala for highlighting how longevity in a city and class privilege influences a sense of entitlement to organize.
4. In 2019–20, members of the Puente Coalition worked with other community members to change the at-large structure of voting in the district to by-area elections. This now ensures greater representation (Coreas et al. 2020).

5. As part of this remembering, I use the names people gave in public venues or the ones they gave me permission to use during the oral histories.
6. For Central Americans, there are many silences surrounding the trauma of civil wars and other forms of violence. This makes it difficult for some to remember—either because of the trauma that remembering invokes or because these histories have been excluded from family knowledge and academic curriculum (Abrego 2017).
7. We drew on local school district resolutions, along with the United We Dream Tool Kit.
8. The DREAM (Development, Relief and Education for Alien Minors) Act was introduced in the U.S. Congress in 2001 as a pathway for citizenship and pushed for by immigrant rights groups (Nicholls 2013, 48). Inspired by this legislation, undocumented students and immigrant organizations used DREAMer to identify (Zimmerman 2016, 1887). This term was more common before 2012 when after pressure then-President Obama issued the DACA executive order when Congress did not pass the DREAM Act.
9. On October 5, 2017, Governor Brown signed the California Values Act (SB 54).

References

Abrego, Leisy. 2017. "On Silences: Salvadoran Refugees Then and Now." *Latino Studies Journal* 15(1): 73–85.

Blackwell, Maylei. 2011. *Chicana Power! Contested Histories of Feminism in the Chicano Movement.* Austin: University of Texas Press.

Cabaniss, Emily R. 2019. "'Shifting the Power': Youth Activists' Narrative Reframing of the Immigrant Rights Movement." *Sociological Inquiry* 89(3): 482–507.

California Department of Education. 2017. "California Safe Haven School District List." Accessed August 31, 2021. www.cde.ca.gov/eo/in/casafehavendistrictslist.asp.

———. 2018. Data Quest Reports Files. California Department of Education. https://dq.cde.ca.gov/dataquest/.

Collins, Patricia Hill. 1990. *Black Feminist Thought: Knowledge Consciousness, and the Politics of Empowerment.* New York: Routledge.

Coreas, Jessica, Bryan Coreas, Eugene Fujimoto, Enrique C. Ochoa, Gilda L. Ochoa, María Oropeza Fujimoto, and Socorro Orozco. 2020. "¡Juntos Podemos! Community Organizing, the California Voting Rights Act (CVRA) and the Struggle for School Transformation in a Southern California School District." *Journal of Latinos and Education* 31: 1–14.

Coutin, Susan Bibler. 2016. *Exiled Home: Salvadoran Transnational Youth in the Aftermath of Violence.* Durham, N.C.: Duke University Press.

Crenshaw, Kimberlé. 1989. "Demarginalizing the Intersection of Race and Sex: A Black Feminist Critique of Antidiscrimination Doctrine, Feminist Theory and Antiracist Politics." *University of Chicago Legal Forum* 1989(1). Art. 8. http://chicagounbound.uchicago.edu/uclf/vol1989/iss1/8.

Deeb-Sossa, Natalia, and Melissa Moreno. 2015. "No Cierren Nuestra Escuela! Farm Worker Mothers as Cultural Citizens in an Educational Community Mobilization Effort." *Journal of Latinos and Education* 15(1): 39–57.

Flores, Williams V., and Rina Benmayor. 1997. "Introduction: Constructing Cultural Citizenship." In *Latino Cultural Citizenship: Claiming Identity, Space, and Rights*, edited by William V. Flores and Rina Benmayor, 1–23. Boston: Beacon Press.

Flores-González, Nilda. 2017. *Citizens But Not Americans: Race & Belonging Among Latino Millennials*. New York: New York University Press.

Gonzales, Alfonso. 2014. *Reform Without Justice*. New York: Oxford University Press.

Gordon, Hava Rachel. 2010. *We Fight to Win: Inequality and the Politics of Youth Activism*. New Brunswick, N.J.: Rutgers University Press.

Latina Feminist Group, ed. 2001. *Telling to Live: Latina Feminist Testimonios*. Durham, N.C.: Duke University Press.

Nicholls, Walter J. 2013. *The DREAMers: How the Undocumented Youth Movement Transformed the Immigrant Rights Debate*. Stanford: Stanford University Press.

Ochoa, Gilda L. 2004. *Becoming Neighbors in a Mexican American Community: Power, Conflict and Solidarity*. Austin: University of Texas Press.

———. 2021. "The Interlocking Processes Constraining the Struggle for Sanctuary in the Trump Era: The Case of La Puente, CA." *Social Sciences* 10(5). www.mdpi.com /2076-0760/10/5/155/html.

Ransby, Barbara. 2018. *Making All Black Lives Matter: Reimagining Freedom the Twenty-First Century*. Oakland: University of California Press.

Seif, Hinda. 2014. "'Coming Out of the Shadows' and 'Undocuqueer': Undocumented Immigrants Transforming Sexuality Discourse and Activism." *Journal of Language and Sexuality* 3(1): 87–120.

Southern Poverty Law Center. 2016. "Over 200 Incidents of Hateful Harassment and Intimidation Since Election Day." November 11, 2016. www.splcenter.org /hatewatch/2016/11/11/over-200-incidents-hateful-harassment-and-intimidation -election-day.

Terriquez, Veronica. 2015. "Intersectional Mobilization, Social Movement Spillover, and Queer Youth Leadership in the Immigrant Rights Movement." *Social Problems* 62: 343–62.

U.S. Census Bureau. 2019. "U.S. Census American Fact Finder." www.census.gov /quickfacts/lapuentecitycalifornia.

Zimmerman, Arely. 2016. "Transmedia Testimonio: Examining Undocumented Youth's Political Activism in the Digital Age." *International Journal of Communication* 10: 1886–1906.

PART IV

Concluding Thoughts

CHAPTER 11

Latinx Belonging and Solidarity in the Twenty-First Century

(Re)Constructing the Meaning of Community in the Era of COVID-19

SUZANNE OBOLER

> It is solidarity which transforms a loose aggregate of individuals into a community;
> it supplements their physical coexistence with a moral one, thereby raising their
> interdependence to the rank of a community of fate and destiny.
>
> —Zygmunt Bauman, 2013

Since the last quarter of the twentieth century, and particularly as a result of the neoliberal ideology that has permeated U.S. culture and society in the post-Reagan years, a general malaise, resulting from a rising antagonism against the very notion of "difference," has increasingly affected daily life across the country. Frequent racial and xenophobic examples of harassment, of raids and ongoing attacks on immigrants, persist, as does the increased domestic violence against Latinx women and LGBTQ+. The violence of the border patrol and growing presence of the national guard continues to reinforce the ongoing militarization of the southern border. At the same time, the nefarious effects of the unrelenting cruelty of the Trump administration's policies against asylum-seeking families and unaccompanied child refugees have persisted well into President Biden's first year in office (Tribuno del Pueblo/People's Tribune 2021; Rodriguez 2021).

The Trump Administration's open embrace of white supremacist ideology, today given a free pass by the nation's state institutions and civic (mis)behavior, was further exacerbated by the public assassination of George Floyd on May 25, 2020. It supports the ongoing impunity, visible to all, of police and state institutions who murder people of color. And it continues unabated, regardless of whether the mainstream media publicly acknowledges it, or generally ignores it, as it is prone to do in the case of the shooting deaths of Latinxs, whether by police in cities and towns, or by the border patrol.[1]

Few would deny the expanding gap in the economic and social disparities in the United States over the past few decades.[2] Fueled by the greed of the elites, and exacerbated by the COVID-19 pandemic, it, too, is overtly driven by the white supremacist, institutional racism that continues to further entrench the nation's long legacy of organized hatred and division based on racial difference. This, in turn, gives credence to Adam Serwer's (2020) assessment of the resulting devastating and otherwise entirely preventable consequences of the coronavirus pandemic among people of color: "The pandemic," he writes, "has exposed the bitter terms of our racial contract, which deems certain lives of greater value than others" (n.p.).

Still, underlying the spiraling weight currently attributed to ideas of difference in American society, is another, perhaps more pressing crisis—a crisis that is not only American, but actually international in scope. It is a crisis that centers on the very notion of national communities, of human collectivities themselves. Already apparent in the 1980s, during the early years of the nation's embrace of neoliberalism, the extent of the impact of its repercussions on the national community has only become fully unveiled today. As the excesses of the still-recent Trump presidency have unambiguously highlighted, what is ultimately at stake is not so much the issue of difference itself, but rather the whole question of what might bind people together into a collectivity. The unprecedented weight currently attributed to difference only makes sense in the broader context of questioning what does, what should, and, actually, what *could* bind people together—particularly in the post-Trump era, as we enter the third decade of the twenty-first century. From this perspective, the very prevalence of the often-virulent debates on, and responses to difference in the public sphere, can best be understood as both a symptom of the extent of the current crisis of community in the United States, and as a contributing factor to it.

In this context of a declining national community, how then can we even approach the question of Latinx belonging in the United States?

Background to the Crisis

Early signs of the crisis of community could already be seen in the years following the civil rights movements of the 1950s to mid-1970s. The racializing labels created in 1977, which ultimately divided the population of the United States, moved the organization of U.S. society away from the very notion of a national community into what are ultimately five official statistical populations, today colloquially referred to as White/European, African American/ Black, Asian American/Pacific Islander, Hispanics or Latinxs, and Native Americans. Created in the immediate aftermath of the civil rights movement, the intention of these labels was at least in part to assist in measuring the nation's progress in integrating racial minorities and ensuring equality to all under the law (Mora 2014; Hattam 2007; Oboler 1995). Yet, today, more than forty years later, the consequences of differentiating racialized and ethnic groups and categorizing them into five arbitrarily-defined statistical populations have been contradictory.

On the one hand, to some extent, the labels undoubtedly allowed for the political inclusion for which racial and ethnic minorities had fought during the 1960s Civil Rights movements. At the same time, as the report by President Clinton's race task force already concluded twenty years after their creation, the racial/ethnic categories have served to reinforce the very idea of the superiority of whiteness and "white privilege" in U.S. society—hence, ultimately fortifying the existing social and racial hierarchy (Holmes 1998).

The response by racialized and ethnic minorities in different parts of U.S. society was to redefine the political reality of these labels. In so doing, they sought to build and/or strengthen their respective group's "imagined communities" (Anderson 1983), even as the mainstream society reinforced its own socio-racial and "ethnic" hierarchy. By the mid-1990s, observing the perception and consequent societal repositioning of Latinxs, Mexican American scholar Leo Chavez (1997) pointed out: "Immigrants, even those who are legal residents and citizens, are being re-imagined as less deserving members of the community."

Indeed, for many Latinxs, particularly undocumented immigrants as well as for U.S.-born or raised children of immigrants, the label "Hispanic" quickly came to provide the only sense of community and belonging they had. Undoubtedly, this sense of belonging—this "cultural citizenship," as scholars Renato Rosaldo, Rena Benmayor, and William Flores (1997) described it at the time—was, in obvious ways, very positive. After all, there is power in numbers, and in this sense, from early on, the labels clearly contributed to mobilizing the respective populations around particular issues. Shunned by U.S. society, whether for racial, linguistic, social, or historical reasons, membership in a broader Latinx community could instead be easily affirmed. For the labels provided the Latinx population with both a temporary sense of belonging and what Felix Padilla's (1985) pioneering study had defined at the time as a "situational identity."

Still, despite the powerful mobilizing and inclusive force that the labels helped to reinforce over time, ultimately, their affirmation through legitimizing membership ("cultural citizenship") in these statistical, imagined communities created by government fiat, has also come to signal the decline of the national community. After all, *all* categories of membership, of citizenship, and of rights, have to be publicly discussed in relation to all the community's members involved, rather than in relation to only one or another population. This idea has been incorporated into the constitutional history of the United States since the Fourteenth Amendment was ratified by Congress in 1868. By the end of the twentieth century, however, it had become clear that it was increasingly up to each particular racialized "ethnic group"—rather than the larger society—to make and/or minimally lead public responses to injustices perpetrated upon its individual members. To this day, for example, it remains up to "Hispanics" to denounce and remind society of the infringement of the rights of people of Latin American descent in the United States, regardless of their citizenship or legal status. This is the case whether the injustices at hand refer to the fate of immigrants, the violation of an individual's rights, the deepening poverty of and discrimination against Latinxs; the killings of Latinxs either by police departments across the nation, by the U.S. Border Patrol, or white supremacist vigilantes, such as the twenty-two-year-old white nationalist who committed premeditated mass murder in El Paso, Texas, on August 3, 2019, killing twenty-three Latinxs, including U.S. and Mexican citizens, in addition to injuring twenty-three other people.

Similarly, the countless murders and senseless deaths of people of African descent at the hands of police have also exemplified the extent to which the response to each racist attack is ultimately the responsibility of the specifically targeted ethnic or racial group. In 2013, the anger of the African American community at the acquittal of George Zimmerman, who murdered Trayvon Martin, led three women organizers to create #BlackLivesMatter (BLM) as a "movement building project" (Black Lives Matter n.d.). By the summer of 2020, the movement's organizers had created BLM chapters across the United States, as well as a global BLM network. The movement's increasingly massive mobilizations finally forced national society to acknowledge its role in the brutal deaths of fellow citizens, including George Floyd in Minneapolis, Breonna Taylor in Louisville, Ahmaud Marquez Arbery in Satilla Shores, Georgia, and so many other African American men and women who have been murdered or, like Jacob Blake in Kenosha, permanently injured by the violence of the police. Protests across the country, particularly following the on-camera murder of George Floyd by a police officer on May 25, 2020, are forcing broader society to recognize the extent to which passivity and inaction on the part of the country's government and citizenry alike are responsible for the ongoing police killings of African Americans and other people of color.[3] As people mobilize and come together, it is highlighting—and making visible to all—the extent to which the racializing ethnic labels have contributed to the ultimately-arbitrary fragmentation and decline of a broader national community to which all members of the society collaborate and in which everyone participates and belongs. In the context of a pandemic, this recognition is also simultaneously being fueled by a growing societal awareness of the invisible contributions that Latinxs, like other people of color, have long made as "essential workers" in U.S. society.

Latinxs as Essential Workers

The Latinx population includes the most vulnerable members of U.S. society. Despite the fact that at least 79 percent of the roughly 60.6 million Latinxs in this country are U.S. citizens either by birth or naturalization, a disproportionate number are poor.[4] Many are unable to emerge from the shadows and are increasingly affected, if not traumatized by the rising societal antagonism against those perceived as "Mexicans" and "immigrants." Certainly, the Latinx population as a whole became significantly more vulnerable in July 2015, when Trump announced his presidential campaign attacking "Mexicans" as criminals and new arrivals. Long a euphemism for those who do not belong—and more specifically for "foreigners," regardless of time of arrival in this country—the term "Mexican" is now also a euphemism for Latinxs, and is increasingly used as a synonym for those who have never been fully acknowledged as members of U.S. society.[5] Instead, perceived as perpetual strangers, "Mexicans" have been invisible in the U.S. public sphere and treated as disposable people—despite their citizenship status, their time of arrival, and their history of multiple political, legal, economic, social, and cultural contributions to this nation (Oboler 2021).

Particularly during 2020, the first year of the COVID-19 pandemic, homogenized as "Mexicans," the very status of people of Latin American descent, while increasingly vulnerable, has created a significant and very public paradox: on the one hand, despite their U.S. citizenship, Latinxs are often perceived as recent immigrants and identified as foreign to the image of "being American." Yet, paradoxically, Latinxs have simultaneously also been declared to be "essential workers" and, as such, are deemed to be "heroes," who are sustaining if not ensuring the very survival of a society that nevertheless continues to deny their belonging.

Essential workers are fundamental to the maintenance of daily life in U.S. society, particularly but not only during this pandemic. They include but are not limited to Latinx farmworkers, meatpacking workers, security guards, grocery store workers, fast food servers; they organize, manage, make deliveries; they work in funeral parlors or cemeteries, or in the country's megastore warehouses; they are the caretakers in retirement homes, the ambulance drivers, doctors, nurses, nurses' aides, and the janitors, and garbage collectors in our society.

As essential workers, Latinxs have borne much of the brunt of this pandemic.[6] Despite its dangers, they are the ones that have had to continue to leave their homes to maintain vital essential services in cities and towns across the country, so that others can shelter in place. On Labor Day, 2020, the League of United Latin American Citizens (LULAC) expressed its gratitude to Latinx essential workers. Drawing on recent data from the U.S. Census, LULAC, the nation's oldest civil rights organization, observed that "Latinos account for 85 percent of all farmworkers, 59 percent of the country's construction crews, 53 percent of all employees in food services and 39 percent of the nation's total workforce." However, the organization emphasized, "Latinos are also experiencing a rate of infection from COVID-19 twice their share of the population because of being on the frontlines daily."

How "essential" are people who are also deemed to be disposable? Referring to the coming economic depression, Matthew Telles unambiguously addresses this very question, as he describes his perception of the status of Latinx essential workers like himself: "Everyone's going to be in the gig economy. You know, it's not just going to be the systemically impoverished minorities, immigrants. They start with them, us—[I'm] Mexican myself. And now we're seeing, you know, more of the middle class being laid off again, just like last time. . . . You know, they call us essential workers . . . it seems more like we're expendable. I guarantee you there's some memos behind closed doors that say, you know, 'When they die, we'll just replace them.' And it's heartbreaking" (Telles 2020).

Disparities in the deaths between whites and people of color were visible relatively early on in the pandemic. By October 2020, awareness of the disproportions in the death rate between white Americans and people of color had led the APM Research labs (2020) to create a "Color of Coronavirus Project" that bluntly and graphically explained the discrepancies in the following terms: "If they had died of COVID-19 at the same actual rate as white Americans, about 21,800 Black, 11,400 Latino, 750 Indigenous and 65 Pacific Islander Americans would still be alive." By March 2, 2021, the project's website reported, "One in 680 Latino Americans has died (or 147.3 deaths per 100,000)" (APM Research Labs 2021, n.p.).

In July 2021, almost a year and a half into the pandemic, UCLA's Jody Heymann and collaborators presented their comparative research on sick leave policies in the United States and various countries around the world. Their publication served to document and highlight the unabated and disproportionate harm that the lack of adequate U.S. leave policies during the pandemic causes in communities of color in the United States (Heymann et al. 2021). Noting that the pandemic has led to a "three-year drop in life expectancy for Latinx and Black Americans," the researchers emphasized that "Latinx workers suffer some of the greatest consequences" of the inequities built into the U.S. health system, including the existing unpaid leave policies under the Family and Medical Leave Act (FMLA) (Heymann and Sprague 2021, n.p.). Because FMLA rules restrict leave "based on employer size, minimum hours and minimum tenure," they ultimately "sharply limit coverage overall and widen racial and gender disparities in access" (Heymann and Sprague 2021, n.p.) As a result, the authors point out, "42 percent of Latinx workers are ineligible for the FMLA because of their employer's size, while 18.7 percent of Latina women don't qualify due to the annual work hours requirement" (Heymann and Sprague 2021, n.p.). Needless to say, the consequences for Latinx essential workers are devastating. Despite their lack of guaranteed paid sick leave, they are forced to work in environments that continuously expose them to high risks of disease, and to confront both the ravages of the pandemic and their own potential health vulnerabilities on a daily basis. These health-related policy inequities also ensure that Latinx families' economic survival is threatened on an ongoing basis (Heyman and Sprague 2021; Gould, Perez and Wilson 2020).

By mid-summer of 2021, the strong presence of the Delta variant across the United States made it clear that the pandemic is far from over. Yet, in the midst of the misery, suffering, and despair that Latinxs, like so many other Americans, continue to experience, there are also significant rays of light. As the examples below suggest, long invisible as full members of this society, Latinx "essential workers" are (re)defining and reconstructing the very meaning of community in the United States, grounded in the mutual aid and the strong sense of solidarity that they visibly and demonstrably contribute at the local level across the country. In the process, Latinxs are shifting the very meaning of belonging, both for themselves and for the broader society.

The Solidarity of Belonging

When the pandemic hit the United States in late February/March of 2020, the rhetoric about the danger of immigrants to the nation and to the economy was at an all-time high. The Immigration and Customs Enforcement agency (ICE), a branch of the U.S. Department of Homeland Security, continued its raids and fearmongering in immigrant communities across the country, particularly in states like California and New York, long at war with then-president Trump.

Of the 2.5 million agricultural workers in the United States, roughly half are undocumented and have no wage protection. Moreover, in the words of Professor Manuel Barajas (2020), these essential workers "live in continuous fear—and some in anger—about their potential deportation."[7] At the same time that the U.S. government was continuing its anti-immigrant rhetoric, Barajas noted, it was simultaneously handing out H-2A seasonal worker visas to agricultural workers. Moreover, in spite of formally "closing the border," the government also made sure that the farmers knew that H-2A visas were available for renewal to agricultural workers who had worked in the United States the previous year. Today, these temporary workers are also ensuring the continuity of the country's food supply. Yet, like other farmworkers across the country, they too lack protective equipment: their contribution is thus often at their expense.

Most are from Mexico, and many are indigenous, Mixteco, Otomi, Nahuatl. As Barajas (2020) pointed out, in California alone, agribusiness is a twenty-plus-billion-dollar industry that relies on and depends on millions of Latinx and other "essential workers" across the country, regardless of legal status and whether they work in related transportation, grocery, or deliveries industries. Yet, despite their categorization as "essential workers," their legal status prevents farmworkers from receiving government assistance or protection, medical insurance, as well as from making doctor's visits, or having access to hospital care. Unable to work, many have lost their life savings; they don't qualify for unemployment insurance and constantly worry about running out of food. According to Irene de Barraicua, Public Relations Manager of *Lideres Campesinas*, even before the pandemic, policies requiring contractors to provide preventive care and clean water, and sanitary bathrooms had never been enforced. Lack of housing has forced many farmworkers to live in their cars; with the pandemic lockdowns, they no longer have access to the shops where they can wash their hands and shower. Despite these and other limitations, farmworkers in California are risking their own health to provide the nation with fruits and vegetables, and playing an essential role in food safety. Using their experience and expertise, they are collaborating with grassroots organizations including the UFW, Lideres Campesinas, the California Rural Legal Assistance Foundation (CRLAF), who include the farmworkers' recommendations in letters they write to the state's governor, often successfully urging him to enact new policies to protect farmworkers—in many cases for the first time. As Juanita Ontiveros of CRLAF points out, the governor has responded because he knows that if the coronavirus ravages the farmworkers' health, the threat is not only to farmworkers but also to the food supply itself. As a result, new laws are being passed in parts of California to address the health and safety needs of all farmworkers in the United States—an example of change grounded in a powerful show of solidarity, coming directly from the demands and needs of the essential workers—in this case, the farmworkers and their grassroots supporters, regardless of legal status.

It's important to note that both fear and distrust of government—whether federal, state, or city—ran high in the spring of 2020. To this day they cloud the lives particularly of undocumented families, those least able to support themselves at home: fear and distrust of ICE, that in the fall of 2020 again resumed raids across the country; fear of COVID-19, particularly given the lack of access to testing and medical support; fear of not finding the means of putting food on the table, given the sudden unemployment many immigrant families have suffered; fear of not being able to send money to their loved ones, themselves surviving COVID-19 related curfews back in their respective homelands. Many have lived in urban areas like New York City for more than a decade, contributing to its daily life in whatever low-paying jobs they could find. The absence of government assistance has led to impressive shows of solidarity and support, an emphasis on humanity grounded in what sociologist Zygmunt Bauman (2013) identifies as the "obviousness of human interdependencies." A Latinx DACA college student described driving in a neighborhood in Queens one Saturday with her undocumented father, and seeing endless lines of people waiting for food and other forms of support from a nearby Ecuadorian neighborhood association. Arriving back home, she raised $1,000 on the internet in three days, allowing her family to cook and deliver enough meals for 750 people, to the neighborhood association the following Saturday.[8]

Latinx essential workers also seek to convey solidarity through their work, while simultaneously trying to survive the neoliberal indifference toward them at their workplace. One young woman who worked in the city's Amazon warehouse, for example, expressed her commitment to "the community"—even as she described her own lonely struggles with her job during this pandemic:

> As a Hispanic woman and an essential worker, I empathize with the struggle of the community. I work at one of the Amazon warehouses as a fulfillment associate. Being an essential worker during these hard times takes a toll on our mental health, it brings a sense of paranoia and depression. Getting on a packed bus in the morning is stressful but if I do not get to work on time, I risk getting an attendance point that can later result in termination. Any feeling of pain or chest discomfort causes an anxiety attack and I immediately isolate myself from my coworkers in case I am infected unknowingly. I had to take an unpaid week off work because of the high number of cases that were being reported at my job. Even so, I am still expected to report to work six days a week for seven to ten-hour shifts. I am still expected to work in a tight space with hundreds of other employees and risk my health and the health of my family members for a low wage. We risk our lives every day to help benefit the CEOs and large corporation bosses who are currently working from home (Cosme 2020).

For this Latinx worker, regardless of how others might perceive her, being an "essential worker" in the era of COVID-19 brings with it a sense of responsibility—one grounded in empathy and a sense of belonging to "the community." It is an identity that is reinforced by her daily acts of solidarity, regardless of whether those acts are socially acknowledged or visible to those around her. At the same time, as a Latinx essential worker she is fully aware of the extent to which, like Matthew Telles, the Mexican essential worker cited above, she too is both "expendable" and has no rights in a society that denies her belonging. In some ways, the experience of Latinx essential workers during this pandemic parallels that of the 200,000 Latinx soldiers in the U.S. armed forces, among whom roughly 40,000 are immigrants raised in this society and were promised a path to citizenship when they volunteered to defend the country, whether in the immediate aftermath of 9/11 or since. Traumatized by war and with no support upon their return home, many Latinx soldiers have had a difficult re-entry period into civilian life. Instead of citizenship, some have found themselves serving time in prisons— retraumatized by the uncaring abandonment they feel from the country they had so eagerly served (Zamudio 2019). As essential as they may once have been to the success of US missions abroad, the full extent of their disposability only becomes apparent once they are released from prison only to be immediately deported from the United States—with little chance of rejoining their families and loved ones, of ever returning to the country where they grew up and for which they were once willing to die (Barajas-Varela 2019). Like these ultimately disposable yet essential soldiers, today's COVID-19 essential workers are also on a mission. It is one which they choose to do voluntarily, their mobilization no longer encouraged by a label, as it may once have been, but rather by a powerful sense of solidarity toward their fellow Americans, regardless of their legal status, race, or ethnicity.

Battling what Bauman (2013) has identified as "the devaluation of human solidarity" created by neoliberalism's ability to dispose of human beings at whim, the very empathy propelling Latinx essential workers to work for others in "the community" whose struggle to survive they recognize as their own, itself manifests their belonging. In so doing, it compels them to reject the currents of neoliberal ideology, and instead to act on a solidarity that, stemming from empathy, serves today as the foundation for the (re)construction of community.

Examples of acts of solidarity by Latinx essential workers, like those of other racialized populations, are visible across the country in urban cities and rural areas alike. Each of these acts alone may not necessarily denote a significant change. However, like the powerful multiracial protests mobilized by Black Lives Matter in response to the public murder of George Floyd by the Minneapolis police, these acts of solidarity are ongoing affirmations of each participant's belonging. No longer tied to (legal) definitions of citizenship—nor to statistically constructed populations—"belonging," in this context, is increasingly grounded in the recognition of the "obviousness of human interdependencies."

Ultimately, this suggests that today, the affirmation of belonging may no longer be a question of identifying with an abstract community. Instead, to assert one's belonging may now be more accurately understood as an expression of a renewed conviction in the power of human solidarity.

Notes

1. In July 2020, *Time* magazine published an article providing a brief history of Latinx murders by state officials, recalling the early twentieth century era of the Texas Rangers, "a racist, repressive and violent force that rained terror on Mexicans and Native people" (n.p.). Noting that since then "the names of Latinos killed by police go on and on," the article's author, Julissa Arce (2020), observes that "nationally 910 Hispanics have been killed since 2015" (n.p.). Arce (2020) goes on to explain that "Latinos are often undercounted in criminal-justice data, since many states report race but not ethnicity" (n.p.). For recent discussion in mainstream media about the neglect of Latinxs murdered at the hands of police, see Contreras (2020) and Santa Cruz, Vives, and Gerber (2015). On the contemporary militarization of the border and the impunity of border patrol agents, see Rios (2021).
2. See Horowitz, Igielnik, and Kochhar (2020).
3. In this respect, Arce's (2020) acknowledgement of the role of Black Lives Matter in providing national visibility to the until recently largely ignored police killings of Latinxs is important to keep in mind. "Thanks to the Black community's arduous work to increase police accountability and awareness, and its bold vision for defunding the police and imagining a system that serves the people, the vicious killings of Latinos are starting to gain national attention. This is the manifestation of 'when Black lives matter, then all lives will matter'" (n.p.).
4. According to John Creamer (2020), an economist with the U.S. Census Bureau, despite the historic low poverty low rates reached in 2019, nevertheless "Hispanics comprised 18.7 percent of the total population, but 28.1 percent of the population in poverty" (n.p.).
5. As Congressman James L. Slayden (1921) emphasized a century ago: "The word Mexican is used to indicate race, not a citizen or subject of the country. There are probably 250,000 Mexicans in Texas who were born in the state but they are Mexicans, just as all blacks are Negroes, though they may have five generations of American ancestors" (125).

6.   It is also important to keep in mind that significant numbers of Latinxs and others who are not essential workers are now unemployed. According to the U.S. Labor Department, at the beginning of the pandemic, only 16 percent of Latinxs could actually work at home, compared to 31.4 percent of non-Latinxs. As a result, already by the end of April of 2020, millions of Latinx people who were not "essential workers" had been fired from their jobs. Latinx unemployment skyrocketed to 18.9 percent (compared to a 14.2 percent white unemployment rate) as roughly 4 million or nearly one in five Latinx lost their jobs. The number of Latinx unemployed was only slightly better in May (17.6 percent), and continued to reflect their relative vulnerability in the job market (Gould, Perez, and Wilson 2020).

7.   I have drawn much of the following information on farmworkers from a highly informative panel discussion on "Essential Labor: Farmworkers During the Pandemic," organized and introduced by Professor Manuel Barajas, Chair of the CRISJ at California State University, on Friday April 17, 2020, and which brought together representatives of grassroots organizations, including Lideres Campesinas, California Rural Legal Assistance Foundation, the Labor Council for Latin American Advancement, UFW union organizers, and other activists to discuss their work and the essential labor of farmworkers during the pandemic.

8.   Private communication.

References

Anderson, Benedict. 1983. *Imagined Communities: Reflections on the Origin and Spread of Nationalism*. New York: Verso Books.

APM Research Labs Staff. 2020. "The Color of Coronavirus: COVID-19 Deaths by Race and Ethnicity in the U.S." APM Research Labs. November 12, 2020. Updated March 5, 2021. www.apmresearchlab.org/covid/deaths-by-race.

Arce, Julissa. 2020. "It's Long Past Time We Recognized All the Latinos Killed at the Hands of Police." *Time*. July 21, 2020. https://time.com/5869568/latinos-police -violence/.

Barajas, Manuel. 2020. "Essential Labor: Farmworkers During the Pandemic." Center on Race, Immigration and Social Justice. California State University-Sacramento. April 17, 2020. https://csus.mediasite.com/Mediasite/Play/826eec57e760481685 9b4ed2c7caa09b1d.

Barajas-Varela, Hector 2019. "Testimony." Congressional Hearing, "The Impact of Current Immigration Policies on Service Members and Veterans, and Their Families." House of Representatives. October 29, 2019. www.congress.gov/116/meeting /house/110150/witnesses/HHRG-116-JU01-Wstate-Barajas-VarelaH-20191029.pdf.

Bauman, Zygmunt. 2013. "Solidarity: A Word in Search of Flesh." *Eurozine*. May 8, 2013. www.eurozine.com/solidarity-a-word-in-search-of-flesh/.

Black Lives Matter. n.d. "Herstory." Accessed September 1, 2021. https://blacklives matter.com/herstory/.

Chavez, Leo. 1997. "Immigration Reform and Nativism: The Nationalist Response to the Transnationalist Challenge." In *Immigrants Out! The New Nativism and the Anti-Immigrant Impulse in the United States*, edited by Juán F. Perea, 61–77. New York: New York University Press.

Contreras, Russell. 2020. "Activists: Police Killings of Latinos Lack Attention." *Associated Press*. August 17, 2020. https://apnews.com/article/shootings-race-and -ethnicity-mexico-immigration-las-cruces-059f64f61b8d348611af6c6a00a71e4e.

Cosme, Alexandra. 2020. "Essential Workers During COVID-19." Unpublished document. May 2020.

Creamer, John. 2020. "Inequalities Persist Despite Decline in Poverty for All Major Race and Hispanic Origin Groups." United States Census Bureau. September 15, 2020. www.census.gov/library/stories/2020/09/poverty-rates-for-blacks-and -hispanics-reached-historic-lows-in-2019.html.

Flores, William, and Rina Benmayor, eds. 1997. *Latino Cultural Citizenship: Claiming Identity, Space, and Rights*. Boston: Beacon Press.

Gould, Elise, Daniel Perez, and Valerie Wilson. 2020. "Latinx Workers—Particularly Women—Face Devastating Job Losses in the COVID-19 Recession." Economic Policy Institute. December 3, 2020. www.epi.org/publication/latinx-workers -covid/.

Hattam, Vicki. 2007. *In the Shadow of Race: Jews, Latinos, and Immigrant Politics in the United States*. Chicago: University of Chicago Press.

Heymann, Jody, and Aleta Sprague. 2021. "The American Economy Cannot Afford to Forgo Paid Medical Leave." *The Hill*. July 28, 2021. https://thehill.com/opinion /healthcare/565249-the-american-economy-cannot-afford-to-forgo-paid-medical -leave.

Heymann, Jody, Aleta Sprague, Alison Earle, Michael McCormack, Willetta Waisath, and Amy Raub. 2021. "US Sick Leave in Global Context: US Eligibility Rules Widen Inequalities Despite Readily Available Solutions." *Health Affairs*. https:// doi.org/10.1377/hlthaff.2021.00731.

Holmes, Steven A. 1998. "Clinton Panel on Race Urges Variety of Modest Measures." *New York Times*. September 17, 1998, 1A.

Horowitz, Juliana Menasce, Ruth Igielnik, and Rakesh Kochhar. 2020. "Trends in Income and Wealth Inequality." Pew Research Center. January 9, 2020. www .pewresearch.org/social-trends/2020/01/09/trends-in-income-and-wealth-in equality/.

Mora, G. Christina. 2014. *Making Hispanics: How Activists, Bureaucrats, and Media Constructed a New American*. Chicago: University of Chicago Press.

Oboler, Suzanne. 2021. "Disposable Strangers: Mexican Americans, Latinxs, and the Ethnic Label 'Hispanic' in the 21st Century." In *Critical Dialogues in Latinx Studies: A Reader*, edited by Ana Y. Ramos-Zayas and Mérida M. Rúa. New York: New York University Press, 67–80.

———. 1995. *Ethnic Labels, Latino Lives: Identity and the Politics of (Re)Presentation in the United States*. Minneapolis: University of Minnesota Press.

Padilla, Felix M. 1985. *Latino Ethnic Consciousness: The Case of Mexican Americans and Puerto Ricans in Chicago*. Notre Dame, Ind.: University of Notre Dame Press.

Rios, Pedro. 2021. "Militarized Border Communities: Documenting the Enforcement Landscape." In "Zooming to the Border for Human Rights: A Fact-Finding Project of the Ongoing Violations of Human Rights Along the US-Mexico Border." Final Report, 16–24. *Tribuno del Pueblo/People's Tribune*, Chicago, IL. January 2021. http://www.tribunodelpueblo.org/wp-content/themes/tribuno_del_pueblo_theme/pdf/ZoomToTheBorder/Zooming_to_the_Border_Report_2021.pdf.

Santa Cruz, Nicole, Ruben Vives, and Marisa Gerber. 2015. "Why the Deaths of Latinos at the Hands of Police Haven't Drawn as Much Attention." *Los Angeles Times*. July 18, 2015. www.latimes.com/local/crime/la-me-0718-latino-police-20150718-story.html.

Serwer, Adam. 2020. "The Coronavirus Was an Emergency Until Trump Found Out Who Was Dying." *The Atlantic*, May 8, 2020. www.theatlantic.com/ideas/archive/2020/05/americas-racial-contract-showing/61138.

Slayden, James L. 1921. "Some Observations on the Mexican Immigrant." *Annals of the American Academy of Political and Social Science* 93(January): 125.

Telles, Matthew. 2020. "Essential or Expendable? Gig Workers at Instacart & Grocery Stores Demand Safety Gear & Hazard Pay." *Democracy Now*. April 20, 2020. www.democracynow.org/2020/4/20/matthew_telles_instacart_gig_workers.

Tribuno del Pueblo/People's Tribune. 2021. "Zooming to the Border for Human Rights: A Fact-Finding Project of the Ongoing Violations of Human Rights Along the US-Mexico Border." Final Report. January 2021. http://www.tribunodelpueblo.org/wp-content/themes/tribuno_del_pueblo_theme/pdf/ZoomToTheBorder/Zooming_to_the_Border_Report_2021.pdf.

Zamudio, Maria Ines. 2019. "Deported U.S. Veterans Feel Abandoned by the Country They Defended." *National Public Radio*. June 21, 2019. www.npr.org/local/309/2019/06/21/733371297/deported-u-s-veterans-feel-abandoned-by-the-country-they-defended.

Contributors

Andrés Acosta is a Queer, first-generation Colombian-American immigrant and U.S. Navy veteran. He is a graduate of Valencia College and UCF, and current coordinator of the Central Florida HIV Planning Council support team at Heart of Florida United Way. He is the Coordinator for Contigo Fund. During the COVID-19 pandemic, Andrés was the main organizer for the Orlando Strong Symposium, which served as a platform for the elected community leaders and organizations fighting the COVID-19 pandemic to better learn the needs of the individuals in Orlando and to tailor their response to the crisis. Through Contigo Fund, Andrés has played a key role in the creation and execution of the Central Florida LGBTQ+ Relief Fund, which has grown into the Central Florida LGBTQ+ Mutual Aid Network, and has provided individual financial assistance, food, clothing, and mental health services to individuals in Central Florida who need assistance during the COVID-19 crisis. He is currently working with Contigo Fund in the future distribution and collection of funds to provide organizational assistance to grassroots organizations and nonprofits providing aid to the LGBTQ+ community during the COVID-19 pandemic.

Jack "Trey" Allen is an epidemiologist at the Center for Health Equity at the Louisville Metro Department of Public Health and Wellness with a PhD from the Department of Sociology at the University of Louisville. In addition to researching the root causes of health inequalities in the city of Louisville,

Trey's research focuses on Islamophobia, racism, and the experiences and agency of immigrant-origin groups in the United States.

Jennifer Bickham Mendez is Professor of Sociology at William & Mary, where she has conducted research and taught for over twenty years. She is the author of *From the Revolution to the Maquiladoras: Gender, Labor and Globalization in Nicaragua* (Duke University Press 2005), and the co-editor (along with Nancy Naples) of *Border Politics: Social Movements, Collective Identity, and Globalization* (New York University Press 2015). Her scholarship has appeared in such academic journals as *Ethnic and Racial Studies, Gender & Society, Journal of Contemporary Ethnography, Mobilization, and Social Problems,* as well as in several edited volumes. Her most recent work examines struggles for racial equity in Virginia public schools and immigrant high schoolers' quest for belonging.

Stephanie L. Canizales is Assistant Professor of Sociology at the University of California at Merced. Her research focuses on the migration and integration experiences of unaccompanied, undocumented Latin American origin youth and young adults in the United States. She writes about Central American and Mexican origin children and youth's migration, labor, transnational lives, and well-being in their transition into adulthood. Her work, most recently funded by the Russell Sage Foundation, the American Sociological Association, and the Institute for Research on Poverty, has been published by *Social Forces, Sociology of Education, Ethnic and Racial Studies* and the *Journal of Ethnic and Migration Studies,* among other publication outlets.

Christopher Cuevas is a lifelong peace practitioner, educator, and community organizer, who leads their work for cultural transformation by centering the unapologetic and unwavering power of radical love. A child of undocumented immigrants and a Queer person of color, Christopher interconnects their lived experience and drives the necessary heart work of building a culture of peace, compassion, and change through advocating for LGBTQ+, immigrant, and racial justice movements. Through their work with state, national, and transnationally recognized initiatives and organizations, Christopher has led conversations and facilitated education campaigns specifically addressing structural racism, health equity, and LGBTQ+ issues. They are the executive director emeritus of QLatinx, a racial, social, and gender justice movement working toward the advancement of intersecting LGBTQ+ Latinx issues. Christopher is currently employed as a grantmaker for the Laughing Gull Foundation, the nation's largest funder of LGBTQ+ initiatives across the U.S. South.

Natalia Deeb-Sossa is Professor of Chicana/o Studies at the University of California, Davis. She is author of *Doing Good: Racial Tensions and Workplace Inequalities at a Community Clinic in El Nuevo South* and editor of *Community-Based Participatory Research: Testimonios from Chicana/o Studies* (2019), both published with the University of Arizona Press. Her research focuses on how Mexican immigrant farmworker families in California rural communities mobilize as cultural citizens and resist local practices and policies of inequity. She is currently exploring how the COVID-19 pandemic is being experienced by so-called Latina/o essential workers and how they endure compounding vulnerabilities. By centering their voices, she is examining their needs, risks, strengths, assets, as well as the role they want to play in building a more just and equitable workplace. Her published work has appeared in such journals as *Latino Studies, Urban Education, Anthropology & Education Quarterly, Journal of Latinos and Education, Aztlán: A Journal of Chicano Studies, Gender & Society, Journal of Ethnic and Migration Studies,* and *Social Forces.*

Yvette G. Flores is a community-clinical psychologist and Professor in Chicana/o Studies at the University of California, Davis. She obtained a doctoral degree in Clinical Psychology at University of California, Berkeley, in 1982 and completed postdoctoral work in health psychology. Her research focus has been substance abuse treatment outcomes, women's mental health, intimate partner violence, and the mental health of immigrant men. Dr. Flores's publications reflect her life's work of bridging community and clinical psychology and Chicano/Latino studies, as she foregrounds gender, ethnicity, and sexualities in her clinical, teaching, and research practice. She is the author of *Chicana and Chicano Mental Health: Alma, Mente y Corazon* (University of Arizona Press 2013), *Psychological Perspectives for Chicano/ Latino Families* (Cognella Academic Publishers 2014), and *Psychological Perspectives on Latinx Children and Adolescents* (Sentia Academic Publishers 2016). Her latest book is entitled *Cultura y Corazón: A Decolonial Methodology for Community Engaged Research* (University of Arizona Press 2020).

Dr. Flores is a national and international consultant on cultural humility, prevention and treatment of trauma, gender, migration and mental health, and self-care for advocates of color.

Melanie Jones Gast is Associate Professor of Sociology at the University of Louisville, Kentucky. Her research focuses on mechanisms of inclusion/exclusion and the structuring of support in schools and community programs serving diverse racial and ethnic groups. In one project, she analyzes coded racial and class stereotypes and social stratification in a diverse high school. Other projects examine intersections of racial, citizenship, and language statuses and immigrant youth and parents in community organizations and school programs. Her published work has appeared in such journals as *Ethnic and Racial Studies*, *Journal of Ethnic and Migration Studies*, *Sociology of Education*, and *Sociology of Race and Ethnicity*.

Monika Gosin is Associate Professor of Sociology and Director of the Latin American Studies Program at William & Mary. Her research and teaching interests include Latinx and Africana studies, race and gender in popular culture and media, and intergroup relations. She is the author of *The Racial Politics of Division: Interethnic Struggles for Legitimacy in Multicultural Miami* (Cornell University Press 2019). Her book situates Afro-Cubans within a historical analysis of African American and (white) Cuban relations in Miami. Her work on Afro-Cuban immigrants has also been published in the edited volumes *Una Ventana a Cuba y los Estudios Cubanos* (Ediciones Callejon, 2010) and *Afro-Latinos in Movement: Critical Approaches to Blackness and Transnationalism in the Americas* (Palgrave 2016) and in journals such as *Latino Studies* and *Anthurium: A Caribbean Studies Journal*.

Pierrette Hondagneu-Sotelo is the Florence Everline Professor of Sociology at the University of Southern California. Her research examines how Latino immigrants negotiate challenges with informal sector work, varied legal status, and changing gender, family, and community relations. She has authored or edited nine books, including *Paradise Transplanted: Migration and the Making of California Gardens* (2014), *God's Heart Has No Borders: Religious Activism for Immigrant Rights* (2008), and *Domestica: Immigrant Workers Cleaning and Caring in the Shadows of Affluence* (University of California Press 2001). She has held research and writing fellowships from the

Rockefeller Foundation for the Humanities, the UCLA Chicano Studies Research Center, UCSD's Center for U.S.-Mexican Studies, the Getty Research Institute, and the School for Advanced Research in Santa Fe, New Mexico.

Nolan Kline is Assistant Professor of Health Behavior and Health Systems in the School of Public Health the University of North Texas Health Science Center. His book, *Pathogenic Policing: Immigration Enforcement and Health in the US South* (Rutgers), is the result of activist anthropological fieldwork with immigrant rights organizations in Atlanta, Georgia, and it describes the multiple, hidden, health-related consequences of immigration enforcement policies and police practices. He has authored several articles and chapters on immigrant policing in the United States, and has worked collaboratively with immigrant rights organizations in Georgia and Florida. His current research focuses on LGBTQ+ Latinx activism following the Pulse shooting in Orlando, Florida, and is supported by the National Science Foundation. As an applied, medical anthropologist, his work overlaps with public health, law, and policy.

Verónica Montes is Associate Professor of Sociology and co-director of the Latin American, Iberian, and Latina/o Studies Minor at Bryn Mawr College. She was an Andrew W. Mellon Postdoctoral Teaching Fellow at the University of Southern California in the Department of Sociology and with the Center for the Study of Immigrant Integration. Her research falls into two areas: immigration from Mexico and Central America to the United States and intersections of gender, belonging, and migration. Currently, her research revolves around the Central American caravan as a new mobility strategy in the North American region, family separation as a result of the U.S. deportation regime and the collective mobilization of deported mothers, as well as the precariousness of the social services provided to the Mexican migrant community in Philadelphia in the context of the COVID-19 pandemic. Her publications have appeared in *Gender & Society; Gender, Place and Culture; Apuntes; Latino Studies;* and *Contexts.*

Yvonne Montoya is a mother, dancemaker, bi-national artist, and the founding director of Safos Dance Theatre. Based in Tucson, Arizona, and originally from Albuquerque, New Mexico, her work is grounded in and inspired by the landscapes, languages, cultures, and aesthetics of the U.S. Southwest.

Montoya is a process-based dancemaker who creates low-tech, site-specific, and site-adaptive pieces for nontraditional dance spaces. From 2017 to 2018, Montoya was a Post-Graduate Fellow in Dance at Arizona State University, where she founded and organized the inaugural Dance in the Desert: A Gathering of Latinx Dancemakers. Montoya is a 2019–2020 Kennedy Center Citizen Artist Fellow, a 2019–2020 Dance/USA Fellow, recipient of the 2020 MAP Fund, and the first Arizona-based artist to receive the 2020 New England Foundation for the Arts (NEFA) National Dance Project Production Grant. www.yvonnemontoya.com.

Michael De Anda Muñiz is Assistant Professor in the Latina/Latino Studies Department at San Francisco State University. He received his PhD in Sociology from the University of Illinois at Chicago in 2020. Broadly, his research focuses on Latinas/xs/os, culture and art, space, and intersectionality. His current research project examines the practices and production of Latina community-engaged artists in Chicago.

Suzanne Oboler is Professor of Latin American and Latinx Studies at John Jay College of the City University of New York. Her current research and teaching interests center on human rights, focusing on racism, immigration, and belonging in the Americas. She is author of *Ethnic Labels, Latino Lives: Identity and the Politics of (Re)Presentation in the United States*, and several articles and book chapters. She has edited several anthologies, including *Latinos and Citizenship: The Dilemma of Belonging* and *Behind Bars: Latino/as and Prison in the United States*. She co-edited *Neither Enemies nor Friends: Latinos, Blacks, Afro-Latinos* with Anani Dzidzienyo; and two encyclopedias on U.S. Latinxs with Deena González, most recently *The Oxford Encyclopedia of Latinos and Latinas in Contemporary Politics, Law and Social Movements*. She is Founding Editor of the journal *Latino Studies* (2002–12). In 2011, she was named Fulbright Distinguished Chair in American Studies at PUC, in Rio de Janeiro, Brazil. She currently serves on the Executive Board of the CUNY-Dominican Studies Institute.

Gilda L. Ochoa is Professor of Chicana/o-Latina/o Studies at Pomona College. Born and raised in Southern California, she writes about where she lives. Her books include *Becoming Neighbors in a Mexican American*

Community (University of Texas Press 2004); *Learning from Latino Teachers* (Jossey-Bass 2007), and *Academic Profiling: Latinos, Asian Americans, and the Achievement Gap* (University of Minnesota Press 2013). She also co-edited *Latino Los Angeles: Transformations, Communities and Activism* (University of Arizona Press 2005) with her brother Enique C. Ochoa. Her latest work focuses on the struggle for sanctuary and other forms of activism in Southern California's San Gabriel Valley.

Dina G. Okamoto is Class of 1948 Herman B Wells Professor of Sociology and Director of the Center for Research on Race and Ethnicity in Society at Indiana University. Her research focuses on the intersection of race, ethnicity, immigration, and social movements. Dina's current projects investigate the civic and political incorporation of immigrants, the formation of new racial categories and identities such as Asian American, and how immigration-related diversity shapes the ways in which immigrant and U.S.-born groups relate to one another. She is author of *Redefining Race: Asian American Panethnicity and Shifting Ethnic Boundaries* (Russell Sage Foundation 2014).

Marco Antonio Quiroga is the Program Director for the Contigo Fund, which launched in response to the horrific shooting at Pulse nightclub in Orlando. The Contigo Fund seeks to partner with existing agencies and support grassroots efforts that focus on healing, educating, and empowering Pulse-affected and historically marginalized communities, particularly LGBTQ and Latinx individuals, immigrants, and people of color in Orlando and across Central Florida. Previously, Marco served as the Director of Public Policy at the True Colors Fund, where he led state and local advocacy efforts to holistically prevent and address LGBTQ youth homelessness. He also served as the National Field Officer at Immigration Equality, a national organization that works to end discrimination in U.S. immigration law, to reduce the negative impact of that law on the lives of LGBTQ and HIV-positive people, and to help obtain asylum for those persecuted and at risk in their country of origin based on their sexual orientation, transgender identity, or HIV-status. Marco has extensive experience organizing with United We Dream and its Queer Undocumented Immigrant Project (QUIP), as well as the AFT and AFL-CIO. Marco is driven as a direct result of his own life experience as an undocumented and Queer person of color.

Michelle Téllez is Associate Professor in the Department of Mexican American Studies at the University of Arizona. Her research examines community formations, gendered migration, and mothering across the US/Mexico borderlands. She co-edited *The Chicana M(other)work Anthology: Porque Sin Madres No Hay Revolución* (University of Arizona 2019) and is the author of *Border Women and the Community of Maclovio Rojas: Autonomy in the Spaces of Neoliberal Neglect* (University of Arizona Press 2021). Dr. Téllez has a long history in grassroots organizing projects, digital media, and community-based arts and performance.

Index

Anzaldúa, Gloria, 217
Apache, 7
Aparicio, Frances, 7
Arbery, Ahmaud, 63, 67, 265
Arce, Julissa, 272n1
Arizona, 21, 212–13. *See also* Dance in the
 Desert (DITD)
Arizona State University, 218, 219, 232n4
Armenians, 83
Arpaio, Joe, 213
arroba, 11
artistic labor: defined, 208n2; devaluation
 of, 190–93, 198–99, 216; resistance
 through (il)legibility of, 201–7. *See also*
 dance
asserting identities. *See* identity-claiming
assimilation theory, 96. *See also* resistance
 strategies
attachment, 119. *See also* belonging

Ballet Hispanico of New York City, 216
banda music, 228
Barajas, Manuel, 268, 273n7
Barraicua, Irene de, 269
Batalla Vidal v. Wolf, 22n1
Bauman, Zygmunt, 261, 270, 271
belonging, 3–6, 116–17; of Afro-Cubans,
 76–78; agents of, 77; defined, 118, 173;
 deservingness politics and, 54–55,
 68–69; immigrant motherhood and,
 120–22, 128; intersectional Latinx
 identities and, 6, 14–17; of Latinx dancers, 213–17; Latinxs and exclusionary
 inclusion, 5–10; Latinx solidarity as,
 159–60, 261, 268–72; politics of, 117–
 18, 131; solidarity of, 268–72; spaces
 of, 79, 80, 110, 214, 239, 242, 246, 254;
 through homemaking, 16–17, 96–98;
 through place-making, 118–19; through
 space-making, 241–42, 248–54; vulnerabilities and, 177, 180–86. *See also*
 citizenship; claims-making; cultural citizenship; solidarity; spaces of belonging

Beltrán, Cristina, 78
Benmayor, Rena, 263
Bickham Mendez, Jennifer, 3–23, 116–38
Biden, Joe, 4, 261
Black Americans: dance organizations
 and projects for, 213, 227, 233n10; ethnoracial identities of, 75–76; violence
 against, 4, 63–64, 67–68, 264–65. *See*
 also Afro-Cubans
Black Lives Matter movement, 3, 63–64,
 68, 255n2, 264–65, 272, 272n3. *See*
 also activism; Black Americans; racism
blackness, 74, 75, 82, 87. *See also*
 identity-claiming
Blake, Jacob, 265
BlakTinx (also BlakTina) Dance festival,
 227, 233n10
"Body Mapping and Community Mapping" class, 100–1
Bondi, Pam, 56
Bootleg Theatre, 233n10
both/and, as concept, 14, 238, 252–53. *See*
 also feminists of color theories
boundary-making, 75–76, 88–89
"Bracero" (Montoya), 220–21
Bracero Program, 163n4. *See also* labor
 migration
bureaucratic disentitlement, 61–62
bureaucratic violence, 61–62. *See also*
 state violence; violence

"Cafe con Leche" (Maya), 221
CalFresh, 175
California: agribusiness in, 268–69; La
 Puente, 21, 235–36, 240, 246–56;
 population of, 6, 212; Prop 187, 237,
 244; San Francisco, 20, 169–71, 184–
 85; SB 54, 256n9; Squire Town (ST),
 116–18, 120–25, 128, 130, 132, 134–37.
 See also farmworkers; Los Angeles,
 California
California Rural Legal Assistance Founda-
 tion (CRLAF), 125, 269